Social and Environmental Disclosure by Chinese Firms

Given the increased social and environmental problems in China, this book looks into the social and environmental disclosure practices of socially responsible Chinese listed firms by constructing a stakeholder-driven, three-dimensional, disclosure index. The book contains a three-part study: the first part explores the current status of social and environment disclosure practices. The second part empirically examines the relationship between corporate social and environmental disclosure and various influencing factors (i.e. stakeholders' power and corporate characteristics). The third part empirically examines the link between corporate social responsibility (CSR) reporting (i.e. publishing a CSR report and the quality of the CSR report) and socially responsible reputation.

The book finds that the CSR report provides more stakeholder-relevant social and environmental disclosure than the annual report. It also finds that corporate characteristics such as firm size, profitability and industry classification are all statistically significant factors influencing the social and environmental disclosure of the Chinese firms studied. The final part of the study reports that publishing a CSR report and the CSR reporting quality have a positive influence on firms' socially responsible reputations and that the CEO/chairman duality negatively influences firms' socially responsible reputations.

This book will be of interest to those who are keen to learn more about corporate social responsibilities in the context of Chinese firms.

Yingjun Lu obtained her PhD from the University of Wollongong, Australia. She is Lecturer in Accounting at the Shanghai University of International Business and Economics, China. Her teaching interests include both financial and managerial accounting. As an accounting academic, she has expertise and research interests in social and environmental accounting and corporate governance. She has published on social and environmental disclosure, internal audit and corporate governance in Chinese and international journals.

Indra Abeysekera is a skilled and committed accounting academic and research leader, having expertise in financial accounting. Professor Abeysekera has an outstanding track record in the accounting discipline, four peer reviewed research books, and publications in excess of 100 articles. He is currently Associate Professor in Accounting at University of Wollongong, Australia.

Social and Environmental Disclosure by Chinese Firms

Yingjun Lu and Indra Abeysekera

LONDON AND NEW YORK

First published 2014
by Routledge
2 Park Square, Milton Park, Abingdon, Oxfordshire OX14 4RN

and by Routledge
711 Third Avenue, New York, NY 10017

First issued in paperback 2017

Routledge is an imprint of the Taylor & Francis Group, an informa business

© 2014 Yingjun Lu and Indra Abeysekera

The right of Yingjun Lu and Indra Abeysekera to be identified as authors of this work has been asserted by them in accordance with sections 77 and 78 of the Copyright, Designs and Patent Act 1988.

All rights reserved. No part of this book may be reprinted or reproduced or utilised in any form or by any electronic, mechanical, or other means, now known or hereafter invented, including photocopying and recording, or in any information storage or retrieval system, without permission in writing from the publishers.

Trademark notice: Product or corporate names may be trademarks or registered trademarks, and are used only for identification and explanation without intent to infringe.

British Library Cataloguing in Publication Data
A catalogue record for this book is available from the British Library

Library of Congress Cataloging in Publication Data
Abeysekera, Indra.
Social and environment disclosure in Chinese firms / Indra Abeysekera and Yingjun Lu.
pages cm
Includes bibliographical references and index.
1. Disclosure of information–China. 2. Corporate governance–China. 3. Social responsibility of business–China. 4. Industries–Environmental aspects–China. 5. Industries–Social aspects–China.
I. Lu, Yingjun. II. Title.
HD2910.A524 2015
338.70951–dc23 2013036772

ISBN 13: 978-1-138-05537-7 (pbk)
ISBN 13: 978-0-415-74056-2 (hbk)

Typeset in Times New Roman
by Wearset Ltd, Boldon, Tyne and Wear

Contents

Figures

Tables

Acknowledgements

Writing this study has been a long journey and many people have contributed in one way or another to its realisation. First, I would like to express a very special and enormous gratitude to my supervisor: Associate Professor Indra Abeysekera, for his professional supervision, invaluable expertise, wise ideas, friendship and support throughout this journey. Even during my depressed time, Indra never gave up on me. He guided me to solve my problems and helped me to rebuild my confidence. For all these reasons, I hope to express my deep appreciation to Associate Professor Indra Abeysekera for his concern, patience and encouragement. I would also like to thank other members in the School of Accounting and Finance, and other people I have met along the way, especially Dr Corinne Cortese, Dr Shiguang Ma, Ms Shirley Xu and Dr Kevin Li, for their support and encouragement. I am also grateful to my friends in China and all the survey participants for their help and time. Finally, thanks to my family, especially my parents for their endless support and constant love.

Dr Yingjun Lu, *Shanghai University of International Business and Economics, China*

I thank Yingjun for inviting me to contribute to this study, which culminated as her doctoral thesis. Leading to develop a stakeholder-relevant, three-dimensional social and environmental disclosure index (SEDI), and theorising a contextually complex phenomenon of social-environmental disclosure in Chinese firms was indeed both challenging and interesting to both of us, and a scholarly journey I cherished. I wish to thank my beloved wife Preethi for her care and support, my children Manil and Minoli whose presence fills me with joy, and my mum and dad for their love and for inculcating the values that are the foundation for becoming a positive contributor to society.

Associate Professor Indra Abeysekera, *University of Wollongong, Australia*

1 Introduction

1.1 Introduction

This chapter provides a background to the research and an overview of three research issues that will be addressed in this study. The study layout is also presented for the reader to visualise the structure and to follow the main thread of the study.

The following sections of this chapter present: the motivation for this study; an overview of three related research issues; an overview of research methods used for the study; research contributions; and an outline of the chapter organisation.

1.2 Motivations for considering China

1.2.1 Economic development and its social and environmental effects

China, as the largest developing country, has made great achievements in its economic development over the past three decades. The average annual growth rate of gross domestic product (GDP) has been close to 10 per cent, which is much higher than the world average level (around 3.5 per cent) during the same period (Wei, 2004). This rapid rate of economic growth is due mainly to the dominant status of industrial development in China's national economy. The Asian Development Bank estimates that, in order to reach the medium term target of China's economic development, which would see China's GDP quadruple by 2020 compared to the 2000 level, the average annual growth rate of China's GDP should be kept at over 7.2 per cent (Wei, 2004). Therefore, China is expected to continue growing and developing at a fast pace. However, along with the rapid economic development, a number of serious social and environmental issues have occurred in China, including energy shortages, environmental pollution, occupational diseases and injuries, and an absence of product liability (Chow, 2007; Chen and Chan, 2010).

Energy is indispensable for economic development. Although China's total energy reserves are considerable, its energy resources are neither diverse enough nor sufficient to support the rapid economic growth, and its pattern of consumption with a heavy dependence on coal is relatively unitary (Voon, 2007). Following the rapid economic development, China's energy consumption has ranked in the second highest position in the world in 2007 (National Energy Administration, 2007). Estimated by the US Department of Energy, between 1997 and 2020, China's energy consumption is expected to increase by 4.3 per cent per annum, compared with 0.9 per cent for industrialised countries and 2.1 per cent for the world average (Klare, 2001). Rapid economic growth and escalating demand for energy have caused a shortage in domestic energy supply; as a result, the Chinese government has adjusted its import and export policies to no longer encourage the export of energy (Voon, 2007).

Rapid economic development has not only caused energy shortages but has also had an adverse effect on China's natural environment. Air emission, water discharge and solid wastes resulting from industrial production have badly polluted the natural environment and even resulted in many abnormal ecological phenomena (Information Office of the State Council, 2006). Smoke, dust and sulphur dioxide emission from burning coal have heavily impacted the air quality. As a result, acid rain has occurred in cities with a high concentration of industries and population. Domestic living and industrial production have also polluted the water. Conventional pollutants like solid particles and wastes are found in the water. Many factories dump non-conventional pollutants like dissolved metals, both toxic and nontoxic, into the water as by-products of their production process (China Water, 2008). Non-conventional pollutants are difficult to remove because they are dissolved in the water; consequently, the water becomes unusable to humans and animals. Industrial and municipal solid wastes like tailings, coal ash and cotton dust, contain a large number of chemicals, some of which are toxic (UNESCAP, 2000). Pollution has affected human health through skin contact, inhalation or ingestion. For example, more than 100 villagers in southern China were poisoned after drinking water contaminated by arsenic from industrial waste (Xinhua News Agency, 2008).

China's occupational health and safety (OHS) is another issue of concern. Unsafe working conditions and occupational diseases and injuries in mining and labour-intensive manufacturing industries are often reported in both Chinese and foreign media. It was estimated by the Ministry of Health that in 2005, 16 million enterprises were using toxic and hazardous materials; 200 million workers were engaged in such hazardous jobs; and five of every 1,000 workers in these jobs suffered from occupational diseases (Ministry of Health, 2006).

The issue of product liability also creates great concerns. In 2008, milk powder produced by some Chinese firms was declared by both Chinese and foreign media as poisonous to human health. As a result, it damaged the reputation of China's food exports, with at least 25 countries stopping all imports of Chinese dairy products (UNESCAP, 2010). This serious reputation crisis has made corporate social responsibility (CSR) a priority for the Chinese government, which has realised that when operating in a globalised society it is essential to do so in a socially responsible manner in order to ensure and propel China's economic growth.

1.2.2 Sustainable development in China

Facing social and environmental problems as a result of rapid economic development, the Chinese government has made sustainable development a priority national strategy. In China, energy conservation work has been developed to address energy shortages and global climate change issues in a variety of ways such as, optimising energy sources, enhancing the utilisation efficiency of energy, encouraging a recycling economy, undertaking energy substitution, and exploiting new renewable energy (Wei, 2004). The government has developed favourable financing and tax policies to encourage energy suppliers and users to actively take energy saving actions. In order to reduce pollution and environmentalhouse gas emissions, the government has also actively encouraged energy substitution and strengthened the research and application of renewable energy such as solar energy, wind energy, geothermal energy and biogas (Wei, 2004).

To address environmental pollution issues, the Chinese government has enacted various laws and regulations regarding environmental protection. Environmental protection authorities have been established under the government at all levels, which has resulted in a comprehensive environmental control system that strengthens the government's role in environmental supervision and administration. In China, environmental education has been popularised to citizens so as to enhance the whole nation's consciousness of the environment. The government treats the prevention and control of industrial pollution as the key to environmental protection. A series of measures have been taken such as readjusting the industrial structure; closing up factories with laggard technology, heavy pollution and high energy consumption; raising efficiency in the use of raw materials and energy; reducing pollutant discharge and developing technical transformation. As a result, although industrial production has increased year by year, the pollutant discharge has declined steadily in recent years (Information Office of the State Council, 2006). At the same time, the government has also encouraged research in environmental science and technology; developed and popularised practical technologies for environmental pollution prevention and control; and fostered the growth of environmental protection industries. In addition, the Chinese government has actively promoted international communication and cooperation with other countries and international firms in the field of environmental protection through participating in international environmental activities and signing a series of bilateral or multilateral environmental conventions and agreements, such as the Basel Convention, Montreal Protocol and Kyoto Protocol (Information Office of the State Council, 2006).

In order to address the issue of occupational diseases and injuries, the Chinese government has improved a series of relevant laws and regulations. The State Administration of Work Safety in conjunction with its agencies at provincial, city and county levels are in charge of the implementation of relevant laws and regulations as well as the monitoring and supervision of work safety. Additionally, many large state-owned enterprises (SOEs) have developed viable OHS systems, worker-management OHS committees, regular health and safety inspections, and workers' and trade unions' oversight and supervision (Chen and Chan, 2010). For example, a nationwide survey of almost 20,000 enterprises in 2002 found that 78 per cent of SOEs provided workers with personal protective equipment, and 57 per cent of SOEs provided medical examinations for workers exposed to occupational hazards (Zhi, 2003).

The Chinese government has also improved laws and regulations regarding product quality control and product liability. The government agency, the General Administration of Quality Supervision, Inspection and Quarantine (AQSIQ) is in charge of the implementation of relevant laws and regulations as well as the supervision of certification, accreditation and standardization of the product. Many Chinese enterprises have established quality control, quality assurance and product testing systems to ensure their product liability to consumers (Li, 2006).

1.2.3 Development of corporate social and environmental disclosure in China

Social and environmental disclosure is a relatively new practice for Chinese firms. Prior to 2005, a very limited number of Chinese enterprises published social and environmental reports (including environmental reports, CSR reports, or sustainability reports). With sustainable development as a priority national strategy, the Chinese government has made great efforts to encourage Chinese enterprises to become more socially and environmentally responsible to their stakeholders. In response, the Shenzhen Stock Exchange (SZSE) promulgated the social responsibility guidelines for listed firms in 2006. The Shanghai Stock Exchange (SSE) also issued guidance documents in 2008 to urge listed firms to publicly disclose social and environmental information in their annual or CSR reports. Consequently, more and more Chinese listed firms started to publish CSR reports or sustainability reports. According to the SSE, in 2008, 290 firms out of about 980 firms listed on the SSE published CSR reports in addition to their financial reports, and of these, 282 firms published them for the first time (*China Securities Journal*, 2009).

1.3 Three research issues

Within the context described above, this study investigates corporate social and environmental disclosure practices in China, covering three interrelated research issues. The first research issue (considered as the first stage of the study), is to undertake an empirical observation on the current state of corporate social and environmental disclosure practices in China. To achieve this objective, the study focuses on socially responsible Chinese listed firms, identified by a widely published social responsibility ranking list in China, and their social and environmental disclosure is examined across two reporting media – annual reports and CSR reports. The primary motivation for this stage of the study is that, despite quite a few studies investigating corporate social and environmental disclosure practices in developed countries (Guthrie and Mathews, 1985; Guthrie and Parker, 1989, 1990; Harte and Owen, 1991; Gray *et al.*, 1995a; Deegan and Gordon, 1996; Campbell, 2004; Frost *et al.*, 2005), there is a general lack of research focusing on developing countries, and in particular, economically rapidly expanding China.

Based on the findings of the first stage of the study, two additional relevant research issues are considered. The findings of the first stage show that social and environmental disclosure varies widely across firms. Therefore, the research objective of the second research issue is to examine what factors influence these firms to make social and environmental disclosure in the reporting period. To achieve this objective, a connection between stakeholders' power, corporate characteristics, and the social and environmental disclosure of these firms is explored. The primary motivation for this stage of the study is that, despite a growing amount of social and environmental disclosure literature that focuses on developing countries (Teoh and Thong, 1984; Andrew *et al.*, 1989; Disu and Gray, 1998; Tsang, 1998; Choi, 1999; de Villiers and van Staden, 2006), there is a general lack of empirical evidence on examining the determinants of corporate social and environmental disclosure in developing countries, and in particular China.

The findings of the first stage of the study also show that the CSR report is a more valuable source of social and environmental disclosure compared to the annual report. Based on this finding, the research objective of a third research issue is considered: to examine the link between publishing a separate CSR report (and the quality of disclosure in the CSR report) and the socially responsible reputation of firms studied. To achieve this objective, a relationship between publishing a CSR report, corporate governance attributes, corporate characteristics, and the socially responsible reputation of firms is explored. The primary motivation for this stage of the study derives from the fact that there is a general lack of empirical evidence in the social and environmental accounting literature on exploring the link between CSR reporting (i.e. publishing a CSR report and the quality of disclosure made in the report) and corporate socially responsible reputation.

1.4 An overview of research methods used for this study

Typically, research can be conducted using quantitative or qualitative methods or a combination of both. To achieve the research objectives of this study, mixed methods were used to approach the research issues from different points of view by using various data sources. They included content analysis, a questionnaire survey, and a panel consultation to collect various data, and the findings were analysed by using nonparametric tests, *t*-test and linear regression statistical techniques.

The first stage of the research analysed the current state of Chinese listed firms' social and environmental disclosure practices through constructing a stakeholder-driven SEDI as the proxy for a firm's social and environmental disclosure in this study. Constructing the disclosure index was aided by three research methods – content analysis, a questionnaire survey, and a panel consultation. This index comprised three dimensions: the quantity measure, the quality measure on disclosure types, and the quality measure on the importance of disclosure items. The quantity dimension of the index was approached by using content analysis to count the frequency of items that are covered in the Global Reporting Initiative (GRI) reporting framework, disclosed in firms' annual reports and CSR reports. The quality dimension of the index relating to disclosure types was approached by conducting a questionnaire survey to collect data about stakeholders' perceptions on the preference of different disclosure types pre-determined from the literature. The quality dimension of the index relating to the importance of disclosure items was approached by conducting a stakeholder panel consultation to collect the data relating to stakeholders' perceptions on the relative importance of the disclosure items covered in the GRI reporting framework. By doing so, this study provided insights into sample firms' social and environmental disclosure from stakeholders' perspectives rather than only from the researcher's perspective.

The second stage of the research designed and tested an empirical model to ascertain the relationship between corporate social and environmental disclosure (SEDI) and various influencing factors identified in this study. Similarly, an empirical model was also designed in the third stage of the research to examine the link between publishing a CSR report and a firm's socially responsible reputation.

The details of the research methods pertaining to each stage of the study will be further explained in Chapter 4.

1.5 Research contributions

This study intends to make contributions to the extant social and environmental accounting literature in the following ways. First, this study makes a methodological contribution to the literature by constructing a stakeholder-driven SEDI with three dimensions. The index comprises a quantity dimension and two quality dimensions – disclosure types and disclosure items' importance. Second, this study contributes to the knowledge of corporate social and environmental disclosure practices by expanding the scope of prior research to the context of China, aiding Chinese policymakers to gain a better understanding of factors contributing to corporate social and environmental disclosure. Third, while there is limited research on investigating the relationship between CSR disclosure and corporate reputation in the extant literature, this study fills a void in current research by examining the link between the CSR report (i.e. publishing a CSR report and the quality of the report) and corporate socially responsible reputation in China, helping Chinese policymakers to develop strategies that make firms more responsible and reputable.

1.6 Overview of remaining chapters

The remainder of this study is organised as follows. Chapter 2 provides an overview of the social and environmental accounting literature. Through reviewing the literature from western developed countries, China, and other developing countries, findings of previous research are summarised. Based on the review of prior literature, this chapter identifies a key research gap in the field. In Chapter 3, the theoretical framework for this study is developed. Legitimacy theory and stakeholder theory are adopted to understand corporate social and environmental disclosure practices in China. Impression management theory, stakeholder theory and legitimacy theory are employed to understand Chinese listed firms' socially responsible reputation. This chapter also develops research hypotheses based on the theoretical framework. Chapter 4 presents the research methodology and methods used in this study; the particular research methods adopted in each stage of the study and the justification of choosing them are discussed. Empirical results for each stage of the study are presented in Chapter 5 (current social and environmental disclosure practices), Chapter 6 (stakeholders' power, corporate characteristics, and social and environmental disclosure) and Chapter 7 (CSR report, corporate governance, and corporate reputation), respectively. Finally, the conclusions of the study are presented in Chapter 8, which also outlines limitations of the study and opportunities for future research.

2 Literature review

2.1 Introduction

The purpose of this chapter is to provide a review of the prior research in social and environmental accounting. To achieve this objective, the development of social and environmental accounting literature is outlined. Key previous social and environmental disclosure studies, focused on developed countries as well as developing countries, are respectively categorised and discussed. In doing so, some significant gaps in the social and environmental disclosure field relating to research within the context of developing countries are identified.

The remainder of this chapter is organised as follows. Section 2.2 describes the definitions of social and environmental accounting. Section 2.3 provides an overview of the development of social and environmental accounting literature. Section 2.4 reviews previous social and environmental disclosure studies focused on developed countries. Section 2.5 reviews previous social and environmental disclosure studies focused on developing countries. Section 2.6 provides a review of the prior research in the context of China. Section 2.7 presents a review of the corporate governance literature relating to social and environmental disclosure and reputation. Section 2.8 highlights some gaps in the literature. Finally, Section 2.9 provides conclusions.

2.2 Definitions of social and environmental accounting

For the purpose of this study, before introducing the definitions of social and environmental accounting, it is necessary to discuss the term CSR first and foremost. CSR is a prominent business issue in the contemporary era and it is a broad concept with no uniform definition yet established. The term CSR came into common use in the early 1970s. The US Committee for Economic Development's (CED) 1971 model described CSR as being 'related to products, jobs and economic growth; related to societal expectations; and related to activities aimed at improving the social environment of the firm' (Wheeler *et al.*, 2003, p. 10). In the 1980s, the popularity of CSR was propelled by the emergence of the concept of sustainable development, which assumed a 'triple bottom line' connection between the economic, environmental and social responsibility of the business

(Carroll, 1979, 1999). Further, a more comprehensive approach to CSR in line with the Commission of the European Communities argued that CSR should integrate the triple bottom line with two other objectives: the need to incorporate short- and long-term gains, and the ability to manage economic, natural and social capital (Commission of the European Communities, 2002). Since CSR is used to describe the social and environmental contributions and consequences of business activities (Jenkins and Yakovleva, 2006), social and environmental accounting, a concept describing the communication of the social and environmental effects of a firm's economic actions to particular interest groups (e.g. regulators, investors and environmental lobby groups) within society and to society at large (Gray *et al.*, 1987), is thus an important aspect of CSR.

Social and environmental accounting is a very broad term that has been refined over many years. Up to now, there has been no single universally accepted definition for social and environmental accounting in the literature. In the 1970s, Mobley (1970, p. 762) first introduced the concept of 'socio-economic accounting', which was defined as:

> Social accounting refers to the ordering, measuring and analysis of the social and economic consequences of governmental and entrepreneurial behavior. So defined, social accounting is seen as encompassing and extending present accounting. Traditional accounting has limited its concern to selected economic consequences – whether in the financial, managerial, or national income areas. Socio-economic accounting expands each of these areas to include social consequences as well as economic effects which are not presently considered.

By the mid-1970s, social and environmental accounting had a thrust on the social dimension, and the term evolved into 'social accounting', which was defined by Ramanathan (1976, p. 519) as 'the process of selecting firm-level social performance variables, measures, and measurement procedures; systematically developing information useful for evaluating the firm's social performance; and communicating such information to concerned social groups, both within and outside the firm'. Anderson (1977, p. 6) extended the concept with an emphasis of accountability as 'social responsibility accounting' and defined it as 'a systematic assessment and reporting on those parts of a company's activities that have a social impact' and argued that social responsibility accounting would describe

> the impact of corporate decisions on environment, the consumption of non-renewable resources and other ecological factors; on the rights of individuals and groups; on the maintenance of public service; on public safety; on health and education; and on many other such social concerns.

During the 1980s, with the increased interest in both social and environmental accountability, the term 'social accounting' was broadened to 'social and environmental accounting' by some scholars. For instance, Gray *et al.* (1987, p. ix) defined social and environmental accounting as:

> the process of communicating the social and environmental effects of organisations' economic actions to particular interest groups within society and to society at large. As such it involves extending the accountability of organisations (particularly companies), beyond the traditional role of providing a financial account to the owners of capital, in particular, shareholders. Such an extension is predicated upon the assumption that firms do have wider responsibilities than simply to make money for their shareholders.

The attempts to develop the concept of social and environmental accounting continued into the 1990s. For example, Mathews (1993, p. 64) defined social responsibility accounting as 'voluntary disclosures of information, both qualitative and quantitative made by organisations to inform or influence a range of audiences. The quantitative disclosures may be in financial or non-financial terms'. With an increasing interest in environmental accounting, the combined term 'social and environmental' was detached by authors to define them separately. For instance, subsequent to Gray *et al.* (1987) offering a definition on social and environmental accounting, Gray *et al.* (1993, p. 6) proposed a definition for environmental accounting in the following terms: 'it can be taken as covering all areas of accounting that may be affected by the business response to environmental issues, including new areas of eco-accounting'. However, there appeared to be a lack of clarity between social and environmental accountability as some defined social accounting with the inclusion of environmental accounting in their definitions. For instance, Mathews and Perera's (1995, p. 364) definition of social accounting says:

> at the very least, social accounting means an extension of disclosure into non-traditional areas such as providing information about employees, products, community service and the prevention or reduction of pollution. However, the term 'social accounting' is also used to describe a comprehensive form of accounting which takes into account externalities.... Public sector organisations may also be evaluated in this way, although most writers on the subject of social accounting appear to be concerned with private sector organisations.

Gray (2002, p. 687) defined social accounting as:

> Social accounting is used here as a generic term for convenience to cover all forms of 'accounts which go beyond the economic' and for all the different labels under which it appears – social responsibility accounting, social audits, corporate social reporting, employee and employment reporting, stakeholder dialogue reporting as well as environmental accounting and reporting.

Despite the diversity among these definitions on social and/or environmental accounting, these definitions have commonly recognised the more comprehensive ambit of social and environmental accounting when compared to conventional accounting.

2.3 An overview of the development of social and environmental accounting literature

As definitions of social and environmental accounting were being developed and refined, academic research in this area flourished. Over the past four decades, the accounting literature has accumulated a substantial number of studies engaged with firms' social and environmental issues. Gray *et al.* (1995a) conducted a review of the literature and showed that these studies involved many different topics and perspectives, such as determinants of social and environmental disclosure, and the relationship between social and environmental disclosure and actual performance (Roberts, 1992; Hackston and Milne, 1996; Patten, 2002; Clarkson *et al.*, 2008); used many different research methods, such as content analysis, case/interview study, and model-testing (Wiseman, 1982; Zeghal and Ahmed, 1990; Guthrie and Parker, 1989; Deegan *et al.*, 2002; Roberts, 1992); and covered many different countries, such as the United States, United Kingdom, Australia, Canada and New Zealand, and a variety of time periods.

Most of the extant studies come from western industrialised countries (Ullmann, 1985; Zeghal and Ahmed, 1990; Harte and Owen, 1991; Hackston and Milne, 1996; Deegan and Gordon, 1996). Among them, American, European and Australian studies are the most frequent, mainly due to the nationality of the empirical investigators (Campbell, 2004). Analysing studies by country is fruitful, but since the purpose of this section is to examine the development of social and environment accounting, a temporal analysis is more appropriate. According to the chronological division, time periods of studies can be classified into: prior to 1980, the 1980s, the 1990s and post-2000.

2.3.1 The period prior to 1980

As summarised in Table 2.1, the early studies prior to 1980 were exploratory in nature (Mathews, 1997). Researchers were interested in the social dimension of accounting, generally more concerned with what should be called 'social accounting' and their works were largely descriptive due to the exploratory undertakings (Mathews, 1997). Environmental interests were not detected as a priority issue pertaining to firms and society during that time, whether by managers, professional accountants, or the majority of other observers (Ernst and Ernst, 1972–1978).

This period started from the introduction of social accounting as a subject for academic research (Mobley, 1970; Ross, 1971; Linowes, 1972; Dilley and Weygandt, 1973; Anderson, 1977; Mathews, 1997). Mobley (1970) first mentioned the concept of socio-economic accounting in the 1970s. Thereafter in the

Table 2.1 Social and environmental accounting studies in different eras

Prior to 1980	*1980s*	*1990s*	*Post 2000*
Exploratory undertakings • Exploring the concept of social accounting (Anderson, 1977; Linowes, 1972; Ross, 1971; Ramanathan, 1976) • Goal-oriented disclosure (Grojer and Stark, 1977)	Beginning of academic inquiry into methdologising • Greater attention to methodological issues • Drivers behind disclosure (Belkaoui and Karpik, 1989; Guthrie and Parker, 1989) • A mindset to theorise as legitimacy (Guthrie and Parker, 1989; Richardson, 1985; 1987) • Environmental disclosure via annual reports (Wiseman, 1982; Rockness, 1985)	Academic advancement into theorising • Domination of environmental accounting over social accounting • Special issue publications in academic journals for environmental accounting (Harte and Owen, 1991; Roberts, 1991; Gibson and Guthrie, 1995; Deegan *et al.*, 1995) • Diverse theoretical frameworks (Arnold, 1990; Patten, 1992; Roberts, 1992) • Diverse research interests such as environmental auditing (Tozer and Mathews, 1994), environmental management accounting (Stone, 1995)	Surging interest in academia and practice into emerging issues • Motivations behind and determinants of disclosure (Cormier and Gordon, 2001; Magness, 2006; Wilmshurst and Frost, 2000) • Investigating social and environmental as separate domains and in combination • Critique and debate into concepts, methods and findings (Tinker and Gray, 2003; Owen, 2008; Unerman, 2000) • International comparisons (Newson and Deegan, 2002; KPMG, 2005) • Using GRI framework to analyse disclosure practices (Frost *et al.*, 2005; Clarkson *et al.*, 2008)

early literature, the concept of social accounting (Ross, 1971; Ramanathan, 1976) was loosely defined and frequently interchanged with the term social responsibility accounting (Anderson, 1977) and socio-economic accounting (Linowes, 1972; Belkaoui, 1980).

As indicated by Mathews (1997), early empirical studies had no specific focus and attempted only to develop methods to measure the incidence of corporate disclosure related to social matters. However, these studies had a variety of motivations (Linowes, 1972; Bowman and Haire, 1975; Grojer and Stark, 1977). Linowes (1972) intended to quantify the interaction of firm with people, products and the environment. Bowman and Haire (1975) was one of the earliest studies that sought to establish a relationship between social responsibility disclosure and corporate income. Grojer and Stark (1977) showed concern with developing goal-oriented reporting, giving explicit consideration to several constituencies, especially employees.

During this period, environmental considerations were not separated from other social matters, with the exception of Ullman (1976) and Dierkes and Preston (1977), whose exclusive focus was on environmental matters. Ullman (1976) introduced a model known as the corporate environmental accounting system to describe non-financial disclosure aimed at disclosing environmental impacts. Dierkes and Preston (1977) critically reviewed several proposals for social accounting and identified three uses of environmental impact costs: (1) to inform taxation proposals; (2) to provide a basis for recognition between affected parties; and (3) to assist in determining effluent charges to be levied against the source of pollution to force internalisation and thus the removal of externalities.

2.3.2 The period of the 1980s

The 1980s witnessed the coming of age of social and environmental accounting research as an area of academic inquiry (Owen, 2008). A further key transformation in social and environmental research came about with an increasing interest in environmental accounting (Mathews, 1997).

During the 1980s, social and environmental accounting research underwent a significant change, with increased sophistication in the social accounting research area and an apparent diversion of interest to environmental accounting (Mathews, 1997). Those empirical studies that continued to examine the incidence of social accounting disclosure started to pay greater attention to methodological issues and to determine the type (Trotman and Bradley, 1981; Cowen *et al.*, 1987), direction (Hogner, 1982; Guthrie and Parker, 1989), and drivers (Belkaoui and Karpik, 1989; Guthrie and Parker, 1989) of social accounting disclosure. As Mathews (1997) noted, attempts to explain the motivation behind corporate social accounting disclosure began with the introduction of concepts such as organisational legitimacy, but were restricted to a limited attempt (Richardson, 1985, 1987; Guthrie and Parker, 1989).

In this period, the public concern in relation to environmental protection increased significantly and this was reflected in some authors' broadening the term 'social accounting' to 'social and environmental accounting' (Gray *et al.*, 1987). The volume of published literature dedicated to social accounting decreased; however there was an expansion of that dealing with environmental matters (Mathews, 1997). Empirical studies in environmental accounting focused primarily on how firms measured and reported environmental issues via their annual reports (Wiseman, 1982; Rockness, 1985).

As Mathews (1997) noted, although there were many attempts to build theoretical models during the 1970s (Linowes, 1972), there were few such studies published in the 1980s, except in the environmental accounting literature (Mathews, 1984; Logsdon, 1985). Mathews (1984) put forward a conceptual model for the classification of various socially oriented disclosure, which might be an early proposal to separate environmental accounting from social accounting. Logsdon (1985) built a model to predict organisational responses to environmental issues through a specific study related to the oil refining industry in the United States.

A further feature of this period was the emergence of philosophical discussion and polemical debate by critical theorists concerning the social and political underpinnings for social and environmental accounting research (Owen, 2008). Critical scholars began to address what had been perceived to be the shortcomings of previous studies in the social accounting literature (Tinker, 1985; Puxty, 1986).

2.3.3 The period of the 1990s

The 1990s witnessed the continuation of advancement in social and environmental accounting research with a significant increase in both the number of publication and the depth of empirical work being undertaken. As Mathews (1997) noted, this period was characterised by the almost complete domination of environmental accounting over social accounting, and some academic journals provided greater opportunities for environmental accounting researchers to report their findings through special issue publications (Harte and Owen, 1991; Roberts, 1991; Gibson and Guthrie, 1995; Deegan *et al.*, 1995).

The increased depth of research was evidenced by more studies attempting to employ theoretical frameworks to explain social and environmental accounting practices (Patten, 1992; Roberts, 1992; Neu *et al.*, 1998). The widely adopted theoretical framework to explain their findings included: political economy theory (Arnold, 1990), legitimacy theory (Patten, 1991, 1992) and stakeholder theory (Roberts, 1992). At the same time, other research interests also gained popularity, like environmental auditing (Tozer and Mathews, 1994) and environmental management accounting (Stone, 1995; Mathews, 1997).

In this period, there were published papers that reviewed the social and environmental accounting literature. For example, Gray *et al.* (1995a) provided a review of the literature on corporate social and environmental disclosure and then attempted to theorise mainstream social and environmental disclosure research. Further, Mathews (1997) provided a detailed review of 25 years of social and environmental accounting research, discussing published articles thematically in terms of empirical studies, normative statements, philosophical discussion, radical/critical literature, non-accounting literature, teaching programmes and texts, regulatory frameworks, and other reviews of the literature, and offering a comprehensive bibliography.

As noted by Mathews (1997), critical literature continued to increase during this period (Maunders and Burritt, 1991; Tinker *et al.*, 1991). Accounting researchers in this field noticed that the new developments often failed to challenge the status quo, and therefore sought to prevent the institutionalisation of social and environmental issues into the accounting mainstream (Power, 1991).

2.3.4 The period post 2000

During the post-2000 period, social and environmental accounting research continued to attract the attention of researchers and witnessed a significant increase in the depth of research and the continuous emergence of new issues in the research arena (Owen, 2008). As O'Connor (2006) indicated, there has once again been a significant increase in the depth of empirical studies being undertaken, evidenced by: (1) a growing number of studies seeking to explain social and environmental disclosure practice; (2) a growing number of studies investigating the faithfulness of social and environmental disclosure practice; (3) the emergence of a number of studies seeking to ascertain the degree to which social and environmental accounting leads to organisational change; and (4) a significant increase in the number of studies using multiple sources of data.

As Owen (2008) noted, numerous empirical studies continuing to explore managerial motivations and determinants for social and environmental disclosure practices have related corporate disclosure to factors such as unfavourable media attention as a catalyst for positive information disclosure (Deegan *et al.*, 2002), ownership status (Cormier and Gordon, 2001), and strategic posture represented by press release activity (Magness, 2006). A small body of work has taken a more direct approach to investigating corporate disclosure practices, via employing questionnaire surveys (Wilmshurst and Frost, 2000) or interview-based methods (O'Donovan, 2002; O'Dwyer, 2002).

In this period, seeking theoretical understanding of corporate social and environmental disclosure practices has continued; particularly evidenced by the appearance of a special issue of *Accounting Auditing and Accountability Journal* (2002) devoted to social and environmental accounting research employing a legitimacy theory lens. Nevertheless, Deegan (2002) identifies the overlapping of a number of social and environmental accounting theories employed to explain corporate disclosure practices. Parker (2005) also indicates that the social and environmental accounting field has developed a range of compatible interpretations of different theoretical perspectives that operate at the deep philosophical level and at the policy implementation level.

Several detailed reviews of the social and environmental accounting literature have appeared in recent years (Gray, 2002; Parker, 2005; Owen, 2008). Each brings a different contribution to the literature based on its task but some agreement is reached on a number of issues related to the current state and future prospects of the field (Owen, 2008). Gray (2002) provides an overview of the development of the social accounting literature, focusing on the role played by *Accounting, Organizations and Society* in its development, and states that social accounting can best operate by opening up a space for new ways of accounting. Parker (2005) investigates and analyses contemporary research in social and environmental accounting, and provides insights into the ongoing theoretical debates within the field. More recently, Owen (2008) presented a critical review of the development of social and environmental accounting research with particular reference to the role of *Accounting Auditing and Accountability Journal*, and also provides some pointers for future possible development.

During this period, a more radical campaign between mainstream social and environmental accounting researchers and critical theorists has commenced. As indicated by Owen (2008), while critical theorists adopt a more interventionist stance in advocating practical accounting change (Cooper *et al.*, 2005), a growing number of mainstream social and environmental accounting researchers have also fundamentally revalued the ethical, social and political beliefs driving their efforts in response to critical theorists. At the same time, a growing level of mutual accommodation between mainstream social and environmental accounting researchers and critical theorists has been perhaps evidenced by joint publications between mainstream and critical researchers (Tinker and Gray, 2003).

2.4 Social and environmental disclosure studies in developed countries

Since its emergence in the 1970s, the western social and environmental accounting literature has embraced quite a number of empirical studies related to social and environmental disclosure. According to Gray *et al.* (1995a), social and environmental disclosure has many virtual synonyms including social (and environmental) disclosure/reporting, social responsibility disclosure/reporting. This study does not consciously consider any differences in nomenclature to be important. Given that, environmental disclosure/reporting is considered to be a facet of social (and environmental) disclosure/reporting, and studies on environmental disclosure/reporting will not be reviewed separately in the study. In order to distinguish the extant studies and appreciate their contributions to knowledge, this review classifies various research questions in this area that have been researched or are currently being researched into the following six groups: (1) what are firms disclosing?; (2) determinants of corporate social and environmental disclosure; (3) managerial motivations to disclose social and environmental information; (4) relationship between corporate social and environmental disclosure and actual performance; (5) value relevance of corporate social and environmental disclosure; and (6) corporate social and environmental disclosure and reputation.

2.4.1 What are firms disclosing?[1]

The existing accounting literature has accumulated many studies providing information about what various firms disclose (Ernst and Ernst, 1972–1978; Trotman, 1979; Hogner, 1982; Gray *et al*., 1987; Guthrie and Parker, 1989, 1990; Harte and Owen, 1991; Deegan and Gordon, 1996; Campbell, 2004; Frost *et al*., 2005; Jose and Lee, 2007). The empirical studies in this area begin with descriptive analyses on the incidence and amount of corporate social disclosure in the 1970s. The typical outcome of many early studies was a 'yes' or 'no' to the existence of information disclosure related to the social dimension of accounting (Ernst and Ernst, 1972–1978). This yes/no analysis was developed over time to include measures of the quantity of disclosure (e.g. pages, sentences, words) on specific social disclosure dimensions (Mathews, 1997). The accounting firm Ernst and Ernst produced a series of analyses of the annual reports of Fortune 500 firms from the year 1971 to 1977 and found that the disclosure rate for socially-oriented information accounted for approximately 90 per cent of the 500 firms, on average the companies' written disclosure amounted to about half a page of text (Ernst and Ernst, 1972–1978). Although the Ernst and Ernst (1972–1978) study is now outdated, much of the empirical research into US practices has tended to utilise the extensive survey evidence of this early study (Hackston and Milne, 1996). In an Australian study, Trotman (1979) examined social responsibility disclosure made by corporations listed on the Sydney Stock Exchange during the period 1967 to 1977 and found an increase in the incidence rate of disclosure across the period.

Although the academic literature began examining corporate social disclosure in the 1970s, this does not mean that such disclosure did not exist before then (Buhr, 2007). Hogner (1982) and Guthrie and Parker (1989) provided evidence of long histories of corporate social disclosure. Hogner (1982) reviewed eight decades of disclosure by US Steel from the year 1901 to 1980 and found that the initial decades reported such information as: dwellings built for workers, community development, worker safety, and mortgage assistance for employees. Guthrie and Parker (1989) reviewed the annual reports of BHP for a 100-year period from 1885 onwards and found that, similar to US Steel, the early decades of BHP disclosure also focused on employee issues over other issues.

The empirical research in corporate social and environmental disclosure since the 1980s has been diversified and sophisticated. Many studies have attempted to explain the pattern, direction and source of disclosure and paid greater attention to methodological issues in order to reduce subjectivity (Mathews, 1997). Guthrie and Parker (1990) undertook an international comparison of corporate social and environmental disclosure practices in the United States, United Kingdom and Australia for 1983. They found that the pattern of social and environmental disclosure appeared to be similar across all countries, with human resources being greatest, followed by community involvement and then environmental issues (Guthrie and Parker, 1990). Roberts (1991) supported this finding by a comparative study of five mainland European countries. Guthrie and Parker

(1990) also found that corporate social and environmental disclosure was typically qualitative in form and predominantly self-laudatory in nature. Deegan and Gordon (1996) confirmed this finding in a study of environmental disclosure practices of Australian corporations.

With an increasing interest in environmental issues, corporate environmental disclosure largely emerged in the 1990s. Gray *et al.* (1996, p. 97) described this change in corporate disclosure with reference to the United Kingdom:

> the early 1970s focused on social responsibility; by the mid-late 1970s the focus shifted to employees and unions; the 1980s saw explicit pursuit of economic goals with a thin veneer of community concern and a redefinition of employee rights as the major theme; while in the 1990s attention shifted to environmental concern.

Accordingly, empirical studies in the 1990s mainly emphasised corporate environmental disclosure (Harte and Owen, 1991; Deegan and Gordon, 1996).

In early studies, the annual report was regarded as the principal means by which a firm communicated its operations to the public (Wiseman, 1982) and it has been the source for almost all existing social and environmental disclosure studies (Harte and Owen, 1991; Gray *et al.*, 1995a; Deegan and Gordon, 1996). However, social and environmental information may be disclosed in a variety of media other than in corporate annual reports (Zeghal and Ahmed, 1990), and therefore it should be recognised that exclusion of other information sources may result in a somewhat incomplete picture of corporate disclosure practices (Roberts, 1991). The KPMG international survey showed that an increasing number of firms were publishing separate environmental and sustainability reports and were also using the Internet as a tool to communicate their environmental performance (KPMG, 2002). Accordingly, some studies have investigated social and environmental disclosure in sources other than the annual report, such as corporate advertisement and brochures (Zeghal and Ahmed, 1990), stand-alone environmental reports or social responsibility reports (Cormier and Magnan, 2003, Frost *et al.*, 2005), and corporate websites (Jose and Lee, 2007; Van Staden and Hooks, 2007). In an Australian survey, Frost *et al.* (2005) found that the annual report was the least valuable source (containing the least amount of disclosure) of information on CSR. Instead, stand-alone environmental or social responsibility reports and corporate websites provided greater levels of such information.

The empirical research on corporate social and environmental disclosure is still continuing, with the focus of the research having changed in the following ways: some studies are shifting to developing countries and to international comparisons (Newson and Deegan, 2002; KPMG, 2005); some studies are focusing on data sources other than annual reports (Frost *et al.*, 2005; Jose and Lee, 2007; Van Staden and Hooks, 2007); and some studies are investigating corporate disclosure based on a widely used sustainable development framework with measures initiated by reporting proponents, such as the GRI (Frost *et al.*, 2005;

Clarkson *et al.*, 2008). By looking at recent corporate disclosure practices, the KPMG (2005) survey revealed that a growing number of firms throughout the world are now publishing social responsibility reports based on the GRI sustainability reporting guidelines.

2.4.2 Determinants of corporate social and environmental disclosure

Beyond the descriptive analyses of corporate social and environmental disclosure practices, further research has been undertaken to examine whether corporate social and environmental disclosure can be linked to some influencing factors (Trotman and Bradley, 1981; Cowen *et al.*, 1987; Belkaoui and Karpik, 1989; Roberts, 1992; Hackston and Milne, 1996; Cormier and Magnan, 1999, 2003; Cormier and Gordon, 2001). The determinants of disclosure typically examined in the literature include firm size, profitability, industry classification, country of origin, firm age, and other firm characteristics. Although some determinants have been repeatedly identified, the findings from prior studies are mixed (see Figure 2.1).

First, an association between firm size and corporate social and environmental disclosure has been examined in a number of previous studies (Cowen *et al.*, 1987; Roberts, 1992; Hackston and Milne, 1996; Cormier and Gordon, 2001). Studies indicate that larger firms undertake more activities and are more likely to be subject to public scrutiny and therefore, will disclose more information to obtain public support for their continuing existence (Cormier and Gordon, 2001). Most empirical studies support that large firms make more social and environmental

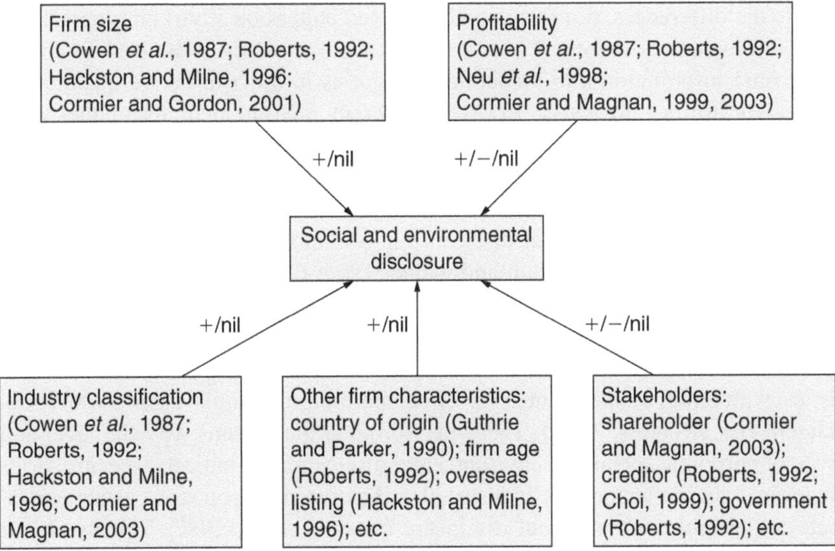

Figure 2.1 Relationships between various determinants and corporate social and environmental disclosure.

disclosure than small firms (Cowen *et al.*, 1987; Hackston and Milne, 1996; Cormier and Gordon, 2001). However, Roberts (1992) found no relationship between size and disclosure in a US sample.

Second, the impact of corporate profitability on social and environmental disclosure has been investigated in many previous studies (Cowen *et al.*, 1987; Roberts, 1992; Neu *et al.*, 1998; Cormier and Magnan, 1999, 2003). As Ullmann (1985) argued, economic performance can influence corporate financial capability to undertake costly programmes related to social demands. Cormier and Magnan (1999) found that profitable firms that have a high level of disclosure are more able to resist stakeholders' pressures and more quickly resolve social and environmental problems. However, generally, empirical findings on the profitability and disclosure relationship are very mixed. Some studies failed to support any relationship between profitability and corporate social and environmental disclosure (Cowen *et al.*, 1987; Hackston and Milne, 1996). Neu *et al.* (1998) found a negative relationship between corporate profitability and voluntary environmental disclosure. Other studies provided evidence for a positive relationship between profitability and corporate social and environmental disclosure (Roberts, 1992; Cormier and Magnan, 1999, 2003).

A possible explanation for the mixed results of the above studies about the relationship between profitability and disclosure is that the way of disclosure being evaluated was different in those studies. For example, some focused on the quantity of disclosure (Cowen *et al.*, 1987; Hackston and Milne, 1996; Neu *et al.*, 1998) and some focused on the quality of disclosure (Roberts, 1992; Cormier and Magnan, 1999). The results of various determinants influencing disclosure accordingly changed. Further, these mixed results of previous studies might be due to the differences in research methods used under objectivist ontological and epistemological assumptions. For example, content analysis is used to codify disclosure information into predefined categories in order to derive quantitative scales for further analysis. However, different measurement techniques (e.g. words, sentences, pages and proportion of pages) used in various research endeavours might lead to diverse quantification of disclosure (Unerman, 2000).

Third, industry classification has been identified as a factor influencing corporate social and environmental disclosure in a number of studies (Cowen *et al.*, 1987; Roberts, 1992; Hackston and Milne, 1996; Cormier and Magnan, 2003). As Patten (1991) stated, industry classification, similar to firm size, influences political visibility and this may drive disclosure in order to avoid undue pressure and criticism from social activists. Different industries have different characteristics, which may relate to intensity of competition, consumer visibility and regulatory risk (Roberts, 1992). These may provide the reasons why the level and type of corporate social and environmental disclosure are industry-specific. Prior empirical studies found that industry classification does appear to affect corporate social and environmental disclosure (Cowen *et al.*, 1987; Roberts, 1992; Hackston and Milne, 1996). For instance, Roberts (1992) found that firms in high-profile industries disclosed more social responsibility information than firms in low profile industries.

Fourth, there appear to be a number of characteristics, other than size, profitability and industry, which may be related to corporate social and environmental disclosure. These include country of origin (Guthrie and Parker, 1990), firm age (Roberts, 1992), overseas listing (Hackston and Milne, 1996), the existence of a social responsibility committee (Cowen *et al.*, 1987), and strategic posture represented by press release activity (Magness, 2006). Hackston and Milne (1996) examined the determinants of corporate social and environmental disclosure in a New Zealand sample and found a positive relationship between overseas listings and corporate social and environmental disclosure. Magness (2006) examined environmental disclosure by Canadian mining firms after a major accident in the mining industry and found that firms with an actively strategic posture by means of press releases made more extensive environmental disclosure.

Finally, the empirical research in this area has been extended to include various stakeholder factors, such as shareholders, creditors, government, special interest groups, and the media (Ullmann, 1985; Roberts, 1992; Deegan and Rankin, 1997; Brown and Deegan, 1998; Choi, 1999; Cormier and Magnan, 2003; Deegan and Blomquist, 2006). An organisation's stakeholders have the power to influence managerial strategic decisions in the form of control over resources required for the organisation to continue to exist (Ullmann, 1985). CSR disclosure has been posited to be an effective management strategy for developing and maintaining satisfactory relationships with various stakeholder groups (Roberts, 1992). Prior studies found that corporate social and environmental disclosure is associated with some stakeholder factors, such as shareholders (Deegan and Rankin, 1997; Cormier and Magnan, 2003), creditors (Roberts, 1992; Choi, 1999), governmental influence (Roberts, 1992), special interest groups (Deegan and Rankin, 1997; Deegan and Blomquist, 2006), and the media (Brown and Deegan, 1998; Deegan *et al.*, 2002).

The influence of shareholders on corporate social and environmental disclosure was examined by Cormier and Magnan (2003), who investigated the determinants of corporate environmental disclosure using a French sample and found that shareholder ownership was a significant determinant of a firm's environmental disclosure. Similarly, Deegan and Rankin (1997) found shareholders were among the groups of users of annual reports who classified environmental information as material to their decision-making. Roberts (1992) also investigated the determinants of CSR disclosure using a US sample and provided evidence that stakeholder factors, both creditors and government, were associated with CSR disclosure. In an Australian study, Deegan and Blomquist (2006) investigated the influence of one of the major environmental organisations in Australia – the World Wildlife Fund (WWF), and found that WWF was able to influence environmental disclosure practices. Another Australian study, Brown and Deegan (1998) found that for the majority of industries studied, higher levels of media attention were associated with higher levels of annual report environmental disclosure.

2.4.3 Managerial motivations to disclose social and environmental information

A stream of the social and environmental disclosure literature has attempted to explain what motivates firms to voluntarily disclose social and environmental information (Guthrie and Parker, 1989; Patten, 1992; Deegan and Rankin, 1996; Neu *et al.*, 1998; O'Donovan, 2002; Milne and Patten, 2002; Van Staden and Hooks, 2007). Voluntary disclosure largely depends on managerial decision-makers' will. As Neu *et al.* (1998) argued, management might adopt disclosure strategies in order to respond to various public pressures and avoid further regulations of their disclosure. On the other hand, Verrecchia (1983) and Dye (1985) argued that decision-makers might withhold some information if they perceived that investors did not need it or could easily find it from alternative sources or that such information could lead to further sanctions by third parties. In reviewing the existing literature, Deegan (2002, pp. 290–291) tentatively summarised:

> a variety of motivations for managers to report social and environmental information:
>
> - the desire to comply with legal requirement,
> - there might be business advantages in appearing to do 'the right thing',
> - a brief in an accountability or responsibility to report,
> - a desire to comply with borrowing requirements,
> - to comply with community expectations,
> - as a result of certain threats to the firm's legitimacy,
> - to manage particular stakeholder groups,
> - to attract investment funds,
> - to comply with industry requirements, or particular codes of conduct,
> - to forestall efforts to introduce more onerous disclosure regulations,
> - and to win particular reporting awards.

Most studies in this area attempted to explain their findings using legitimacy theory in two different approaches: reactive (Patten, 1992; Deegan and Rankin, 1996; Deegan *et al.*, 2002) and proactive (O'Donovan, 2002; Milne and Patten, 2002; Van Staden and Hooks, 2007). The application of legitimacy theory in these two approaches will be particularly discussed in the theoretical framework chapter (Chapter 3).

In addition, some studies examining the relationship between environmental disclosure and environmental performance (reviewed in the next section) often demonstrated a reactive approach if the findings indicated a negative relationship between environmental disclosure and performance – firms with higher levels of toxic releases had higher levels of environmental disclosure (Patten, 2002; Cho and Patten, 2007). Such findings implied that the motivation of firms' disclosure was to alleviate public concerns regarding their high levels of negative environmental activity. The proactive approach was also indicated by the empirical research in this field, which found a positive correlation between environmental disclosure and environmental performance (Al-Tuwaijri *et al.*, 2004; Clarkson *et al.*, 2008). A positive relationship implied that the motivation of firms' proactive disclosure was to prevent possible threats to their legitimacy.

2.4.4 Relationship between corporate social and environmental disclosure and actual performance

Research on the reliability of social and environmental disclosure has examined the correspondence between corporate social and environmental disclosure and actual corporate performance (Wiseman, 1982; Rockness, 1985; Bewley and Li, 2000; Hughes *et al.*, 2001; Patten, 2002; Al-Tuwaijri *et al.*, 2004; Clarkson *et al.*, 2008).

Some early studies found that voluntary disclosure was not significantly correlated with firms' actual performance (Ingram and Frazier, 1980; Wiseman, 1982; Rockness, 1985; Freedman and Wasley, 1990). For instance, Wiseman (1982) examined the association between corporate environmental disclosure and environmental performance. She used a performance index devised by the Council for Economic Priorities (CEP) to represent corporate environmental performance, and designed an environmental disclosure index covering 18 items in four categories to evaluate corporate environmental disclosure. The results found no association between the CEP environmental performance rankings and the Wiseman (1982) environmental disclosure index rankings. The Wiseman (1982) index was developed to measure the quality of corporate environmental disclosure by means of putting more weight on quantitative disclosure and this index has been widely used in later environmental disclosure studies (Freedman and Wasley, 1990; Bewley and Li, 2000; Hughes *et al.*, 2001; Patten, 2002). Most of these early studies employed quite similar methodologies. They used the CEP rankings as a proxy for environmental performance and then measured the extent of environmental disclosure by means of content analysis. Since the environmental performance rankings published by the CEP were restricted to specific types of pollution, industries and geographical area, reliance on the CEP rankings for sample selection might be problematic (Ilinitch *et al.*, 1998).

Although previous studies failed to find an association between corporate social and environmental disclosure and actual performance, some further investigation indicated a negative association between environmental disclosure and environmental performance (Bewley and Li, 2000; Hughes *et al.*, 2001; Patten, 2002). Bewley and Li (2000) examined factors associated with voluntary environmental disclosure by Canadian manufacturing firms, and found that firms with more news media coverage, higher pollution propensity (i.e. environmental performance), and more political exposure were more likely to disclose general environmental information. This finding suggested that there was a negative association between environmental disclosure and environmental performance.

Hughes *et al.* (2001) also examined environmental disclosure made by US manufacturing firms and then evaluated whether environmental disclosure were associated with environmental performance ratings (good, mixed and poor) by the CEP. They found no difference in environmental disclosure between good and mixed groups, but firms rated with poor performance by the CEP were inclined to make more environmental disclosure.

Further, Patten (2002) identified three issues that existed in previous studies in this field (i.e. failure to consider other factors, inadequate sample selection, and inadequate measures of environmental performance). In order to overcome the limitation of environmental performance measures by the CEP, Patten (2002) employed the Toxic Release Inventory (TRI) data as a proxy for environmental performance. He found that controlling for firm size and industry classification, two factors influencing the extent of disclosure, there was a negative relation between corporate environmental disclosure and environmental performance.

In contrast, more recently researchers have found a positive association between corporate environmental disclosure and environmental performance (Al-Tuwaijri *et al.*, 2004; Clarkson *et al.*, 2008). Al-Tuwaijri *et al.* (2004) explored the relations among environmental disclosure, environmental performance and economic performance using a simultaneous equations approach. Similar to Patten (2002), Al-Tuwaijri *et al.* (2004) also used TRI data as a proxy for corporate environmental performance, and found a positive relation between environmental performance and environmental disclosure.

Clarkson *et al.* (2008) revisited the relationship between environmental performance and environmental disclosure by focusing on purely discretionary environmental disclosure. They developed a content analysis index based on the GRI Sustainability Reporting Guidelines (2002) to assess the level of discretionary environmental disclosure in stand-alone social responsibility reports and corporate websites. This index differed from the Wiseman (1982) index, focusing on disclosure related to a firm's actual performance indicators rather than those easily imitated items. Clarkson *et al.* (2008) found a positive association between environmental performance and the level of discretionary environmental disclosure, i.e. the better a firm's environmental performance, the more it voluntarily disclosed.

The possible reasons for the mixed findings of previous studies are due to the different choices of social and environmental disclosure indices employed for evaluating corporate disclosure and the different proxies used for measuring actual environmental performance (Clarkson *et al.*, 2008).

2.4.5 Value relevance of corporate social and green disclosure

Studies on the value relevance of social and environmental disclosure, intend to explore the capital market reactions to social and environmental information disclosed by firms. This issue has been investigated by some empirical researchers (Ingram, 1978; Jaggi and Freedman, 1982; Shane and Spicer, 1983; Blacconiere and Patten, 1994; Richardson and Welker, 2001; Magness, 2002; Murray *et al.*, 2006; Cormier and Magnan, 2007). The findings of extant studies in this field are still relatively inconclusive.

Ingram (1978) examined the value relevance of information disclosed by firms on social responsibilities and found that, on average, there was no significant difference between the variance of returns of firms that did or did not disclose environmental information in their annual reports. Jaggi and Freedman (1982) examined the content of environmental information disclosed in annual reports and 10K reports, and found that there was no significant difference in abnormal returns between firms that disclosed and did not disclose environmental information in the month when their 10K reports were filed. However, the cumulative mean abnormal returns for the ten months prior to the filing of 10K reports were significantly different. Results from these studies indicated that there is no immediate or obvious reason for shareholders to have any interest in the social and environmental aspects of their investment except where those aspects present potential risk to their investment (Murray *et al.*, 2006).

One possible reason for previously inconclusive results is that assessing the impact of a firm's social and environmental disclosure on its stock market performance is rather difficult as most of them are not immediately visible. Therefore, a recent investigation by Murray *et al.* (2006) explored whether there was any relationship between social and environmental disclosure and the financial market performance of the United Kingdom's largest firms on a longitudinal basis. They did not find a direct relationship between share returns and disclosure, but the longitudinal data showed a convincing relationship between consistently high returns and the propensity to high disclosure.

Many studies of the value relevance of social and environmental disclosure have focused on specific events that might or might not influence firms' overall social and environmental disclosure strategy (Shane and Spicer, 1983; Blacconiere and Patten, 1994; Magness, 2002). Most of these studies suggested a negative association between environmental performance information and stock market value. In other words, higher pollution levels or environmental accidents translate into lower stock market values. For instance, Shane and Spicer (1983) investigated the relationship between stock price movements and environmental information disclosed by polluting firms that were announced by the CEP, and showed that stock prices of those firms went down and the extent of the drop depended on firms' pollution records. Similarly, Magness (2002) examined the association between environmental disclosure and stock market value for Canadian listed firms following the Placer Dome mine leak and found that the ecological accident did cause the stock prices of Canadian gold mining firms to go down. However, evidence also showed that a firm disclosing some concern about environmental management prior to an environmental event experienced a less severe drop in share price following the event (Blacconiere and Patten, 1994; Magness, 2002).

Although it is still unclear whether a firm's voluntary social and environmental disclosure strategy affects the stock market valuation of its earnings, investors' expectations, as they are implicitly reflected in current stock market valuations, are likely to influence a firm's social and environmental disclosure (Cormier and Magnan, 1999). Likewise, by responding to such demands through increased social and environmental disclosure, firms are also bound to influence investors' appreciation of their future financial performance (Cormier and

Magnan, 2007). Several more recent studies provided some evidence for this argument (Richardson and Welker, 2001; Cormier and Magnan, 2007). Richardson and Welker (2001) examined the relationship between social disclosure and the cost of equity capital and found a positive relationship between them. Cormier and Magnan (2007) investigated the impact of environmental disclosure on the relationship between a firm's earnings and its stock market value and found that decisions to report environmental information had a moderating impact on the stock market valuation of a German firm's earnings.

2.4.6 Corporate social and environmental disclosure and reputation

The literature has suggested that it is necessary to take into account the complexity of external and internal factors that might lead firms to disclose social responsibility information (Adams, 2002). One emerging explanation for corporate social and environmental disclosure, suggested by reporting proponents (GRI, 2006; KPMG, 2005) and researchers (Friedman and Miles, 2001; Toms, 2002; Hasseldine *et al.*, 2005), is that it could be viewed as both an outcome of and part of reputation risk management processes (Bebbington *et al.*, 2008).

As noted in Figure 2.2, although corporate reputation is ubiquitous, it remains relatively understudied (Fombrun, 1996). The literature has conceptualised reputation in diverse ways (Fombrun and Van Riel, 1997). These conceptualisations have originated from economic, strategic management, marketing, organisational, sociological, and accounting perspectives. For example, from the economic perspective, reputation is regarded as either traits or signals, in other words the perceptions held by the external observers of the firms (Fombrun and Van Riel, 1997). From the strategic management perspective, reputation is viewed as an intangible asset with the potential for value creation (Fombrun, 1996; Little and Little, 2000). From the marketing perspective, reputation is often labelled as a 'brand image', which focuses on the nature of information

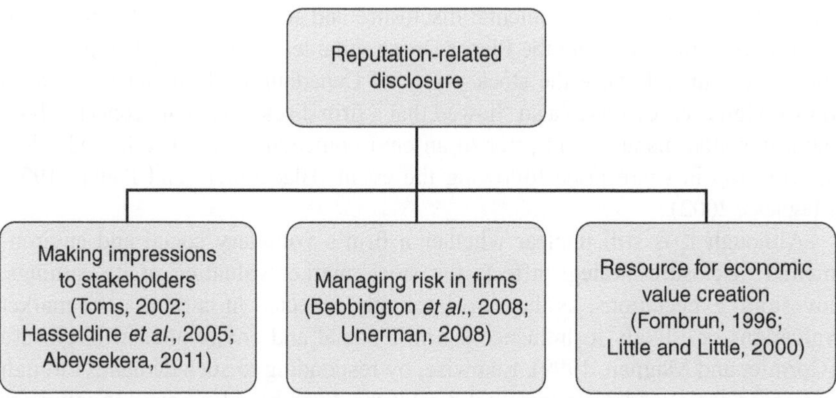

Figure 2.2 Facets of firm reputation examined in reputation-related disclosure literature.

processing and results in 'pictures in the heads' of external subjects (Fombrun and Van Riel, 1997). From the organisational perspective, corporate reputation is rooted in the sense-making experiences of employees (Fombrun and Van Riel, 1997). From the sociological perspective, reputation is viewed as the outcome of shared socially constructed impressions of a corporation (Fombrun and Van Riel, 1997; Bebbington *et al.*, 2008). Finally, from the accounting perspective, many researchers call for broad-based efforts to develop better measures of investments in intangible assets (Barney, 1986; Rindova and Fombrun, 1999).

Fombrun and Rindova (1996) summarised that reputation has the following characteristics: (1) external reflection of a firm's internal identity – itself the outcome of sense-making by employees about the firm's role in society; (2) summarising assessments of past performance by diverse evaluators; (3) deriving from multiple but related images of firms among all of a firm's stakeholders; and (4) embodying two fundamental dimensions of firms' effectiveness: economic performance and fulfilling social responsibilities. Consistent with these characteristics, Fombrun and Van Riel (1997, p. 10) presented the following definition:

> A corporate reputation is a collective representation of a firm's past actions and results that describes the firm's ability to deliver valued outcomes to multiple stakeholders. It gauges a firm's relative standing both internally with employees and externally with its stakeholders, in both its competitive and institutional environments.

In extant literature, the most popular way to measure corporate reputation is via reputation ranking studies and various reputation indices (Abeysekera, 2011). An examination by Bebbington *et al.* (2008) of six worldwide reputation ranking surveys revealed that they mainly focus on five elements of reputation: financial performance, quality of management, social and environmental responsibility performance, employee quality and the quality of the goods/services provided. However, reputation is a complex organisational characteristic, it is impossible for ranking studies to include all the aspects of reputation and any one aspect of reputation possibly lost by the firm is often framed as reputation risk (Bebbington *et al.*, 2008). As Fombrun *et al.* (2000) argued, a firm's reputation is 'at risk' in everyday interactions between firms and their stakeholders, with risks having many sources, such as strategic, operational and financial.

The identification of reputation risk is closely linked to making efforts to manage such risks. There has been evidence showing that firms attempt to manage their reputation risks by means of their social and environmental disclosure. For example, KPMG's (2005) survey of corporate sustainability reporting claimed that one of the business drivers for social and environmental disclosure is to have a good brand and reputation. Specifically, as firms become increasingly aware of the need to manage a wide range of environmental, social and ethical risks, they begin investing in activities likely to create a positive social and environmental reputation; however, to realise the value of the reputation, firms must make associated disclosure (Hasseldine *et al.*, 2005). The existence of a linkage between corporate reputation and corporate disclosure strategy has been investigated in several empirical studies (Friedman and Miles, 2001; Toms, 2002; Hasseldine *et al.*, 2005; Bebbington *et al.*, 2008).

First, Friedman and Miles (2001) examined the relationship between corporate social and environmental disclosure and socially responsible investment (SRI) through interviews with experts in the SRI field, and they suggested that reputation risk management is at the core of the corporate governance agenda, which will create a greater demand for corporate social and environmental disclosure. This is the first study to profess the potential of social and environmental disclosure in managing firms' environmental, ethical and social reputation, but it fails to empirically test the relationship between corporate social and environmental disclosure and corporate social reputation.

Toms (2002), examined the relationship between environmental disclosure and environmental reputation and found that quality of disclosure, institutional shareholder power and low systematic risk are associated with corporate environmental reputation. In Toms' (2002) study, corporate environmental reputation was determined using the corporate reputation rankings for the community and environmental responsibility aspect of the *Management Today* survey of Britain's most admired firms for 1996 and 1997. This study provided strong support for the relationship between corporate disclosure strategy and environmental reputation.

Hasseldine *et al.* (2005) retested the work of Toms (2002) and confirmed that the quality of environmental disclosure rather than mere quantity had a strong effect on the creation of environmental reputation. They also extended Toms' (2002) model by including two potentially relevant variables, and found that research and development (R&D) expenditure, and under certain circumstances diversification, also contributed to environmental reputation.

More recently, Bebbington *et al.* (2008) explored the proposition that CSR disclosure could be viewed as both an outcome of, and part of, reputation risk management processes by way of a three-stage investigation. They developed a reputation risk management explanation of CSR disclosure in an empirical setting through reading Shell's 2002 report, and concluded that the concept of reputation risk management could assist in the understanding of CSR disclosure practice.

Based on practitioners' surveys and academic studies, it can be seen that the notion of reputation is becoming an increasingly popular explanation for corporate social and environmental disclosure. Although this area has increasingly attracted attention and interest, there is a significant scope for further research in this area. In this regard, Toms (2002) and Hasseldine *et al.* (2005) only tested the relationship between environmental disclosure and environmental reputation in the United Kingdom, but there is a lack of research that examines the relationship between corporate social and environmental disclosure and corporate social reputation in a developing country.

2.5 Social and environmental disclosure studies in developing countries

As reviewed above, in the extant literature most empirical studies of social and environmental disclosure focus on the developed countries. Only a handful of studies are available from the developing countries, especially the newly industrialised countries. These will be reviewed in the following sections.

2.5.1 Studies on South Asia

Studies by Singh and Ahuja (1983), Hegde *et al.* (1997) and Belal (2000) have investigated the corporate social and/or environmental disclosure practices of South Asia. Singh and Ahuja (1983) and Hegde *et al.* (1997) examined the entire social disclosure practices of public sector organisations in India. Hegde *et al.* (1997) indicated that public sector undertakings operated for the purpose of social gain rather than profit maximisation in India, therefore these organisations published social balance sheets, social income statements and human resources accounts. These two studies did not include environmental disclosure practices. In order to bridge this gap, Belal (2000) examined the environmental disclosure practices of Bangladeshi firms by analysing 30 annual reports of Bangladeshi firms for the year 1996. The study showed that the quantity and quality of disclosure seemed inadequate and poor as compared to the environmental disclosure in the developed countries.

2.5.2 Studies on South East Asia

The studies by Teoh and Thong (1984), Andrew *et al.* (1989), Tsang (1998) and Smith *et al.* (2007) have made significant contributions to the social and environmental disclosure literature from the South East Asian context. Teoh and Thong (1984) investigated the CSR disclosure of Malaysian firms based on personal interviews and survey data. They found that corporate social disclosure lagged behind social involvement and that firms paid most attention to activities relating to employees and products or services. In addition, the results also indicated that corporate size and national origin of corporate ownership were relevant in reflecting the extent of social commitments undertaken by firms. Andrew *et al.* (1989) examined 119 annual reports of listed firms in Malaysia and Singapore for the year 1983, and found that the overall number of firms disclosing social information was only 31 (26 per cent). Again, they found that a higher proportion of large or medium sized firms made social disclosure compared with small firms. In another study, Tsang (1998) undertook longitudinal research of social and environmental disclosure by 33 listed firms in Singapore over the period from 1986 to 1995, and the results showed that although only 17 (52 per cent) firms made social and environmental disclosure, a steady increase in social and environmental disclosure was captured during the late 1980s, which stabilised in 1993. More recently, Smith *et al.* (2007) examined the extent to which environmental disclosure in the annual reports of Malaysian listed firms was associated with corporate characteristics. They found a significant negative association between environmental disclosure and return on assets, and such a finding suggested that environmental disclosure was negatively associated with corporate financial performance.

2.5.3 Studies on East Asia (other than China)

A Korean study by Choi (1999) examined corporate environmental disclosure in their audited semi-annual financial reports for the year 1997 and also tested the possible associations between the propensity to disclose and a variety of corporate characteristics. The results indicated that 64 (8.3 per cent) out of 770 Korean listed firms made environmental disclosure and that industry classification was significantly associated with both the quality and the quantity of disclosure. Further, if industry classification was controlled, firm size, financial performance and auditors' influence were significantly associated with corporate disclosure decisions (Choi, 1999). More recently, Dasgupta *et al.* (2006) examined the stock market reaction to the list of firms failing to comply with national environmental laws and regulations published by the Ministry of the Environment of the Republic of Korea. They found that firms on the list experienced a significant reduction in their market values, and the larger the extent of coverage by newspapers, the larger the reduction in market value.

2.5.4 Studies on Africa

In addition, several researchers have undertaken studies on social and environmental disclosure in the African context (Savage, 1994; Disu and Gray, 1998; Kisenyi and Gray, 1998; de Villiers and van Staden, 2006). In a study of 115 South African firms, Savage (1994) found that approximately 63 per cent of firms made social disclosure, but the average length of disclosure was only half a page. Disu and Gray (1998) made a study of 22 large multi-national corporations (MNCs) in Nigeria for the years 1994 and 1995, and they found that less than a quarter of corporations made disclosure in the areas of environment, equal opportunities and consumer concerns. In another study of social and environmental disclosure in Uganda, Kisenyi and Gray (1998) noted that none of four surveyed firms made any environmental disclosure. Although the sample size of this study was small, the results still suggested that social and environmental disclosure was scant in Uganda. More recently, de Villiers and van Staden (2006) investigated the environmental disclosure practices in South Africa over a nine-year period and found a reduction in environmental disclosure after an initial period of increase. They proposed that legitimacy theory can also explain reductions in disclosure as it explains maintaining or increasing disclosure.

In sum, social and environmental disclosure research is scarce in the developing countries when compared to the western developed countries. Even in the few studies conducted in developing countries, most only investigated what the firms are disclosing. Very few studies explored the determinants of social and environmental disclosure, attempted to explain motivations for disclosure, or investigated other issues associated with social and environmental disclosure.

2.6 Social and environmental disclosure studies in China

China, as the largest developing country, has been experiencing rapid economic growth. At the same time, along with its rapid economic development some serious problems have arisen, such as environmental pollution, energy shortages, occupational diseases and death, and an absence of product liability. Facing these troubles, social and environmental accounting studies focused on China have become more and more necessary. Since the 1990s, some scholars have begun to include China (including Hong Kong) in their investigations (Lynn, 1992; Gamble *et al.*, 1996; Qu and Leung, 2006; Taylor and Shan, 2007). However, in the extant literature, social and environmental disclosure studies focused on China are far fewer than those on other developing countries as mentioned above, let alone the developed countries.

2.6.1 International comparison studies including China

A minority of researchers have covered China in their international comparison studies on corporate social and environmental disclosure practices (Gamble *et al.*, 1996; Adnan *et al.*, 2010). For instance, Gamble *et al.* (1996) conducted an international comparison on corporate environmental disclosure through investigating the annual report environmental disclosure of 276 firms from 27 countries for the years 1989 to 1991. They indicated that China did not have specific disclosure requirements for environmental concerns at that time and that sample firms within China did not disclose any environmental information for the period. Recently, Adnan *et al.* (2010) provided an international comparison on CSR disclosure practices of 70 large corporations in four countries: China, India, Malaysia and the United Kingdom. They found that the quality of CSR disclosure varied across countries, with UK corporations being the best reporters and Chinese corporations being the last when annual reports were compared.

2.6.2 Studies on Hong Kong (special administrative region of China)

Compared with studies focused on the social and environmental disclosure practices of Chinese mainland firms, studies on Hong Kong firms are relatively greater (Lynn, 1992; Jaggi and Zhao, 1996; Gao *et al.*, 2005). For example, Lynn (1992) provided a study of corporate social and environmental disclosure practices in Hong Kong through an analysis of 264 Hong Kong public firms' annual reports for 1989. He found that only 17 firms made disclosure and that the whole Hong Kong economy paid less attention to social issues and public interests. Lynn (1992) also found that industry membership had a significant relationship with corporate social and environmental disclosure, but firm size had no impact on disclosure in Hong Kong. Another study by Jaggi and Zhao (1996) reported that, among 100 Hong Kong firms examined, only 13 had been consistently disclosing environmental information, for the years 1992 through 1994, only three provided quantitative information, and most firms did not disclose any financial information on their environmental activities. Again, considering the substantial changes in the Hong Kong economy in the 1990s (including the 1997 handing over of Hong Kong sovereignty back to China), which influenced corporate behaviours and disclosure practices in Hong Kong, Gao *et al.* (2005) reinvestigated the patterns and determinants of corporate social and environmental disclosure in Hong Kong through an analysis of 154 annual reports prepared by Hong Kong firms from 1993 to 1997. Compared with the earlier study by Lynn (1992), they found that Hong Kong firms had increased social and environmental disclosure between 1993 and 1997, and the level of corporate social and environmental disclosure varied with both firm size and industry membership.

2.6.3 Studies on Chinese firms' disclosure covering information on the social dimension

Some studies on Chinese firms' disclosure practices have included social and environmental information when assessing the level of voluntary disclosure (Qu and Leung, 2006; Xiao and Yuan, 2007). In a study of the voluntary disclosure behaviour of Chinese listed firms, Qu and Leung (2006) explored the impact of a changed cultural environment on corporate voluntary disclosure from a corporate governance perspective and analysed six areas of voluntary disclosure in the 2003 annual reports provided by 120 sample firms, including employee-related issues and stakeholder interest. They found that Chinese listed firms disclosed more information related to stakeholder interest and employee issues than other sensitive information such as related party transactions in order to legitimate their social status. Another study by Xiao and Yuan (2007) examined the impact of ownership structure and board composition on corporate voluntary disclosure in China through an analysis of the 2002 annual reports prepared by 559 sample firms. Xiao and Yuan's (2007) study included non-financial information such as employee training, social welfare and environmental protection when constructing their voluntary disclosure index, and the results of their study indicated that the level of corporate voluntary disclosure was positively associated with blockholder ownership, foreign listing and independent directors.

2.6.4 Studies on social and environmental disclosure of Chinese firms

Despite being few in number at present, the number of studies focused on the social and environmental disclosure of Chinese firms is on the increase (Guo, 2005; Taylor and Shan, 2007; Liu and Anbumozhi, 2009). For example, Guo (2005) summarised three surveys on corporate environmental disclosure in China conducted in 2001, 2003 and 2004 respectively, and reported that corporate environmental disclosure in China was still at an initial stage but had increased from 2001 to 2004; firms in heavy polluting industries showed the greatest interest in environmental disclosure; and corporate pressure for disclosure mainly came from government agencies.

Taylor and Shan (2007) investigated the social and environmental disclosure practices of Chinese firms listed on the Hong Kong Stock Exchange and attempted to address the issue of whether the drivers of corporate disclosure practices could be explained by western-developed theories. The results of their study indicated that voluntary disclosure in the annual reports of the sample firms was quite limited and that organisational legitimacy was less effective than stakeholder expectations in explaining voluntary social and environmental disclosure in the Chinese context. They also suggested that government and its agencies in China need to prescribe detailed social and environmental disclosure requirements and make it mandatory for listed firms because the soft approach of encouraging voluntary disclosure had not been effective.

Recently, Liu and Anbumozhi (2009) examined the determinant factors affecting the level of environmental disclosure by Chinese listed firms under a stakeholder theory framework through analysing the sample firms' 2006 annual reports, separate environmental (sustainability or CSR) reports and websites. They found that corporate environmental disclosure appears to be marginal in the current Chinese context; the sample firms' environmental sensitivity and size are currently the major significant factors influencing their environmental disclosure, and the role of stakeholders like shareholders and creditors in influencing environmental disclosure is still weak.

2.7 Corporate governance – a related literature to social and environmental disclosure and corporate reputation

Similar to social and environmental disclosure, corporate governance is also a topic of growing concern to various stakeholders. The term 'corporate governance' is a relatively new one in both the public and academic debates, although the issues relating to corporate governance have been reported in the media for a much longer time, at least since Berle and Means (1932). John and Senbet (1998, p. 372) defined corporate governance by stating that it 'deals with mechanisms by which stakeholders of a corporation exercise control over corporate insiders and management such that their interests are protected'. Fombrun (2006, p. 267) closely shared this view as he claimed that 'corporate governance is the system of structural, procedural and cultural safeguards designed to ensure that a firm runs in the best long-term interests of its stakeholders'.

In the corporate governance literature, the widely investigated research issues include: corporate governance and corporate performance (Grossman and Hart, 1983; Zahra and Pearce, 1989; Boyd, 1995; Cole and Mehran, 1998; Dalton *et al.*, 1999; Denis and Sarin, 1999), corporate governance and voluntary disclosure (Haniffa and Cooke, 2002; Eng and Mak, 2003; Gul and Leung, 2004; Qu and Leung, 2006; Xiao and Yuan, 2007), and corporate governance and corporate reputation (Fombrun and Shanley, 1990; Radbourne, 2003; MacMillan *et al.*, 2004; Wu, 2004; Musteen *et al.*, 2010).

The studies related to the relationship between corporate governance and corporate performance are abundant but their findings are mixed. For example, Gales and Kesner (1994) and Dalton *et al.* (1999) found a positive association between board size and corporate performance, but some other studies found that a smaller board was related to better corporate performance (Yermack, 1996; Denis and Sarin, 1999). Some studies have examined the relationship between ownership structure and corporate performance but with no conclusive directional evidence. For example, Kaplan (1989) and Cole and Mehran (1998) found a positive relationship between the increase in insider ownership by managers or directors and an improvement in corporate performance. However, some studies failed to find evidence of a relationship between insider ownership and corporate performance (Holderness and Sheehan, 1988; Loderer and Martin, 1997). A possible explanation for these mixed results is that many studies have not taken into account the possibility that several different governance mechanisms for the alignment of interests with shareholders are used simultaneously with the substitution effects of insider ownership of reducing agency costs. It is conceivable that different firms may use different mixes of corporate governance devices (e.g. outside directors, insider ownership and compensation packages) (Rediker and Seth, 1995).

Studies that examined the relationship between factors relating to corporate governance and voluntary disclosure provide mixed results (see Figure 2.3). Gul and Leung (2004) and Xiao and Yuan (2007) found a negative association between CEO duality and voluntary corporate disclosure, but Haniffa and Cooke (2002) found no relationship between CEO duality and voluntary disclosure. Eng and Mak (2003) found that lower managerial ownership and significant

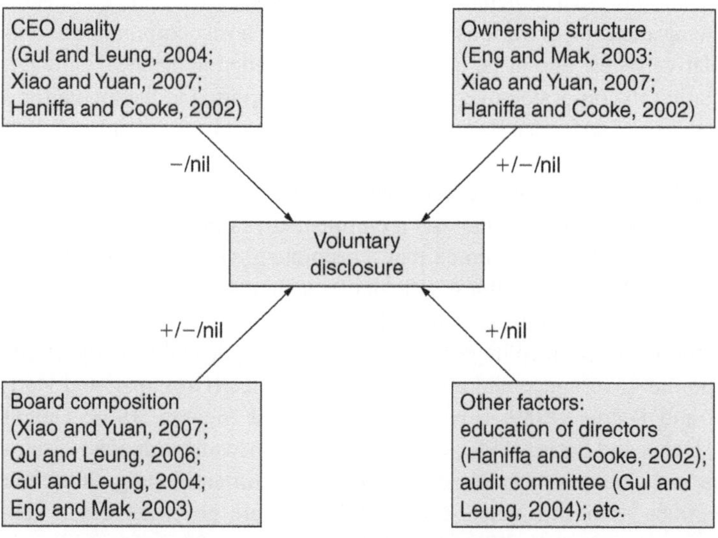

Figure 2.3 Relationships between corporate governance factors and voluntary disclosure.

government ownership were associated with increased disclosure. However, Xiao and Yuan (2007) found that managerial ownership and government ownership were not associated with disclosure but that they provided evidence that higher blockholder ownership and foreign listing ownership were associated with increased disclosure. These mixed findings may be due to different disclosure indices and different proxies for governance variables used in studies.

Recent corporate failures have damaged the reputation of the corporate sector as a whole and have brought corporate governance to the attention of academics as well as practitioners (Fombrun, 2006). As noted in Figure 2.4, the number of studies investigating the relationship between corporate governance and corporate reputation has increased during the recent time period due to the emphasis placed on organisational reputation (Fombrun and Shanley, 1990; Radbourne, 2003; MacMillan *et al.*, 2004; Musteen *et al.*, 2010). As Radbourne (2003) stated, the term corporate governance is used in two ways: one is that a firm relates to others in the external environment through its disclosure, business performance and demonstration of its responsibility, which are reputational measures; the other is that governance is concerned with the mechanism by which firms are directed and controlled, which relates to the internal performance of the board within the firm. Those corporate failures have exemplified the failed process of the board in managing corporate reputation among other things, reinforcing the fact that corporate governance through managing stakeholder expectations can influence the relationship of CSR reporting to enhance corporate reputation (Fombrun, 2006; MacMillan *et al.*, 2004). Good governance is expected to ensure corporate effectiveness and strategic development as well as leading to better performance over time, which in turn contributes to the firm's reputation (Radbourne, 2003).

Fombrun and Shanley (1990) empirically examined what influences corporate reputation by using a sample of 292 large US firms. They found that institutional

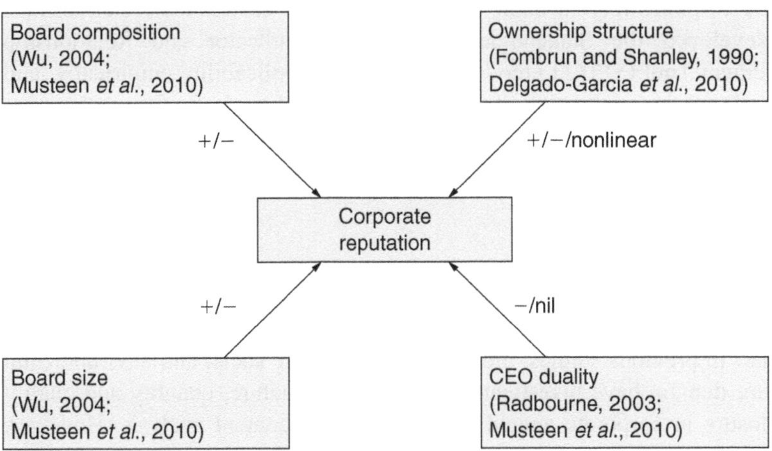

Figure 2.4 Relationships between corporate governance factors and corporate reputation.

ownership positively affects corporate reputation, indicating that the public tends to assign higher reputations to firms with a high proportion of shares held by banks, insurance firms and mutual funds. They also found that profitability and firm size are positively associated with corporate reputation.

Radbourne (2003) investigated the relationship between board performance and corporate reputation by proposing a qualitative model of good governance and testing the model through interviews with board chairs and general managers of performing arts organisations in Australia. The findings of the study indicated that reputation is an important factor to non-profit arts organisations and that arts boards can establish reputation through good governance.

Although Radbourne (2003) claimed that good governance facilitates reputation, there is a lack of empirical evidence to support it. Wu (2004) provided empirical evidence on the relationship between governance and reputation through labelling firms as having good versus poor corporate governance. The study found that such labelling reduced the reputation of those firms labelled as having poor corporate governance.

More recently, Musteen *et al.* (2010) also examined the relationships between board characteristics and corporate reputation based on a sample of 324 firms featured in Fortune's list of most admired firms in the United States. They found that board characteristics significantly influence the assessment of corporate reputation by the business community. Firms with a greater proportion of outside directors exhibited better reputations. Consistent with Fombrun and Shanley (1990), Musteen *et al.* (2010) found that corporate profitability and firm size are positively associated with reputation. However, different from Wu (2004), they found a positive association between board size and corporate reputation. A possible explanation for the above mixed results is that different reputation measures and different governance mechanisms were used in different samples.

Extending the literature of corporate governance and corporate reputation, MacMillan *et al.* (2004) linked corporate governance, corporate reputation and corporate responsibility through an examination of stakeholder relationships. They developed the Stakeholder Performance Indicator and Relationship Improvement Tool (SPIRIT) model, examined its applicability empirically, and concluded that the application of SPIRIT allows the board of a firm to improve its governance and then both enhance its reputation and demonstrate its responsibility.

2.8 Gaps in the literature

As reviewed above, there is a relative shortage of social and environmental disclosure literature in the context of developing countries in general and China in particular. In previous studies, most researchers in the social and environmental disclosure domain have investigated the incidence, nature, quantity and quality of disclosure in corporate annual reports by using content analysis. However, there are several shifts that have occurred in the literature over time. First, the data sources for examining social and environmental disclosure have extended beyond the annual report to include various other reporting media. Second, the coding framework for content analysis has been updated to a widely accepted reporting framework (e.g. GRI Sustainability Reporting Guidelines). Along with these shifts, the research approaches and tools have changed, and the updated approaches and tools have been applied to the social and environmental disclosure research in developed countries. Third, the relative power positions have changed due to the forces pertaining to globalisation, which is particularly significant to China as it recently opened up to the forces of globalisation. The research on corporate social and environmental disclosure in the developing countries including China is still sparse, and it is a perceived gap in Asian in the twenty-first century that has been assumed to propel responsible corporate growth in the globe. Fourth, even in the extant literature focusing on a Chinese context, most studies are only descriptive, showing what firms disclose, and fail to analyse in-depth the determinants of firms' disclosure and explain their disclosure behaviour from theoretical perspectives. On the other hand, the extant literature that investigates the determinants influencing corporate social and environmental disclosure in developed countries still has mixed findings. Fifth, studies on examining the relationship between corporate social and environmental disclosure and reputation are relatively deficient in the literature. As reviewed, corporate governance influences corporate reputation, but there have been no previous studies that examined whether dedicated social and environmental disclosure (e.g. CSR report) in the presence of various corporate governance factors can influence corporate reputation.

Against this background, this study attempts to bridge the gap by conducting an updated empirical observation on the current state of the social and environmental disclosure practices of socially responsible Chinese listed firms. Further, with corporate characteristics identified in the literature as having an influence on social and environmental disclosure, this study empirically examines the effect of stakeholders' power on firms' social and environmental disclosure. Additionally, with corporate governance factors identified in the literature as having an influence on corporate reputation, this study empirically examines the link between publishing a CSR report (and also the quality of disclosure in the report) and corporate socially responsible reputation.

2.9 Conclusions

This chapter reviewed and summarised social and environmental accounting studies in general. The development of social and environmental accounting literature was briefly introduced, followed by a discussion on the major areas within social and environmental disclosure research. The studies within the context of developing countries in general, and China in particular, were discussed respectively. Corporate governance studies as a related literature to social and environmental disclosure studies as well as reputation studies were also reviewed. In doing so, gaps in the social and environmental disclosure literature were highlighted and research objectives were identified. Based on a relative shortage of social and environmental disclosure studies in the context of China, this study seeks to undertake an empirical investigation into the social and environmental disclosure practices of socially responsible Chinese listed firms by observing the current state of their disclosure practices, examining the determinants influencing their disclosure practices, and testing the link between publishing a separate CSR report (and also the quality of the CSR report) and their socially responsible reputation.

Note

1 The corporate reporting system covering social and environmental issues experienced an evolutionary process, which begins with employee reporting and then moves on to social reporting, environmental reporting, social responsibility reporting and finally, sustainability reporting (Buhr, 2007).

3 Theoretical framework

3.1 Introduction

The purpose of this chapter is to present the theoretical framework through which relevant constructs are identified, operational variables are developed based on those constructs, and findings are interpreted in this study. A joint consideration of legitimacy and stakeholder theories is adopted to understand Chinese listed firms' social and environmental disclosure practices. A joint consideration of impression management, stakeholder and legitimacy theories is adopted to understand firms' socially responsible reputation statuses.

The remainder of this chapter is organised as follows. Section 3.2 provides a brief overview of theorising in the prior social and environmental disclosure literature. Section 3.3 discusses legitimacy theory. Section 3.4 discusses impression management theory. Section 3.5 then discusses stakeholder theory. Following this, Section 3.6 presents a theoretical framework of legitimacy and the stakeholder to study corporate social and environmental disclosure. Section 3.7 presents a theoretical framework of impression management, the stakeholder and legitimacy to study corporate socially responsible reputation. Section 3.8 justifies the application of these frameworks in the Chinese context. Section 3.9 presents the research hypotheses. Finally, conclusions are provided in Section 3.10.

3.2 A brief overview of theorising in social and environmental disclosure studies

Empirical investigations of corporate social and environmental disclosure are usually undertaken in some sort of theoretical context. According to Gray *et al.* (1995a), theoretical frameworks for explaining corporate social and environmental disclosure can be arranged into two groups. One group regards social and environmental disclosure as an addendum to conventional accounting and its reports for aiding decision-usefulness through greater transparency. This stream has grounded their findings through agency theory, stakeholder theory and legitimacy theory (Gray *et al.*, 1995a). The other group treats social and environmental disclosure as 'residing at the heart of the role of information in the organisation-society dialogue' (Parker, 2005, p. 845), and the findings have been grounded in political economy theory, deep environmental ecology theory and feminist-based theory (Gray *et al.*, 1995a). These theories point out that social and environmental disclosure is a means of entering into dialogue with society to mask conflicts between firms and society rather than to increase transparency through better stewardship (Spence, 2007). Although different theories offer different analytical insights and understandings, a number of them overlap and provide mutually compatible interpretations of the same empirical evidence (Gray *et al.*, 1995a). The existence of both similarity and difference in explaining the same research issue has enriched the social and environmental disclosure literature.

For instance, political economy theory has identified interest groups of firms as constituents. These constituents from the stakeholder theoretical perspective can be postulated as broad stakeholder groups. Williams (1999) examined the influence of constituents on the quantity of firms' social and environmental disclosure across nations. Using an objectivist ontological and epistemological position, the study noted that the political constituent and social constituent had an influence on firms' social and environmental disclosure. Using operational variables to represent each constituent treated in the study as separate constructs in the political economy theory, Williams (1999) demonstrated that socio-political and economic constituents in each nation interacted to shape the quantity of firms' social and environmental disclosure. The study concluded that firms' self-interests were paramount in social and environmental disclosure and firms were motivated to avoid government regulation and to meet social expectations through such disclosure.

The use of political economy theory in explaining the social and environmental disclosure by Williams' (1999) study also demonstrated how political economy theory can overlap with agency theory and stakeholder theory. The agency theory argues that information asymmetry is a result of managerial/corporate self-interest. The stakeholder theory argues that stakeholders are interest groups of firms who can either influence firms or be influenced by firms. The constituents have similarity with stakeholders and a point of difference can be that constituents are larger/broader groups of stakeholders. Political economy theory demonstrates how firms use social and environmental disclosure to respond to the competing pressures between firms and constituents. This also has some overlaps with legitimacy theory where it demonstrates that firms disclose social and environmental information to meet primarily social expectations so as to receive support from social groups for their continuing operations.

Institutional theory attends to deeper and more resilient aspects of social structure. It investigates how the processes of structures (e.g. schemes, rules, norms and routines) have become authoritative guidelines for social behaviour. It also enquires into how these processes of structures are developed, embraced and augmented in firms, and then decline and are disused over time. Institutional theory therefore attends to examinations of consensus and conformity and also conflict and change in social structures (Scott, 2004). For instance, activities such as staff work arrangements and the social and environmental disclosure of firms are not pre-ordained by laws and regulations, but are shaped by social, cultural and political processes. The differentiation of firms' social and environmental disclosure to different stakeholder groups helps firms to sustain competitive advantage, but the conformity of firms' social and environmental disclosure to all stakeholders' interests becomes necessary in establishing legitimacy (Fernandez-Alles and Valle-Cabrera, 2006). Firms can respond to such pressures by combining substantive (e.g. social environmental disclosure in annual reports) and symbolic (e.g. publishing a CSR report as a supplementary report) disclosure. Institutional theory therefore has some overlaps with legitimacy theory (conforming to the expectations of all stakeholders) and impression management theory (symbolising disclosure for an intended purpose).

Among the theories mentioned above, social and political theories, and most specifically, legitimacy theory and stakeholder theory, have provided insightful perspectives on corporate social and environmental disclosure. These complementary theories explicitly recognise that firms evolve within a society that includes many political, social and institutional frameworks (Patten, 1991, 1992; Roberts, 1992; O'Donovan, 2002; Deegan *et al.*, 2002). In fact, Gray *et al.* (1995a, p. 52) suggested that legitimacy theory and stakeholder theory are better seen as two overlapping perspectives that 'are set within a framework of assumptions about "political economy" ' and the differences between them are 'in levels of resolution of perception rather than arguments for and against competing theories as such'.

Recently, some scholars have adopted impression management theory from sociology and social psychology and applied it to corporate social and environmental disclosure studies (Hooghiemstra, 2000; Ogden and Clarke, 2005). As an imported theory in accounting, impression management theory can help to understand the role of social and environmental disclosure as a way of making impressions to enhance firms' reputations.

Confined to a summary of nomological relations among agency, impression management, institutional, legitimacy, stakeholder and political economy theories, it is noted that although each theory offers its distinct theoretical position, there are overlaps with other theoretical positions, which places each theory in the wider nomological network of theories. As depicted in Figure 3.1, the distinct aspect of information asymmetry in agency theory has a nomological relation with impression management and legitimacy theories. The disclosure made to reduce information asymmetry can result in making intended impressions and legitimising activities towards particular stakeholder groups. The disclosure made to reduce information asymmetry, especially other than for economic efficiency considerations, can help to meet stakeholder expectations, and can be explained by legitimacy theory. Firms' disclosure relating to rationalising (consensus, conformity and conflict) a set of social structure processes under institutional theory can be explained by using legitimacy theory (conformity) (Deephouse, 1996) and impression management theory (consensus and conflict resolution). Impression management and legitimacy are two disclosure activities that firms can undertake towards stakeholders, and when they are investigated,

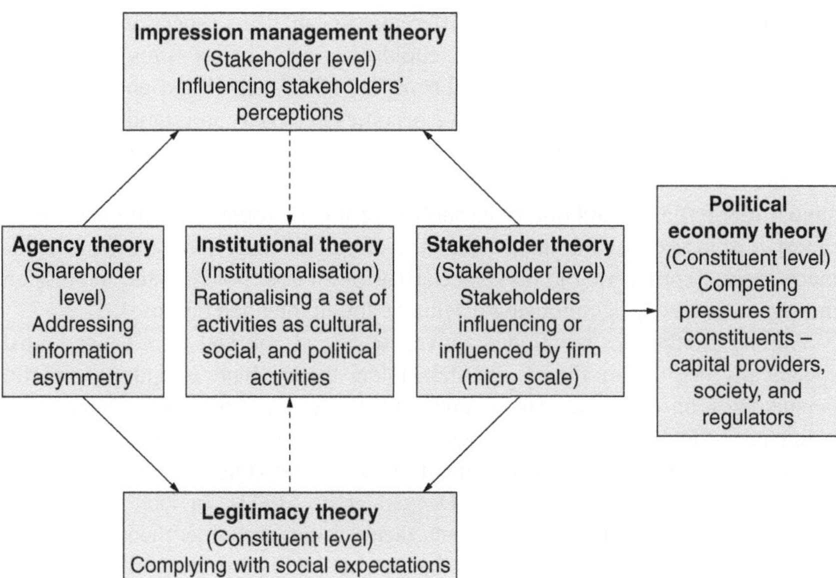

Figure 3.1 Nomological network of theories.

stakeholder theory comes into the forefront as those stakeholders can influence or be influenced by firms. Political economy theory helps in broadening these stakeholder groups into three constituents as social, political and economic.

The following sections will discuss these theoretical perspectives – legitimacy, impression management and stakeholder – in greater detail as they are the chosen theoretical frameworks for this study, acknowledging the fact that they are members of the nomological network and have relations with other theoretical underpinnings.

3.3 Legitimacy theory

3.3.1 What is legitimacy?

Accepting legitimacy as a theoretical perspective requires an acknowledgement that firms are open systems that interact with their outer environment. The outer environment is co-constructed by actors in firms with structures (such as norms and procedures) that influence or are influenced by the environment. The environment is defined as the social, political and economic systems that make firms respond to their context. Since legitimising actions either direct to, or are directed by firms to, the environment that has several broad systems (social, political and economic) and is contextual, defining legitimacy has been problematic and diverse. Noticing the broad and fuzzy possibilities by which a firm can legitimate its actions, Suchman (1995) posed two questions: what is legitimacy, and legitimacy for what? Suchman's questions not only identify the definition of legitimacy as being a challenge, but also demand that the reasons behind firms' legitimation are accounted for. As a result, the literature has not agreed upon a uniform definition. The reasons behind firms' legitimation have been numerous, and Suchman (1995) made an effort to conceptualise them from the literature to that date. Nevertheless, it is necessary to visit some of the more cited definitions and explanations offered in the literature to appreciate the diversity and division among them, acknowledging that they are neither wrong nor comprehensively correct.

From an organisational perspective, Lindblom (1993, p. 2) defined legitimacy as:

> a condition or status which exists when an entity's value system is congruent with the value system of the larger social system of which the entity is a part. When a disparity, actual or potential, exists between the two value systems, there is a threat to the entity's legitimacy.

Lindblom's (1993) definition is consistent with Suchman's (1995, p. 574) definition about legitimacy in that: 'Legitimacy is a generalised perception or assumption that the actions of an entity are desirable, proper, or appropriate within some socially constructed system of norms, values, beliefs, and definitions.' As both definitions suggest, legitimacy is related to the social system in which the entity operates and it is time and place specific (Deegan, 2007). Lindblom's definition has an accent on 'fear' and Suchman's definition has an accent on 'duty', it is a point of division between the two. Consistent with Suchman's (1995) view that legitimacy is based on perceptions, Nasi *et al.* (1997, p. 300) defined legitimacy with a connotation that 'duty is imposed' on firms:

> Legitimacy is a measure of the attitude of society toward a corporation and its activities, and it is a matter of degree ranging from highly legitimate to highly illegitimate. It is also important to point out that legitimacy is a social construct based on cultural norms for corporate behaviour. Therefore, the demands placed on corporations change over time, and different communities often have different ideas about what constitutes legitimate corporate behaviour.

According to Lindblom (1993), legitimacy is a condition, it is a perception to Suchman (1995), and it is a measure to Nasi *et al.* (1997). In contrast, Dowling and Pfeffer (1975) viewed legitimacy as a resource on which a firm is dependent for survival (Dowling and Pfeffer, 1975). However, unlike many other resources, it is a resource that firms can impact or manipulate through various disclosure-related strategies (Woodward *et al.*, 2001).

3.3.2 An overview of legitimacy theory

Legitimacy theory attempts to explain why a firm's management undertakes certain actions, such as disclosing social and environmental information, which seeks to explain or predict particular managerial activities, and therefore it is generally accepted to be a positive theory (Deegan, 2007). Legitimacy theory is also considered to be a systems-based theory (Deegan, 2002). As Gray *et al.* (1996, p. 45) state: 'a systems-oriented view of the organisation and society ... permits us to focus on the role of information and disclosure in the relationship(s) between organisations, the State, individuals and groups.' Within a systems-oriented perspective, the organisation is supposed to be influenced by, and in turn be able to influence, the society in which it operates (Deegan, 2002).

A firm seeking legitimacy should make its actions accountable to meet the expectations that society has with regard to how a firm should act, as there is an implicit 'social contract' between the firm and society (Deegan, 2007). Specifically, it is argued that if society perceives that a firm has breached its expectations then the firm's survival would be threatened as the social contract is not satisfied (Deegan, 2007). Mathews (1993, p. 26) explained the concept of social contract:

> The social contract would exist between corporations (usually limited companies) and individual members of society. Society (as a collection of individuals) provides corporations with their legal standing and attributes and the authority to own and use natural resources and to hire employees. Organisations draw on community resources and output both goods and services and waste products to the general environment. The organisation has no inherent rights to these benefits, and in order to allow their existence, society would expect the benefits to exceed the costs to society.

The concept of social contract is a core theoretical construct in legitimacy theory, but how firms meet the social contract is firm-specific as managers have different perceptions about how society expects the firm to behave, and this therefore explains why some managers take actions that are different from those of other managers (Deegan, 2007).

The concept of social contract can be directly linked to the utilisation of legitimacy theory. A central premise of legitimacy theory is that firms can sustain their operations only to the extent that they meet social expectations and have the support of the community (Deegan, 2007). On the contrary, if society is not satisfied with the firm that is operating, then society will effectively revoke the 'contract' for the firm to continue to operate (Deegan, 2002). When there is a lack of congruence between a firm's activities and society's expectations and perceptions of what these activities should be, a 'legitimacy gap' arises (Deegan, 2007). At a broad level, Wartick and Mahon (1994) suggested the reasons that legitimacy gaps may occur: first, corporate performance changes while societal expectations of corporate performance remain the same; second, societal expectations of corporate performance change while corporate performance remains the same; and third, both corporate performance and societal expectations change, but they either move in different directions, or move in the same direction but with a time lag. In order to be legitimate, firms need to adopt relevant legitimation strategies to reduce the legitimacy gap (O'Donovan, 2002).

3.3.3 Managing organisational legitimacy – the choice and communication of legitimation strategies

When talking about legitimacy theory, it is argued that we must first distinguish between legitimacy (a status or condition) and legitimation (a process seeking that state) (Lindblom, 1993). The choice of legitimation strategies may differ depending on whether the firm is trying to gain, maintain or repair legitimacy (Suchman, 1995). The task of gaining legitimacy occurs when a firm moves into a new area of operations where it has no prior reputation, and thus it needs to proactively undertake activities to win acceptance (Deegan, 2007). Maintaining legitimacy is typically considered to be easier than either gaining or repairing legitimacy (Suchman, 1995; O'Donovan, 2002) and the challenge for management in maintaining legitimacy is to forecast future changes of community perceptions and protect the firm's past accomplishments (Suchman, 1995). As to repairing legitimacy, related legitimation strategies tend to be reactive responses to often unforeseen crises (Suchman, 1995).

Lindblom (1993) identified four strategies that an firm may adopt in the process of seeking legitimacy: first, the firm may seek to educate and inform its relevant publics about actual changes in its performance and activities; second, the firm may seek to change the perceptions of the relevant publics, but not change its actual behaviour; third, the firm may seek to manipulate perception by deflecting attention from the issue of concern to other related issues through an appeal to, for example, emotive symbols; fourth, the firm may seek to change external expectations of its performance. According to Lindblom (1993), disclosure can be employed by a firm in each of the above strategies. For instance, a firm may provide disclosure to inform the interested parties about its attributes that were previously unknown, or it may provide information to offset negative media exposure about its activities, such as pollution, by drawing attention to its strengths, such as environmental awards (Deegan, 2002).

3.3.4 The application of legitimacy theory in social and environmental disclosure studies

Legitimacy theory has been widely applied in the social and environmental accounting literature (Patten, 1992; Deegan *et al.*, 2002; Milne and Patten, 2002; Magness, 2006; Van Staden and Hooks, 2007). The legitimacy framework has provided useful insights into corporate social and environmental disclosure practices. As Lindblom (1993) and Suchman (1995) demonstrated, legitimation strategies adopted by firms to gain, maintain or repair legitimacy may be proactive or reactive. Accordingly, as briefly outlined in the literature review (Chapter 2), corporate social and environmental disclosure studies in the extant literature have employed legitimacy theory with two different approaches: reactive (Guthrie and Parker, 1989; Patten, 1992; Deegan *et al.*, 2002) and proactive (O'Donovan, 2002; Milne and Patten, 2002; Van Staden and Hooks, 2007).

3.3.4.1 Reactive approach to legitimacy

According to Suchman (1995, p. 572), there are in fact two layers of legitimacy theory – 'strategic' and 'institutional':

> the strategic tradition adopts a managerial perspective and emphasises the ways in which firms instrumentally manipulate and deploy evocative symbols in order to garner societal support. In contrast, the institutional tradition adopts a more detached stance and emphasises the ways in which sector-wide structuration dynamics generate cultural pressures that transcend any single organisation's purposive control.

The reactive approach to legitimacy resonates with Suchman's (1995) institutional approach to legitimacy. Firms' social and environmental disclosure is operationalised as a set of constitutive beliefs and managerial decisions for the construction of disclosure are empathised by the same belief systems that determine audience reactions. In this respect, the reactive approach to legitimacy has some overlapping with an institutional theoretical perspective. This approach has an accent on firms' 'disclosure for fear' and is consistent with Lindblom's (1993) definition of legitimacy.

The reactive approach shows that firms increase social and environmental disclosure in reaction to a specific ecological accident or socio-political event (e.g. Exxon Valdez accident, lawsuits, and environmental lobby group pressures) (Hogner, 1982; Guthrie and Parker, 1989; Patten, 1992; Deegan and Rankin, 1996; Walden and Schwartz, 1997; Deegan *et al.*, 2002; Cho, 2009). One of the early studies to embrace legitimacy theory was Hogner (1982), who examined corporate social disclosure in the annual reports of US Steel Corporation over a period of 80 years. Hogner (1982) indicated that the extent of social disclosure varied from year to year and speculated that such variation could present a response to community's changing expectations of corporate activities.

Another early and influential study utilising the reactive approach was Guthrie and Parker (1989). Guthrie and Parker (1989) attempted to match the social disclosure practices of BHP Ltd (a large Australian company) across the period from 1885 to 1985 with major events related to the company's history. They argued that if corporate disclosure was reactive to major social and environmental events, there should be correspondence between peaks of disclosure and events that were significant in the company's history.

Patten (1992) tested the effect of the Exxon Valdez oil spill on the environmental disclosure of petroleum firms other than Exxon and concluded that threats to a firm's legitimacy do compel the firm to disclose more environmental information in its annual report. An Australian study by Deegan and Rankin (1996) also found an increase in the level of environmental disclosure by those firms prosecuted by Australian environmental protection authorities.

As an extension of Guthrie and Parker (1989), Deegan *et al.* (2002) reinvestigated the social and environmental disclosure practices of BHP for the years 1983 to 1997. The results of their study support legitimacy theory by showing that those issues that attracted the largest amount of media attention were also those issues that were associated with the largest amount of annual report disclosure.

Although the results of these studies supported legitimacy theory, critics were quick to question whether 'such disclosures highlight positive environmental actions, obfuscate negative environmental effects, or both' (Neu *et al.*, 1998, p. 266). Several empirical studies also confirmed that such disclosure was misleading because firms appeared to provide positive disclosure in response to increased exposures that were threats to firms and because such disclosure did not appear to be an accurate measure of their actual performance (Deegan and Rankin, 1996; Deegan *et al.*, 2002).

3.3.4.2 Proactive approach to legitimacy

The proactive approach to legitimacy resonates with Suchman's (1995) strategic approach to legitimacy. The social and environmental disclosure is purposive, comprises calculated managerial decisions to reduce conflicts between firms and their constituents, and the disclosure has become an operational resource to legitimate firms' actions. In this respect, the proactive approach to legitimacy has some overlapping with the political economy perspective (neo-classical strand). This approach has given rise to a stream of legitimacy definitions with an emphasis on 'duty' to disclose (Suchman, 1995), and 'duty being imposed' to disclose (Nasi *et al.*, 1997).

The proactive approach, where disclosure is designed to prevent a legitimacy gap rather than to narrow such a gap, has been found in more recent empirical studies (Wilmshurst and Frost, 2000; O'Donovan, 2002; Milne and Patten, 2002; Van Staden and Hooks, 2007). If the reactive approach attempts to repair legitimacy, managerial tactics to gain or maintain legitimacy are usually proactive (O'Donovan, 2002). In an Australian study, O'Donovan (2002) interviewed senior managers from three large public firms to investigate their perceptions about disclosure choices. The findings of the study supported legitimacy theory as an explanation for the managerial decision to disclose environmental information in the annual report and also enhanced the predictive power of legitimacy theory through a proactive approach.

Milne and Patten (2002) explored the role that environmental disclosure might play in producing a legitimating effect on investors by conducting an experimental investment scenario under both a long-term and short-term investment time horizon. The results of the study indicated that those investors who received 'legitimising disclosure', when adopting a long-term investment horizon, tended to invest more in the poorly performing company than those who did not receive that kind of disclosure.

More recently, Van Staden and Hooks (2007) examined whether there was an association between firms that were identified as environmentally responsive and their environmental disclosure using a proactive approach, and they found a positive association between firms' environmental disclosure and their environmental responsiveness, supporting the argument that responsive firms may be taking a proactive legitimacy strategy.

The conceptual dissection of legitimacy as proactive and reactive approaches, and strategies adopted to gain, maintain and repair legitimacy in the two approaches are useful in understanding specific strategies employed by firms for a given circumstance, but going forwards the firm needs to intermingle these three strategies and two approaches concurrently. Therefore, when investigating a phenomenon using a positivist ontological and epistemological stance, these legitimacy strategies and approaches do not become clearly evident as they congregate into the phenomenon garnered for analysis by the positivist method. For instance, when investigating the association between firms' social and environmental disclosure and various stakeholder groups and firm characteristics, firms' disclosure responds to several past events that have taken place over the disclosure period or to possible future events. The social and environmental disclosure therefore becomes an aggregation of all disclosure strategies and approaches that account for those past and future circumstances. Although these circumstances can be isolated by legitimacy strategies and approaches, the exercise is outside the objectives of this study, which investigates the total social and environmental disclosure rather than facets of disclosure driven by legitimacy for a given event. Although Deegan (2007) noted that the majority of accounting research utilised legitimacy theory to explain social and environmental disclosure informed by the strategic approach of legitimacy theory, this study takes a more 'fluid' approach to legitimacy in that it draws out appropriate legitimacy strategies (gaining, maintaining and/or repairing) and approaches (reactive and/or proactive) in interpreting corporate social and environmental disclosure (please see Chapter 5). It is necessary for this study to have such a fluid approach for two reasons. First, from a broader perspective, China is thrusting global trade for its exports and liberalising the economy while maintaining a degree of state control on public affairs with a lacklustre history on social and environmental accountability, the Chinese political, social and economic environment can influence firms' social and environmental disclosure practices. Second, the sample firms being socially responsible firms also characterises their social and environmental disclosure practices. The complex forces in the contextual setting in which the sample firms function can influence those firms to use both proactive and reactive approaches to legitimacy; and use gaining, maintaining and/or repairing legitimation strategies. This study also tests legitimacy in terms of the legitimating role of corporate characteristics in the process of social and environmental disclosure from the public pressure perspective (please see Chapter 6).

3.4 Impression management theory

3.4.1 What is impression management?

Impression management, originated by Goffman (1959), refers to the process by which people attempt to control or manipulate the reactions of others to achieve their intended aims and objectives (Schlenker, 1980; Tedeschi, 1981; Leary and Kowalski, 1990; Rosenfeld *et al.*, 1995). It has received considerable attention in sociology and social psychology (Schlenker, 1980; Tedeschi, 1981) but only recently received attention in the accounting literature. Schlenker (1980, p. 6) defined impression management as 'the conscious or unconscious attempt to control images that are projected in real or imagined social interactions'. According to Goffman's (1959) dramaturgical perspective of social interactions, people are viewed as actors engaging in performances in various settings before the audiences. Basically, the environment provides the setting and context within which actors perform for audiences, and actors and audiences interact to develop a definition of the situation that guides their behaviours (Goffman, 1959). Using their definition as a guide, the actors consciously select specific behaviours that they expect will make the most desirable impression (Gardner and Martinko, 1988). These behaviours are self-presentations and can take many forms, including verbal (e.g. self-description), nonverbal (e.g. facial expressions) and artifactual (e.g. manipulation of physical appearances) (Gardner and Martinko, 1988; Hooghiemstra, 2000). The success of an actor's self-presentation is influenced by the degree to which the actor's performance is perceived as being accordant with the audience's definition of the situation, and when accordance is high, the actor is more likely to create the desired impression (Gardner and Martinko, 1988).

Increasingly, scholars have adopted impression management and applied it to organisational settings, for example to explain the reactions of firms facing legitimacy threats (Elsbach and Sutton, 1992; Elsbach, 1994), and to account for changes in firms' performance in the annual reports (Staw *et al.*, 1983; Aerts, 1994). Gardner and Martinko (1988) developed a conceptual framework of impression management in firms. In the framework, they described that employees, as actors, consciously selected specific impression management strategies to create desirable images for their audiences within the constraints set by their firms (Rao *et al.*, 1995).

Gardner and Martinko (1988) argued that four aspects are crucial to the impression management process, which are (1) the motivation for managing the impression of oneself, (2) the construction of the impression, (3) the audience or target to whom the impression is addressed, and (4) the organisational context in which impression management is performed. (1) The impression motivation describes why actors attempt to control the impressions of their audiences and involves the goals people seek, the value of these goals and the discrepancy between current and sought images (Leary and Kowalski, 1990). (2) The impression construction focuses on the strategies used to create the desired impression by altering the audiences' perceptions (Rao *et al.*, 1995). (3) In the process of impression management, the relative attractiveness, status, power and familiarity of the audience are typically considered by actors (Gardner and Martinko, 1988). (4) The organisational context factors include the opportunity for impression management, the existence of formal rules and procedures, task and role ambiguity, and the scope for novelty in the firm (Gardner and Martinko, 1988).

3.4.2 Impression management theory and its application at the organisational level

Impression management theory has been applied at both the individual level and the organisational level. Under this theory, any individual or organisation must establish and maintain impressions that are congruent with the perceptions they want to convey to the public (Goffman, 1959). Impression management theorists suggest that a primary motive for such behaviour, both inside and outside of organisations, is to be viewed by others favourably and to avoid being viewed unfavourably (Rosenfeld *et al.*, 1995).

Schlenker (1980) indicated two main motives that individuals engage in impression management: one is 'instrumental', where people want to influence others and gain rewards; and the second is 'expressive', where people construct an image of themselves to claim personal identity and present themselves in a manner that is consistent with that image. The motivation to manage impressions is likely to be influenced by certain factors, for example the goal relevance of impressions, the value of image enhancement, and the discrepancy between current and desired images (Leary and Kowalski, 1990). Individuals are more motivated to manage impressions when they view such impressions as instrumental in achieving their goals (Leary and Kowalski, 1990) and the value of achieving the goal images is salient. An implication of this dichotomy is that an 'instrumental' motive has a manipulative connotation in impression management and an 'expressive' motive has an honest connotation in impression management. This dichotomy highlights the two broad pathways, and the choice of the two by a given actor is dependent upon the level of intrinsic morality of the actor. For instance, how does one distinguish strategically moral action from intrinsically moral action? According to Frank (1988), reputable actors are likely to convey honest intentions more sincerely than others. For firms, reputation will be the most important means of conveying intrinsic honesty as their conducts are likely to contribute to greater competitive advantage.

To accomplish the goal, individuals and organisations use a variety of impression management strategies – specific behaviours designed to create a desired image (Bolino *et al.*, 2008). Impression management theorists have identified many tactics that individuals may employ in organisational settings (Schlenker, 1980; Jones and Pittman, 1982; Tedeschi and Melburg, 1984). According to Schlenker (1980), impression management tactics include two main categories: acquisitive (or proactive) and protective (or reactive). The most interesting acquisitive tactics are acclaiming tactics, comprising of enhancements and entitlements, which are adopted to explain a desirable event in a way that maximises their desirable implications for the actor (Schlenker, 1980). In contrast to acclaiming tactics are accounting tactics, including excuses and apologies, which are a form of remedial tactics aimed at offering the audience an explanation of, or an apology for, a predicament with the actor's attempts to minimise the negative repercussions of the predicament (Schlenker, 1980). Both acquisitive (or proactive) and protective (or reactive) tactics can be used with the two main motives – instrumental and expressive, as Schlenker (1980) indicated.

Jones and Pittman (1982) reviewed the impression management tactics that individuals may employ in organisational settings and classified them into five categories: (1) ingratiation, whereby individuals seek to be viewed as likeable; (2) exemplification, whereby individuals seek to be seen as dedicated; (3) intimidation, whereby individuals seek to appear dangerous or threatening; (4) self-promotion, whereby individuals hope to be viewed as competent; and (5) supplication, whereby individuals seek to be seen as needy or in need of assistance. The literature indicates that some of these behavioural tactics seem to have more in common than others, for example, ingratiation, self-promotion, and exemplification are all tactics utilised by individuals attempting to make a positive impression on others (Turnley and Bolino, 2001). The superimposition of these tactics for firms must be conceptualised with empirical evidence only as some tactics employed by individuals may not be used by firms because firms are a collection of individuals, and they collectively act rather than individually act. For instance, it is unlikely that firms use intimidation tactics as such a tactic can be costly to firms if firms are taken to court under a legal framework that provides protection to consumers against unfair trade practices. Supplication may be useful for charitable organisations, but is unlikely to be utilised by a private profit making firm to gain stakeholder support. Conceptually, ingratiation, exemplification and self-promotion are tactics that firms can use for impression management, as firms like to be viewed as likeable, dedicated and competent. As Schlenker (1980) pointed out, whether firms use these tactics with instrumental or expressive motives depends on the level of corporate morality, and reputation can be a proxy for their sustained moral standards.

Just as individuals employ impression management to influence others' perceptions of them, organisational representatives and spokespersons also use impression management in an effort to influence the way that others view the organisation as whole (Bolino *et al.*, 2008). The most frequently referenced classification of organisational impression management tactics was developed by Mohamed *et al.* (1999). They suggested that organisational impression management tactics may be characterised, using a 2×2 matrix, as either direct or indirect and as either assertive or defensive (Mohamed *et al.*, 1999). Direct impression management tactics involve techniques for presenting information about the organisation's characteristics, abilities or accomplishments, and in contrast, indirect tactics seek to manage information about activities with which the organisation is associated (Mohamed *et al.*, 1999). Assertive tactics are proactive and attempt to improve the organisation's image in some particular way, and in contrast, defensive tactics are reactive and used in response to situations that threaten to damage the organisation in some way (Mohamed *et al.*, 1999).

In general, the number of studies on organisational impression management is relatively small (Bolino *et al.*, 2008). Reviewing the limited number of studies on impression management at an organisational level, Bolino *et al.* (2008) classified them into five streams – restoring legitimacy after controversies, preventing controversies, creating a specific image, the role of audience, and hedging defamation against existing image. First, some studies have examined how firms use impression management tactics reactively to restore legitimacy as a result of controversial or image-threatening events (Elsbach and Sutton, 1992; Elsbach, 1994). For instance, Elsbach and Sutton (1992) found that defensive impression management tactics could be used to shift attention away from illegitimate actions and toward socially desirable goals. A second stream of research has examined how firms use assertive or proactive impression management tactics in an attempt to prevent controversies or complaints (Elsbach *et al.*, 1998; Arndt and Bigelow, 2000). For example, Arndt and Bigelow (2000) examined how hospitals used proactive impression management tactics preceding a change in the organisational structure to increase the acceptance of the change. Third, some studies have investigated how firms use a variety of impression management tactics in an effort to create a specific image or to accomplish a specific goal (Bansal and Kistruck, 2006; Davidson *et al.*, 2004). For example, Bansal and Kistruck (2006) examined firms' websites to determine the effect of illustrative and demonstrative forms of impression management on observers' perceptions of the firm's commitment to the natural environment. Fourth, a few studies have focused on the importance of the audience as to the use of organisational impression management (Rindova and Fombrun, 1999; Carter, 2006). For instance, Carter (2006) found that firms selectively increase the use of impression management by directing most impression management attempts at their most visible stakeholders. Finally, there is limited research on issues like defamation, whereby firms use impression management in an attempt to harm the image of their competitors. For example, Mohamed and Gardner (2004) inductively developed a model of organisational defamation by studying the contents of defamation lawsuits.

3.4.3 The application of impression management theory in social and environmental disclosure literature and corporate reputation literature

It is acknowledged that it is easier to manage a firm's image through communication than through changing the firm's output, goals, or methods of operations (Neu *et al.*, 1998). The image-building communication can be used tactically to manage a firm's relationship with stakeholders to influence their perceptions. The tactics of communication can include 'echoing, enlisting and harmonising with other discourses' (Lehman and Tinker, 1987, p. 509; Neu *et al.*, 1998, p. 266). Prior research pointed out the importance of corporate communication as self-presentational devices (Elsbach, 1994; Hooghiemstra, 2000). As a kind of corporate communication media, annual reports that have been described as a means of communicating a particular corporate image (McKinstry, 1996; Preston *et al.*, 1996), can be regarded as an 'instrument of impression management' (Arndt and Bigelow, 2000, p. 501). Corporate managers have increasingly reported financial information to shareholders beyond the legal requirements in order to celebrate corporate achievements and present favourable images of the firm and thereby enhance the legitimacy with which corporate activities are viewed (Patten, 1992; Brown and Deegan, 1998; Neu *et al.*, 1998). Corporate disclosure is frequently informed by impression management (Neu and Wright, 1992), as is the disclosure of social and environmental issues (Gray *et al.*, 1995a; Mathews, 1997; Ogden and Clarke, 2005). As reviewed in the previous chapter, the social and environmental disclosure literature shows that corporate management has preferred to report 'good news' rather than to disclose 'bad news', implying that social and environmental disclosure was mainly self-laudatory (Hackston and Milne, 1996; Deegan and Gordon, 1996). In this regard, Elkington (1997, p. 171) commented that 'a large part of firms engaging in corporate social disclosure view their reports as public relations vehicles, designed to offer reassurance and to help with "feel-good" image building'. By use of social and environmental disclosure, firms provide information aimed at influencing stakeholders' perceptions and eventually society's perceptions about the firm. In such a way, the firm is then likely to be viewed as a 'responsible corporate citizen' whose actions justify its continued existence (Guthrie and Parker, 1989). Therefore, corporate social and environmental disclosure as a form of impression management can contribute to firms' images or reputations (Hooghiemstra, 2000).

Based on corporate communication and impression management perspectives, Hooghiemstra (2000) discussed the application of impression management strategies in Shell's social reporting. Consistent with the earlier findings that corporate social and environmental disclosure was self-laudatory (Hackston and Milne, 1996; Deegan and Gordon, 1996), it was found that the use of proactive acclaiming tactics (e.g. entitlements, enhancements) was more prominent than the use of reactive accounting tactics (e.g. excuses, justifications) in Shell's reports in order to build a positive image of a socially and environmentally aware firm (Hooghiemstra, 2000).

In the emerging corporate reputation literature, the theoretical underpinnings of organisational impression management have been proposed to view the formation of corporate reputation (Highhouse *et al.*, 2009). Firms, like people, are viewed as social actors with self-presentation goals (Whetten *et al.*, 2009) to gain approval and status from their relevant constituents (Highhouse *et al.*, 2009). Firms' struggling for both approval and status maps on to individual impression management strategies (Highhouse *et al.*, 2009), such as exemplification (i.e. convincing others that you are a good person) and self-promotion (i.e. convincing others that you deserve respect) (Jones and Pittman, 1982). A collective of relevant constituents' impressions on a firm constitutes its reputation (Fombrun, 1996; Barnett *et al.*, 2006), which necessitates a view of impression formation as a foundation for understanding corporate reputation (Highhouse *et al.*, 2009). Although individual impressions make up the collective reputation, the collective reputation is not viewed as more than the sum of individual impressions, but rather a shared impression: the resulting average of all individual impressions (Highhouse *et al.*, 2009).

Through reviewing the literature relating to the formation and foundation of corporate reputation, Highhouse *et al.* (2009) presented an illustrative model of the individual impression development process as applied to the formation of corporate reputation. In the illustrative model, environmental cues that are specific pieces of information about a firm (e.g. corporate CSR policy) signal certain images of the firm (e.g. CSR image) in the minds of constituents, and then images of the firm held by constituents can have an impact on their perceptions of the firm's respectability (i.e. regarded as having honour and integrity) and impressiveness (i.e. regarded as having prominence and prestige) (Highhouse *et al.*, 2009). These respectability and impressiveness dimensions are aligned with Rindova *et al.*'s (2005) view of reputation – a perceived quality and prominence.

3.5 Stakeholder theory

3.5.1 What is a stakeholder?

Freeman (1984, p. vi) defined a stakeholder as: 'any group or individual who can affect or is affected by the achievement of a firm's purpose'. The stakeholders of a firm include its shareholders, employees, customers, suppliers, creditors, government, environmentalists and special interest groups (Freeman, 1984).

By reviewing the historical roots of the stakeholder approach, Freeman (1983) categorised the development of the stakeholder concept into a corporate planning and business policy model and a CSR model of stakeholder management. The corporate planning and business policy model of the stakeholder concept emphasises developing the approval of corporate strategic decisions by groups (stakeholders) whose support is required for the firm to continue to exist; stakeholders in this model are comprised of customers, owners, suppliers and employees, who are not adversarial in nature (Freeman, 1983). The CSR model of the stakeholder concept extends the corporate planning model to include external influences on the firm that may present adversarial positions, and such adversarial groups are characterised as regulatory or special interest groups concerned with social issues (Freeman, 1983).

After Freeman (1983, 1984), Clarkson (1995) made continuing efforts to define stakeholders. As Clarkson (1995, p. 106) argued,

> stakeholders are persons or groups that have, or claim, ownership, rights, or interests in a firm and its activities, past, present, or future. Such claimed rights or interests are the result of transactions with, or actions taken by, the firm, and may be legal or moral, individual or collective. Stakeholders with similar interests, claims, or rights can be classified as belonging to the same group: employees, shareholders, customers, and so on.

Clarkson (1995) also dichotomised stakeholders into categories as primary and secondary. A primary stakeholder group was defined by Clarkson (1995, p. 106) as 'one without whose continuing participation the firm cannot survive as a going concern'. Primary stakeholder groups typically include shareholders, employees, customers and suppliers, together with what are defined as public groups: governments and communities (Clarkson, 1995). A high level of interdependence is expected between the firm and its primary stakeholder groups (Clarkson, 1995). Secondary stakeholder groups were defined by Clarkson (1995, p. 107) as 'those who influence or affect, or are influenced or affected by, the firm, but they are not engaged in transactions with the firm and are not essential for its survival'. According to Clarkson (1995), the media and a wide range of special interest groups are viewed as secondary stakeholders.

3.5.2 An overview of stakeholder theory

In the management literature, Freeman's (1984) work provided a solid and lasting foundation for many succeeding efforts to define and to construct stakeholder models, frameworks and theories (Clarkson, 1995). One of the essential premises of stakeholder theory is that it focuses on managerial decision-making (Jones and Wicks, 1999). An organisation's stakeholders have the power to influence managerial strategic decisions in the form of control over resources required for the organisation to continue to exist (Ullmann, 1985). Freeman (1984) justified consideration of stakeholders for their contribution to the strategic management of companies. Generally stakeholder theory has been approached from the point of view of business ethics, corporate financial performance, corporate governance and/or corporate social performance (Friedman and Miles, 2002).

Stakeholder theory has been presented and used in three different ways in its evolution: descriptive, instrumental and normative (Donaldson and Preston, 1995). According to Donaldson and Preston (1995), the descriptive aspect of stakeholder theory reflects and explains specific affairs of corporations and their stakeholders; the instrumental aspect of the theory makes a connection between stakeholder management and the achievement of various corporate performance goals; and the normative uses of the theory attempt to interpret the function of the corporation and offer moral or philosophical guidelines for the operation and management of corporations. All the three aspects of the theory are also found in the work of Freeman (Freeman, 1984, in Donaldson and Preston, 1995).

Turning to the accounting literature, Deegan (2000) argued that there is an ethical (or normative) branch as well as a managerial (or positive) branch of stakeholder theory. The ethical branch provides prescriptions in terms of how organisations should treat their stakeholders and this view focuses on the responsibilities of organisations, by contrast, the managerial branch of the theory focuses on the need to manage those particular stakeholder groups, who are deemed to be powerful by controlling the resources necessary to the organisation's operations (Ullmann, 1985; Deegan, 2002). According to Gray *et al.*

(1996), from the managerial perspective of stakeholder theory, the more important the stakeholder to the organisation, the more effort will be made in managing the relationship, with information being a major element that can be employed by organisations to indicate that they are conforming to the stakeholders' expectations.

3.5.3 The application of stakeholder theory in social and environmental disclosure studies and corporate reputation studies

The stakeholder perspective has also been widely applied in the social and environmental disclosure literature. A firm's stakeholders have the power to influence managerial strategic decisions in the form of control over the resources required for the firm's continued existence (Ullmann, 1985). To ensure its continued existence, a firm must seek and maintain the support of its stakeholders (Freeman, 1984). Corporate social and environmental disclosure is seen as part of the dialogue between the firm and its stakeholders (Gray *et al.*, 1995a).

Based on Freeman's work, Ullmann (1985) developed a conceptual model with three dimensions – stakeholder power, strategic posture and economic performance – and used the model to study CSR activities. Ullmann (1985) concluded that the stakeholder approach provides an appropriate justification for incorporating strategic decision-making into studies of CSR activities. Following this study, Roberts (1992) empirically tested Ullmann's (1985) framework by investigating the determinants of CSR disclosure. The results of this study showed that measures of stakeholder power, strategic posture and economic performance were significantly associated with corporate social disclosure, and provided support for the application of stakeholder perspective in corporate social disclosure research.

In recent years, the stakeholder approach has been employed by researchers to investigate a firm's stakeholder engagement in the social and environmental disclosure process and external stakeholder perceptions of corporate social and environmental disclosure (Unerman, 2007; Tilt, 2007). Unerman and Bennett (2004) employed Habermas' discourse ethics as a theoretical framework to investigate stakeholder engagement in practice through conducting an in-depth analysis of the use of an internet-based stakeholder dialogue mechanism employed by Shell – 'web forum', which is in the form of a bulletin board of social and environmental issues hosted on Shell's website. They found that this web-forum had not been utilised in practice by either Shell or many of its external stakeholders to engage in a debate about the social and environmental responsibilities and accountabilities of Shell. Although seldom used by stakeholders, they suggested that such internet stakeholder dialogue should be more widespread to establish greater transparency about firms' accountabilities towards society and environment.

To understand why stakeholder engagement is a crucial factor of social and environmental disclosure, Deegan and Unerman (2006) developed a staged hierarchical model of the social and environmental disclosure process. Deegan and

Unerman (2006, p. 311) argued that there are four broad hierarchical stages, expressed as 'why – who – for what – how', involved in the social and environmental disclosure process. The 'why' stage determines a firm's motivations for engaging in social and environmental disclosure; the 'who' stage identifies the stakeholders to whom a firm considers itself responsible and need to be addressed in the social and environmental disclosure process; the 'for what' stage is the stakeholder engagement and dialogue stage, where stakeholders' expectations are identified and prioritised; and the 'how' stage comprises the mechanisms and reports that a firm uses to address stakeholders' expectations.

Since reputation is assessed and controlled by multiple stakeholders in a shared institutional environment (Fombrun and Van Riel, 1997), the stakeholder perspective has been utilised to study corporate reputation (Walker, 2010). For example, Cable and Graham (2000) examined the determinants of job seekers' perceptions about firm's reputation using the stakeholder perspective, and found that some factors influencing job seekers' reputation perceptions were quite different from the factors that had been examined in previous research focusing primarily on executives. The findings suggested that stakeholders can differ in their perceptions about a firm's reputation as different factors influence their perceptions.

3.6 A joint consideration of legitimacy theory and stakeholder theory to investigate corporate social and environmental disclosure

3.6.1 Political economy theory and its implications for legitimacy theory and stakeholder theory

As mentioned above, legitimacy theory and stakeholder theory are two overlapping perspectives since the insights provided by them build on those that emanate from another theory – political economy theory (Benson, 1975). The 'political economy' theory has been defined by Gray *et al.* (1996, p. 47) as 'the social, political and economic framework within which human life takes place'. The essence of political economy theory is that society, politics and economics are inseparable and economic issues cannot be investigated in isolation from the political, social and institutional framework within which the economic activity takes place (Gray *et al.*, 1995a).

Political economy theory has two categories: bourgeois and classical. The distinction between them is crucial because classical political economy (also called Marxian political economy) places class interests, structural conflict and the role of state at the heart of its analysis; bourgeois political economy, however, largely ignores these elements and is inclined to perceive the world as pluralistic comprising social, economic, and political interest groups (Gray *et al.*, 1995a). In reality, political economy has become a code for Marxism (Abercrombie *et al.*, 1984), whereas, in its accounting applications, it is often used in its bourgeois formulation (Arnold, 1990). For instance, as Guthrie and Parker

(1990, p. 166) state, 'the political economy perspective perceives accounting reports as social, political, and economic documents' and 'disclosures have the capability to transmit social, political, and economic meanings for a pluralistic set of report recipients'.

Under the bourgeois political economy framework, there are two theories that can be seen more clearly in its context: stakeholder theory and legitimacy theory (Gray *et al.*, 1995a). Consistent with the political economy theory that firms are part of a broader social system, legitimacy theory often emphasises 'society' and compliance with the expectations of society and indicates that firms exist to the extent that the particular society considers that they are legitimate (Deegan, 2002). Also consistent with the political economy theory recognising various groups within society, stakeholder theory explicitly accepts that different groups have different views about how a firm should operate and have different levels of power or ability to affect a firm's operation (Deegan, 2002). Consequently, both legitimacy theory and stakeholder theory are linked to the political economy theory.

3.6.2 The overlapping and differences between legitimacy theory and stakeholder theory

The overlap between legitimacy theory and stakeholder theory has been found in several social and environmental disclosure studies. For instance, when some researchers who embrace legitimacy theory, such as Lindblom (1993) and Neu *et al.* (1998), discuss the concerns of relevant publics, they change the focus from 'society' to particular groups therein, and indeed borrow insights from stakeholder theory (Deegan, 2002).

Although, both legitimacy theory and stakeholder theory build on those insights from political economy theory, they may offer explanations with different focuses. Stakeholder theory is typically bourgeois in that it focuses on the economic motivations, whereas legitimacy theory, which does reflect a bourgeois perspective but goes beyond a simple bourgeois view and is inclined to be classical to some extent, focuses primarily on the social motivations of corporate behaviours (Gray *et al.*, 1995a).

As discussed above, when legitimacy theory and stakeholder theory have a shared objective to explain corporate activities, legitimacy theory emphasises the expectations of 'society' in general – that is, the average expectations of all stakeholder groups in a society; stakeholder theory, however, recognises the different expectations of different stakeholder groups. Because there is a deal of overlap between legitimacy theory and stakeholder theory, and because they can provide different and useful points of view, it is possible and necessary to join them to provide more insightful explanations for particular corporate activities.

In this study, legitimacy theory is employed from the report preparers' perspectives to explain why a firm makes social and environmental disclosure, and stakeholder theory is employed from the users' perspectives to investigate how the firm pays attention to those specific and identifiable stakeholder groups in the process of corporate social and environmental disclosure practice.

3.7 A joint consideration of impression management theory, stakeholder theory and legitimacy theory to study corporate reputation

As emerges from the preceding discussion, since reputation relates to the shared stakeholder impressions of a firm (Fombrun, 1996; Fombrun and Van Riel, 1997; Highhouse *et al.*, 2009), the building of a firm's reputation may prompt the firm to engage in impression management to gain favourable impressions from the stakeholders. The emergence of CSR as an area of scholarship has placed corporate reputation as one of the central links between CSR and competitive advantage (McGuire *et al.*, 1988). In this regard, reputation is a product of a firm's attention to environmental, social justice and ethical concerns (Highhouse *et al.*, 2009). From the theoretical underpinning of impression management, the CSR report as part of the dialogue between the firm and its stakeholders (Gray *et al.*, 1995a) can be used as an instrument of impression management (Arndt and Bigelow, 2000) to contribute to the firm's reputation (Hooghiemstra, 2000). According to Highhouse *et al.*'s (2009) illustrative model of impression formation, the CSR report with the information showing corporate efforts toward behaving responsibly and ethically to their stakeholders signals a socially responsible image in the minds of stakeholders, and then such an image of the firm held by stakeholders positively contributes to these individual perceptions of the firm's reputation. As Fombrun and Shanley (1990) concluded, most important to a firm's reputation building are the cues that signal financial performance, conformity to social norms, and strategic management. Further, impression management can enhance a firm's reputation by increasing the firm's positive visibility and distinctiveness (Fombrun, 1996). For a firm, publishing a CSR report as an instrument of impression management increases its visibility and distinctiveness in the eyes of stakeholders.

From the perspective of stakeholder theory, publishing a CSR report is assumed to be responsibility-driven, which implies that people in society have a right to be informed about certain facets of a firm's operation (Deegan, 2009). On the other hand, how a firm is governed is a means for the firm to manage its relationships with particular stakeholders (MacMillan *et al.*, 2004) toward desirable images of the firm in the eyes of those stakeholders.

In the accounting literature, legitimacy and reputation are sometimes used interchangeably (Chalmers and Godfrey, 2004). Both concepts are social constructions with stakeholders assessing firms, both are linked with similar characteristics, such as firm size and financial performance, and both create an improved ability to obtain resources (Deephouse and Carter, 2005). Legitimacy relies on 'meeting and adhering to the expectations of social system's norms, rules and meanings', however reputation relates to 'a comparison of firms to determine their relative standing' (Deephouse and Carter, 2005, p. 331). Legitimacy informs firms' reputation-seeking activities, meeting and adhering to social systems' norms, rules, and meanings, and corporate characteristics are an important dimension in this regard (King and Whetten, 2008). Therefore, corporate characteristics (e.g. firm size, industry and financial performance) can play legitimating roles in the process of reputation-seeking.

In this study, impression management theory is used to investigate the effect of publishing a CSR report on the formation of a corporate socially responsible reputation. Stakeholder theory helps to understand the roles of the governance towards the stakeholders who control the resources necessary to firms' operations or are involved in the assessment of firms' reputations, in the process of reputation-building. Legitimacy theory helps to understand the legitimating roles of corporate characteristics played in the process of reputation-building.

3.8 The application of the theoretical framework in the Chinese context

3.8.1 Introduction

Legitimacy theory, stakeholder theory and impression management theory have been applied to investigate corporate social and environmental disclosure practices in developed countries. Can these western-developed theoretical perspectives be used to explain the social and environmental disclosure practices of Chinese listed firms? To answer this question, it is very important to understand the Chinese context in which firms function – (1) the reform of the economic system, (2) the traditional culture, and (3) the social change in China. The rapid economic growth and governmental efforts toward sustainable development have been generally discussed in the introductory chapter. The internal social, political, economic and cultural context for developing and studying corporate social and environmental disclosure practices in China will be analysed in-depth in the following sections.

3.8.2 The reform of the economic system in China

In general, the development of Chinese economy can be divided into two stages by the reform of economic system. The first stage started from 1949, the foundation of the People's Republic of China, up to the end of the 1970s, before the economic system reform. In this period, the Chinese economy was mainly an agricultural economy, characterised by the planned development controlled by the government. At that time, the key tasks were to develop heavy industry, which was viewed as the base of national economy, and to carry out land reform for Chinese peasants to own lands and work for themselves. In this stage, most Chinese enterprises were 100 per cent state-owned under the planned economy. Enterprises' operation and production had to be carried out in accordance with governmental planning and the government was the only external user of enterprises' performance information. There was no need for enterprises to consider social and environmental issues incidental to their production.

The second stage started at the end of the 1970s, the beginning of economic reform. During this period, the Chinese economy changed from an agricultural to a more industrialised one. Based on the strategy of economic reform and openness to the world initiated by Chairman Deng Xiaoping, a socialist market economy system was established. Although the government has kept predominant ownership of large enterprises and control of some crucial industries (e.g. energy, transportation and financial services), there has been the emergence of private ownership accompanied by the reform of the economic system and the transition to market economy. Especially the privatisation of SOEs since the mid-1990s has led to an increase in the private economy. Joint ventures with Chinese enterprises have been allowed for foreign participation. The occurrence of private ownership, securities markets and a modernised accounting profession in China calls for internationally acceptable disclosure practices by Chinese enterprises (Taylor and Shan, 2007). The modernised corporate system as a substitute for the former SOE system and the development of securities markets have helped to facilitate China's economic expansion. The economic expansion has been coincident with growing public concerns and governmental supervisions about social and environmental issues incidental to economic growth. Simultaneously, multinational firms and foreign economic participation have brought western CSR into the Chinese market. Chinese firms have passively begun to accept western standards, regulations and codes of conduct relating to CSR, to consider relevant stakeholders' concerns (e.g. working conditions, health and safety issues) when maximising their profits, because their foreign purchasers require them to do so (Wang and Juslin, 2009). As Chinese firms went through this transition, ideas such as stakeholder engagement for the purpose of fulfilling CSR can help them to better understand how to meet new political, economic and cultural expectations when they access new foreign markets (Zhou, 2006).

3.8.3 The traditional culture of CSR in China

Although the term CSR originated from the West, the core principles of CSR can be shown in China for a long history. The traditional culture of the responsible business can be traced back more than 2,500 years ago to Confucianism (Wang and Juslin, 2009). The Confucian virtues, such as 'righteousness – yi' and 'sincerity – xin', strongly influenced Chinese ancient merchants, who pursued profits with integrity and commitment to the community's prosperity (Huang, 2008). The meaning of 'yi' implies that businesses should consider a broad range of stakeholders who may affect or be affected by their operations. The Confucian family values of leaving the best for their children have been known to play a role in protecting the environment (Rowe, 2007). Looking back on the history of China, the Chinese community was strongly affected by the Confucian values, which resonated with western CSR. Chinese businesses constantly followed and developed Confucian virtues to legitimise their existence by achieving the community's expectations. However, Confucianism was seriously denounced during the Cultural Revolution[1] period (1966–1976) (Laurence *et al.*, 1995; Pang *et al.*, 1998). The traditional culture of the responsible business was replaced by the obligatory responsibilities that were authorised by the government under the planned economy (Wang and Juslin, 2009). Further, during the reform of the economic system prior to the mid-1990s, CSR was absent and the only target for Chinese enterprises was to maximise profits. This situation did not change until the entrance of western CSR into the Chinese market. Recovering and developing business ethics have been urgently needed by current enterprises in China.

3.8.4 Social change in China

Chinese society has experienced large changes since the foundation of the country. Considerable progress has been made in improving social conditions (e.g. education, health and social security) by the implementation of a series of policies and measures established by the government. Environmental education has been provided to citizens so as to enhance the whole nation's awareness of the environment, specifically including: widely undertaking environmental publication work, gradually popularising environmental education in secondary and primary school, developing vocational education in environmental protection and training specialised personnel in environmental science and technology as well as environmental administration (Information Office of the State Council, 2006). The public and media concerns on CSR are increasing with the reform and openness. A milestone in the development of CSR in China is the proposed overall national strategic goal 'constructing a harmonious society', which has Confucian roots and demonstrates the localisation of CSR in China (Wang and Juslin, 2009).

3.8.5 The application of western-developed theories in the Chinese context

Increasing the governmental role, public and media concerns, related laws, regulations and standards, and CSR requirements from the global market environment, are all effective drivers for making Chinese firms more publicly responsible to their various stakeholders. Accordingly, more and more Chinese firms have used social and environmental disclosure to communicate with stakeholders and to demonstrate their social legitimacy. Since the western CSR concept was introduced to Chinese society, Chinese academics have carried out comprehensive studies and worked on CSR extensions to China (CNTAC, 2006).

Overall, CSR disclosure and practices are not exotic. CSR is a term that can be legitimately interpreted within the Chinese social value system. Various interest groups concerned with CSR within Chinese society propel the development of corporate social and environmental disclosure practices in China. The Chinese culture and values of supporting CSR appear to resonate with western-developed legitimacy theory and stakeholder theory, which are used in this study to explain corporate social and environmental disclosure practices. Several studies on Chinese firms' social and environmental disclosure have discussed the application of legitimacy theory and stakeholder theory in the Chinese context (Taylor and Shan, 2007; Rowe, 2007; Liu and Anbumozhi, 2009).

Taylor and Shan (2007) examined what drives the social and environmental disclosure practices of Chinese firms listed on the Hong Kong Stock Exchange. They concluded that western-developed theories only partially explained the voluntary social and environmental disclosure practices of Chinese firms, and legitimacy theory was less effective than stakeholder theory as an explanation of the quantity and quality of corporate social and environmental disclosure in the Chinese context. Rowe (2007) explored the normative assumptions underpinning corporate environmental disclosure in China focusing on Shanghai through interviewing senior managers and executives from 15 enterprises operating in Shanghai. The findings of the study indicated that 33 per cent of participating enterprises that produced environmental disclosure in Shanghai appeared to be motivated by ideas associated with legitimacy theory and stakeholder theory. Liu and Anbumozhi (2009) examined the determinants influencing Chinese listed firms' environmental disclosure under a stakeholder theory framework. The findings of the study implied that stakeholder theory only partially explained corporate environmental disclosure in China. However, Liu and Anbumozhi acknowledged that the pressure from stakeholder groups continued to grow, implying the emergence of social contract between firms and stakeholders for disclosure.

Although the above studies have investigated the cross-cultural transferability of western-developed legitimacy and stakeholder theories in the context of China, the findings of these studies are inconclusive. Taylor and Shan's (2007) study focused on Chinese firms listed on the Hong Kong Stock Exchange, which has some different laws and regulations from mainland China. Rowe (2007) and Liu and Anbumozhi (2009) only focused on corporate environmental disclosure and failed to view the whole picture of social and environmental disclosure. Therefore, this study will further examine the application of legitimacy and stakeholder theories in explaining corporate social and environmental disclosure in the Chinese context.

In addition, it has been found that reputation is also a main driver for Chinese firms' social and environmental disclosure practices. Rowe (2007) found that 40 per cent of participating companies in her in-depth study identified reputation as a major incentive for corporate environmental disclosure. Taylor and Shan (2007) indicated that the disclosure of socially and environmentally responsible activities can convey the image of a well-managed and responsible firm. They also supported that charitable donations in China occur in a culture that emphasises 'face', and in this culture rich enterprises 'buy' prestige by assisting their poor (Acs and Dana, 2001). Therefore, reputation can be viewed as an incentive for corporate socially and environmentally responsible activities and their disclosure in China. However, the above studies did not employ a theory to examine the relationship between corporate social and environmental disclosure and corporate reputation in the Chinese context. As emerges from the preceding discussion, impression management theory can be used to explain how firms provide social and environmental disclosure to convey socially responsible images to their stakeholders and then to influence the stakeholders' assessment on their reputation. Accordingly, this study will employ impression management theory to examine the effect of firms' publication of a CSR report (and also the quality of the CSR report) on their socially responsible reputation in the Chinese context.

3.9 Research hypotheses

3.9.1 Hypotheses to study the determinants of corporate social and environmental disclosure

Based on a joint consideration of legitimacy and stakeholder theories, the second empirical stage of this study will examine the influence of various stakeholders' power (i.e. government, shareholder, creditor and auditor) on the social and environmental disclosure of socially responsible Chinese listed firms, as well as some corporate characteristics (i.e. firm size, profitability, industry and overseas listing) frequently examined in prior studies, or deemed to influence corporate social and environmental disclosure in the context of China (reviewed below). As embraced by previous studies, legitimacy theory suggests that a firm's motivation to disclose social and environmental information will be positively related to public concern over these issues (Deegan, 2002). The extent of the likelihood that firms are subject to public scrutiny may be influenced by some corporate characteristics, such as firm size and industry (Patten, 1991; Neu *et al.*, 1998). When changing the focus from the concern of the public to particular groups within the society, stakeholder theory provides powerful insights into firms' social and environmental disclosure. Neu *et al.* (1998) found support for the view that particular stakeholder groups can be more influential than others in demanding social and environmental disclosure, such as financial stakeholders and government regulators. Specifically, the following hypotheses are proposed to represent various constructs under the two theoretical underpinnings as operational variables for empirical testing, which are schematically summarised in Figure 3.2.

3.9.1.1 Stakeholders' power

GOVERNMENT

The stakeholder perspective proposed by Freeman (1984) recognises the ability of the government to influence corporate strategy and performance via regulations. Roberts (1992) provided empirical evidence to support Freeman's (1984) perspective. In a Chinese study, Liu and Anbumozhi (2009) found that the Chinese government had positive and significant influence on corporate environmental disclosure. In China, in early 2008 the State-owned Assets Supervision and Administration Commission of the State Council (SASAC) issued recommendations to guide the social responsibility activities of the central SOEs (SASAC, 2008). As a result, CSR disclosure was used as a strategic tool for central SOEs to satisfy government demands. Thus, it is expected that the higher the level of perceived government influence on corporate activities, the greater the effort by management to meet the requirements of government. For this reason, it is hypothesised that:

H1.1: There is a positive association between government power and corporate social and environmental disclosure.

SHAREHOLDERS

Shareholders are expected to have important effects on corporate social and environmental disclosure. Keim (1978) stated that as the distribution of ownership of a firm becomes less concentrated, the demands placed on the firm by shareholders become broader. The less concentrated ownership encourages the management to disclose more relevant information to meet various shareholders' demands. Disperse corporate ownership, especially by investors concerned with CSR activities, increases pressure for management to disclose social responsibility information (Ullmann, 1985). Previous studies have examined the effects of shareholders on corporate social and environmental disclosure (Roberts, 1992; Choi, 1999), and similar to previous studies, it is hypothesised that:

H1.2: There is a negative association between concentrated ownership and corporate social and environmental disclosure.

CREDITORS

Creditors control access to financial resources that may be essential for the continuing operation of a firm, and thus creditors are important stakeholders whose influences should be managed. Roberts (1992) argued that the greater the degree to which a firm relies on debt financing, the greater the degree to which corporate management would be expected to respond to creditor expectations concerning the firm's role in socially responsible activities. Some empirical evidence on the creditor influence and disclosure relationship is, however, contradictory (Cormier and Magnan, 1999, 2003). A negative association between financial leverage and disclosure could be explained by arguing that only firms that are financially sound (low leverage) may be able to trade off the benefits from additional disclosure with the proprietary costs of revealing potentially damaging information with respect to their social and environmental performance (Cormier and Magnan, 2003). It seems that firms with low leverage are more likely to engage in corporate social and environmental disclosure as a precautionary measure to ensure proper assessment of their financial risk by market participants. Considering the mixed findings from prior studies, this study will re-examine the effects of creditors on corporate social and environmental disclosure to identify whether a positive or a negative relationship exists between creditor power and corporate social and environmental disclosure, and it is hypothesised without a directional form. Therefore, it is hypothesised that:

> *H1.3: There is an association between corporate financial leverage and corporate social and environmental disclosure.*

AUDITORS

Auditors play an important role in assisting their clients with initiating new accounting practices (e.g. social responsibility accounting). For fair and impartial audit opinions, the auditor's independence is crucial. If we say larger audit firms such as the Big Four are relatively more independent (DeAngelo, 1981), it could be argued that larger audit firms are less likely to be affected by their client firms and therefore they are in a position to exercise more discretion over the accounting practices of their client firms (Choi, 1999). Further, larger audit firms have greater expertise and experience to influence companies to disclose additional information (Wallace *et al.*, 1994). Craswell and Taylor (1992) found a positive association between auditor and voluntary reserve disclosure in the Australian oil and gas industry. In a Malaysian study, Ahmad *et al.* (2003) also found that firms audited by the (then) Big Five auditors disclosed more environmental information in their annual reports. To test the relationship between the auditor and corporate social and environmental disclosure, this research proposes the following hypothesis:

> *H1.4: There is a positive association between financial audits by the Big Four and corporate social and environmental disclosure.*

3.9.1.2 Corporate characteristics

FIRM SIZE

Legitimacy theory literature suggests that larger firms are more likely to be subject to public scrutiny and therefore will disclose more information to obtain public support for their continuing existence (Cormier and Gordon, 2001). In addition, larger firms have more shareholders who may be interested in corporate social activities and are more likely to use disclosure to communicate the results of corporate social endeavours (Cowen *et al.*, 1987). Firm size has been found to be a strong indicator for influencing corporate social and environmental disclosure in previous studies (Hackston and Milne, 1996; Choi, 1999; Cormier and Gordon, 2001). Therefore, this research proposes the following hypothesis:

> *H1.5: There is a positive association between firm size and corporate social and environmental disclosure.*

FINANCIAL PERFORMANCE

As Ullmann (1985) argued, economic performance can influence corporate financial capability to undertake costly programmes related to social demands. High profitability increases corporate credibility in the market and thus a firm with good financial performance disclosing more information will be expected to have the means to better resist stakeholders' pressures and more quickly resolve social and environmental problems (Cormier and Magnan, 1999). Prior studies support a positive association between corporate financial performance and corporate social and environmental disclosure (Bowman and Haire, 1976; Roberts, 1992). Therefore, it is hypothesised that:

> *H1.6: There is a positive association between corporate profitability and corporate social and environmental disclosure.*

INDUSTRY

The public pressure perspective of legitimacy theory suggests that industry, like firm size, influences political visibility and may drive disclosure as firms seek to avoid undue pressure and criticism from social activists (Patten, 1991). Different industries have different characteristics, which may relate to the intensity of competition, consumer visibility and regulatory risk (Roberts, 1992). These may provide the reasons why the level and type of corporate social and environmental disclosure are industry-specific. For example, Dierkes and Preston (1977) found that extractive industries are more likely to disclose information about their environmental impacts than are firms in other industries. Prior empirical studies

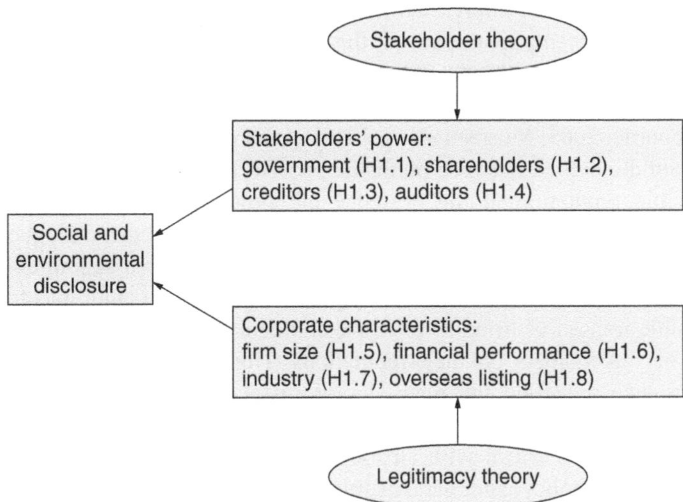

Figure 3.2 The relationship between social and environmental disclosure and various determinants.

have found a positive association between industry classifications and corporate social and environmental disclosure (Roberts, 1992; Hackston and Milne, 1996). As Roberts (1992) suggested, firms in high-profile industries (i.e. high consumer visibility, high regulatory risk, or concentrated intense competition) are expected to have higher levels of social responsibility disclosure. Of course, such industry classifications are, to an extent, subjective and ad hoc (Hackston and Milne, 1996). In this research, it is hypothesised that:

> *H1.7: There is a positive association between industry classification and corporate social and environmental disclosure.*

OVERSEAS LISTING

Firms whose shares are cross-listed on other developed stock markets may face additional social and environmental regulations and disclosure requirements (Gray *et al.*, 1995a; Hackston and Milne, 1996). Consequently, firms with overseas listings are expected to disclose more social and environmental information to the public for legitimising their operations (Hackston and Milne, 1996). To test this, the following hypothesis is proposed:

> *H1.8: There is a positive association between overseas listing and corporate social and environmental disclosure.*

3.9.2 Hypotheses to study corporate reputation

Based on a joint framework of impression management, stakeholder and legitimacy theories, the third empirical part of this study will examine the link between publishing a CSR report and a corporate socially responsible reputation. As reviewed in the literature chapter, good governance also facilitates corporate reputation (Radbourne, 2003; Musteen *et al.*, 2010). Accordingly, this part of the research will examine the link between publishing a CSR report and a corporate socially responsible reputation in the presence of corporate governance. As emerges from the preceding discussion, CSR reports as part of the dialogue between firms and their stakeholders (Gray *et al.*, 1995a) can be used as impression management instruments (Arndt and Bigelow, 2000) to communicate socially responsible images of firms to their stakeholders and then to influence the assessment of stakeholders on their reputations (Highhouse *et al.*, 2009). Corporate governance reflecting the internal performance of the board (Radbourne, 2003) might influence the assessment of its performance by diverse stakeholders. The board of a firm with attributes of good governance is more likely to adopt a CSR policy and demonstrate its social and environmental responsibility to relevant stakeholders through CSR reporting, which in turn leads to the enhancement of corporate reputation. CSR reports as well as corporate governance are means to manage relationships with particular stakeholders

(MacMillan *et al.*, 2004) for the purpose of influencing their perceptions on corporate reputation. Therefore, corporate reputation is expected to be a major driving force for firms to operate within a framework of good governance and demonstrate their commitments to social responsibility through CSR reports. In this research, the publication of a CSR report and good governance (measured by board characteristics) are expected to have positive effects on the socially responsible reputation of a firm. Corporate characteristics (i.e. financial performance, firm size and industry) are expected to play legitimating roles in the firm's reputation-seeking process. Therefore, a corporate socially responsible reputation comprises three theoretical dimensions: arising through impression management (i.e. CSR reporting), arising through stakeholder engagement (i.e. governance activities), and arising through firms' legitimation (i.e. corporate characteristics). Specifically, the following hypotheses are proposed to represent various constructs under the theoretical underpinnings as operational variables for empirical testing, as summarised in Figure 3.3.

3.9.2.1 CSR report

Since reputation derives from an external collective assessment of firms (Fombrun and Van Riel, 1997), one way in which it can be created and managed is through the disclosure process (Toms, 2002). Reputation includes two fundamental dimensions of firms' effectiveness: an evaluation of firms' economic performance and an evaluation of firms' fulfilment of social responsibilities (Fombrun and Van Riel, 1997). Firms can use separate CSR reports as impression management instruments to demonstrate their fulfilments of social responsibility and to influence stakeholders' perceptions on their reputations. In this study, the first stage of the research (Chapter 5) found that separate CSR reports are the more valuable source of information on CSR than traditional annual reports. Empirical studies confirmed that stakeholders usually view CSR disclosure as important or useful (Harte *et al.*, 1991; Deegan and Rankin, 1997; Milne and Chan, 1998) and found a positive relationship between CSR disclosure and corporate reputation (Toms, 2002; Hasseldine *et al.*, 2005). Therefore, in this study, it is hypothesised that the publication of a separate CSR report (as a valuable source of CSR disclosure) has a positive effect on the socially responsible reputation of a firm.

> *H2.1: There is a positive association between publishing a separate CSR report and corporate socially responsible reputation.*

3.9.2.2 Corporate governance

Since corporate governance is often a matter for the board (MacMillan *et al.*, 2004), board characteristics are usually considered as important determinants of corporate governance in the literature (Brickley *et al.*, 1997; Haniffa and Cooke, 2002; Eng and Mak, 2003; Musteen *et al.*, 2010). The stakeholder theoretical perspective has been considered in corporate governance (focusing on board characteristics) literature (Wang and Dewhirst, 1992; Hillman *et al.*, 2001). According to the stakeholder perspective, a firm's objectives are to identify the various powerful stakeholders concerned, to balance the conflicting interests of all these stakeholder groups and manage them, and to enhance corporate social performance through the board of directors who represent the various stakeholder groups (Wang and Dewhirst, 1992). In this research, the impact of governance on the link between CSR reporting and corporate reputation will be examined in terms of various board characteristics, including CEO/chairman duality, board size, board ownership and board committees.

CEO/CHAIRMAN DUALITY

CEO/chairman duality means that both CEO and chairman positions are occupied by the same individual, in other words, that the CEO is also the chairman of the board. Fama and Jensen (1983) pointed out that CEO/chairman duality signals the absence of separation of decision control and decision management. When the CEO is also the chairman, the board's effectiveness in performing its governance function may be compromised due to the concentration of decision making and control power (Haniffa and Cooke, 2002), which is expected to have a negative effect on the quality of management and thereby corporate reputation. Duality is often equated with weak governance and has been criticised by investors and other stakeholders (Boyd, 1995). Separation of the two roles has been advocated as a way of providing essential checks and balances over managerial performance (Argenti, 1976). In addition, splitting the two positions is likely to enhance the external stakeholders' perceptions of a firm as being worthy of support (Suchman, 1995). Prior studies have found that stakeholders view firms that have a clear separation between the two positions as being more reputable (Musteen *et al.*, 2010; Mazzola *et al.*, 2006). In China, this issue has been considered by the Chinese Securities and Regulations Commission (CSRC) as sufficiently important to suggest that large listed firms should separate the roles of CEO and chairman (Xiao and Yuan, 2007). Therefore, the following hypothesis is proposed:

> *H2.2: There is a negative association between CEO/chairman duality and corporate socially responsible reputation.*

BOARD SIZE

Board size has been considered prominently in the corporate governance literature (Abeysekera, 2010; Dalton *et al.*, 1999). According to Pfeffer and Salancik (1978), members of corporate boards have been regarded as important links to critical resource providers. Larger boards are viewed as being more desirable as they can provide firms with more ways to connect with the external stakeholders controlling the resources necessary to the firms' operations (Musteen *et al.*, 2010). Moreover, larger boards are more likely to include directors with greater diversity in education and industry experience and this diversity allows the board members to provide management with high quality advice (Zahra and Pearce, 1989) and to influence boards' decisions on better serving stakeholders' needs (Hafsi and Turgut, 2012). This could then improve the firm's image and relationships with stakeholders. Some empirical management studies have found a larger board to be better in firm performance (Gales and Kesner, 1994; Dalton *et al.*, 1999). Musteen *et al.* (2010) have found that board size is positively associated with corporate reputation. Therefore, it is hypothesised that:

> *H2.3: There is a positive association between board size and corporate socially responsible reputation.*

BOARD OWNERSHIP

Bhagat *et al.* (1999) proposed board ownership as a new measure of corporate governance. It is plausible that board members with appropriate stock ownership will have the incentive to provide effective monitoring and oversight of important corporate decisions, and thus efforts to improve corporate governance should include a consideration of board ownership (Bhagat *et al.*, 1999). Grossman and Hart (1983) also pointed out that ownership by managers or directors may be used to induce them to act in a manner that is consistent with the interests of shareholders. Directors may also see CSR as desirable because improved relations with stakeholders have a positive long term effect (Hafsi and Turgut, 2012). Previous studies found a positive relationship between insider ownership by managers or directors and corporate performance (Kaplan, 1989; Cole and Mehran, 1998). In this study, it is expected that board ownership as a proxy for good governance will have a positive effect on corporate reputation. Therefore, it is hypothesised that:

> *H2.4: There is a positive association between board ownership and corporate socially responsible reputation.*

BOARD COMMITTEES

The board of a firm may wish to establish a number of committees to maximise board efficiency and effectiveness, and thereby to enhance the assessment of its performance by diverse stakeholders. Solomon and Palmiter (1994) stated that the role of board committees is becoming more and more critical in the United States, especially in public listed companies. In China, the CSRC has established regulations to assist listed firms to develop board committees that will improve their corporate governance (CSRC, 2002). In this study, the following hypothesis is proposed:

> *H2.5: There is a positive association between board committees and corporate socially responsible reputation.*

3.9.2.3 Corporate characteristics

FINANCIAL PERFORMANCE

As Bebbington *et al.* (2008) stated, financial performance is a major element of reputation rankings. Strong financial performance may predispose stakeholders to regard firms more favourably (Fombrun and Shanley, 1990). Firms with strong financial performance are more likely to communicate their legitimacy to the public and seek reputation as a competitive advantage. Prior studies on corporate reputation have indicated a strong positive relationship between corporate financial performance and reputation (McGuire *et al.*, 1988; Fombrun and Shanley, 1990; Musteen *et al.*, 2010). Therefore, it is hypothesised that:

> *H2.6: There is a positive association between corporate profitability and corporate socially responsible reputation.*

FIRM SIZE

Firm size provides a proxy for the degree of pressure and visibility. According to legitimacy theory, larger firms are more likely to be subject to public scrutiny (Fombrun and Shanley, 1990), and therefore more likely to seek legitimacy and then reputation. Firm size has been found to be a strong indicator for influencing corporate reputation in previous studies (Fombrun and Shanley, 1990; Hasseldine *et al.*, 2005; Musteen *et al.*, 2010). Thus, following previous research, the following hypothesis is proposed:

> *H2.7: There is a positive association between firm size and corporate socially responsible reputation.*

INDUSTRY

Similar to firm size, industry also influences political visibility, which drives firms to become more legitimate so as to avoid undue pressure. Different industries have different characteristics, which may relate to intensity of competition, consumer visibility and regulatory risk (Roberts, 1992). It has been found that firms in high-profile industries (i.e. high consumer visibility, high regulatory risk, or concentrated intense competition) have higher levels of CSR disclosure (Roberts, 1992; Hackston and Milne, 1996). Prior studies have controlled potential industry effects on corporate reputation (Toms, 2002; Hasseldine *et al.*, 2005; Musteen *et al.*, 2010). In this study, it is hypothesised that:

> *H2.8: There is a positive association between industry classification and corporate socially responsible reputation.*

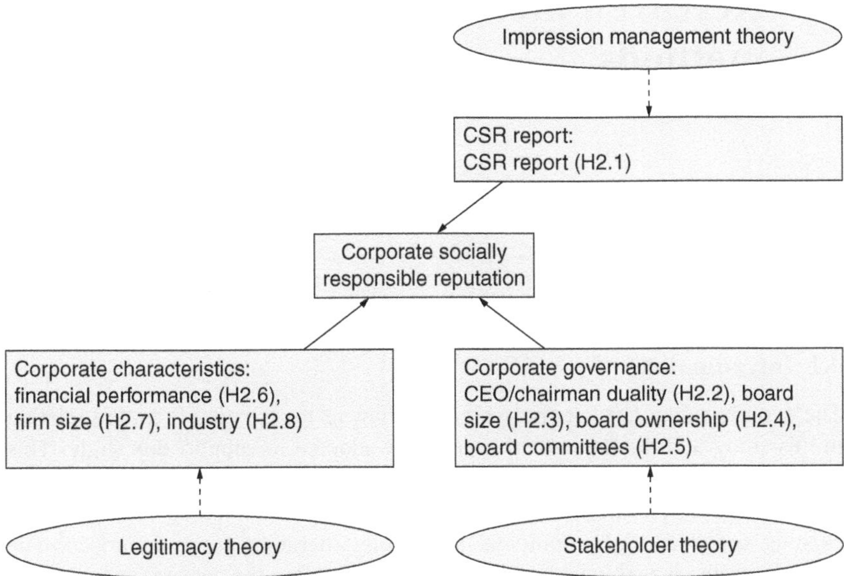

Figure 3.3 The relationship between corporate socially responsible reputation and publishing a CSR report.

3.10 Conclusions

This chapter has provided a theoretical discussion of legitimacy, impression management and stakeholder perspectives. Legitimacy theory and stakeholder theory have been presented to aid the understanding of corporate social and environmental disclosure practices in the Chinese context. The theoretical framework suggests that firms disclose social and environmental information in response to particular stakeholder expectations and general public pressures. Impression management theory, stakeholder theory, and legitimacy theory have been employed to investigate the link between Chinese listed firms' publication of a CSR report and their socially responsible reputation. The theoretical framework suggests that firms' publishing a CSR report that discloses social and environmental information to their stakeholders is symbolic for impression management and facilitates the formation of their socially responsible reputation. In this chapter, research hypotheses based on the theoretical framework have been developed. The research methods used to collect data and test hypotheses are one of the key parts of this study, which will be discussed in the following chapter.

Note

1 It was a socio-political movement that was initiated to further consolidate socialism and remove all capitalist elements from Chinese society.

4 Research methodology and methods

4.1 Introduction

The two preceding chapters presented a review of the existing literature relating to this study and the theoretical framework adopted to support this study. This chapter outlines the research methodology and methods that are applied in undertaking the research endeavours. The research methodologies used in the existing social and environmental accounting literature are summarised. The research methods that have been chosen to inquire into the research questions in this study and the justification of choosing them are discussed in this chapter.

The remainder of this chapter is organised as follows. Section 4.2 provides a discussion of the research methodology. Section 4.3 presents different research methods that can be used to conduct the research. Section 4.4 then summarises the methods used in the social and environmental accounting literature. Section 4.5 presents an outline of the research design for this study. The particular research methods adopted in the three stages of this study are discussed respectively in Sections 4.6, 4.7 and 4.8. Finally, conclusions are presented in Section 4.9.

4.2 Research methodology

4.2.1 Overview

Research methodology describes an approach to a research problem that can be put into practice in a research programme or process, which could be formally defined as an operational framework within which the facts are placed so that their meaning may be discerned clearly (Ryan *et al.* 1992). In brief, research methodology refers to the procedural framework within which the research is conducted. It is far more than the methods employed in a particular research and includes the rationale and the philosophical assumptions that underpin a particular research. A scientific research can be approached based on some philosophical assumptions and rationales relating to the underlying ontology and epistemology (Chua, 1986). The decision on the philosophical assumptions provides the direction for the design of all phases of any research (Creswell, 2008).

Hence, the primary step in defining the methodological framework of the research is to identify the philosophical positions. The two dimensions of research philosophy: ontology and epistemology will be discussed as follows.

4.2.2 Research philosophy

4.2.2.1 Ontology

Ontology is concerned with the very nature of reality. The central point of ontology concerns whether social entities exist in a reality external to social actors or are constructed from the perceptions and actions of social actors. The former position is referred to as objectivism and the latter is referred to as constructionism (Bryman, 2008). Both ways of seeing the world have devotees in most academic areas, but none of them is considered to be superior to the other (Saunders *et al.*, 2009).

Objectivism is the objective view of ontology and it holds that 'social phenomena and their meanings have an existence that is independent of social actors' (Bryman, 2008, p. 19). Take firms as an example, objectivists view firms as tangible objects with their own rules and regulations and firms exert pressure on individuals to conform to their requirements (Bryman, 2008).

Constructionism is the subjective view of ontology and it asserts that 'social phenomena and their meanings are continually being accomplished by social actors' (Bryman, 2008, p. 19). It implies that this is a continuous process, in that social phenomena are produced through social interaction and then they are in a constant state of construction and reconstruction. Instead of taking the view that firms are pre-existing, constructivists argue that firms and the social order are in a constant state of change and rules and regulations of firms are much less like commands and much more like general understandings (Strauss *et al.*, 1973).

4.2.2.2 Epistemology

Epistemology is referred to as the way of obtaining knowledge in a given nature of reality. It concerns what constitutes acceptable knowledge in a field of study and whether the social world can and should be studied scientifically as the natural science (Bryman, 2008). Since assuming that social entities exist external to social actors, the objective aspect of epistemology holds the position that social science researchers can take a philosophical stance as natural scientists and work with observations of social reality. It implies that the researcher is independent of and neither affects nor is affected by the subject of the study (Remenyi *et al.*, 1998). In contrast, the subjective aspect of epistemology argues that the social science researcher's knowledge and understanding of the world they observe are subjective and play an important role in the process of interpreting the social world (Blumberg *et al.*, 2005).

To sum up, ontological and epistemological positions concern what is commonly referred to as a researcher's worldview, which has significant influence on the perceived relative importance of the aspects of the social world. Questions of ontology and epistemology cannot be isolated from the conducting of social research. Researchers' ontological and epistemological positions can influence both the selection of different approaches to research and judgements about the value of outcomes. The different research approaches based on ontological and epistemological positions will be discussed in the following section.

4.2.3 Different approaches

4.2.3.1 Positivistic approach

Based on ontological and epistemological positions, there are three main approaches that can be applied to scientific research, i.e. positivistic, interpretive and critical (Neuman, 2006). Positivistic research generally assumes that reality is objectively given and can be described by measurable properties that are independent of the observer and his or her instruments (Myers, 2009). Positivism reflects the objective view of both ontology and epistemology. The positivistic approach is dominant in accounting literature (Chua, 1986), which is based on experiments, quantitative measurements and logical reasoning to search for ways to test theories of human behaviour (Neuman, 2006). The typically positivistic process begins with developing hypotheses and then measuring variables operationalised as proxies for constructs and finally statistically analysing the hypothesised relationship between variables. Positivists believe that it is possible to generalise from the specific sample to the wider population since a sample can be representative of the whole.

4.2.3.2 Alternative approaches

In contrast to the positivistic approach, the interpretive approach focuses on interpreting reality through the researcher's own knowledge, thoughts, feelings and motivations (Neuman, 2006). It is 'the systematic analysis of socially meaningful action through the direct detailed observation of people in natural settings in order to arrive at understandings and interpretations of how people create and maintain their social worlds' (Neuman, 2006, p. 88). Interpretivism reflects the subjective view of ontological and epistemological positions. Interpretivists believe that a simple assumption cannot be applied to each social phenomenon since social reality is produced and reconstructed by social actors. Accordingly, generalisation from a sample to the whole is less emphasised in interpretive research.

Another alternative, the critical approach assumes that social reality is historically constituted and focuses on fundamental conflicts in contemporary society and seeks to bring social justice (Chua, 1986). It defines social science as 'a critical process of inquiry that goes beyond surface illusions to uncover the real structures in the material world in order to help people change conditions and build a better world for themselves' (Neuman, 2006, p. 95). Interpretive and critical approaches take a subjective philosophical position that invariably introduces the researchers' own biases in analysing actors and structures situated in the social construction.

4.2.4 Summary

As emerges from the preceding discussion, different philosophical positions and different research approaches selected based on ontological and epistemological positions have been reviewed. The positivistic methodology believes there is an objective world waiting to be discovered and seeks for ways to test defined theories and hypotheses and is more concerned with generalising findings to a population. Researchers, who adopt an interpretive methodology, are more concerned with their understandings and interpretations of a given social phenomena but are less concerned with generalising their findings to a population. Although different methodological views exist, methodologies, like theories, cannot be true or false, only more or less useful (Silverman, 2009). Therefore, as Broadbent and Unerman (2011) argued, both positivist and interpretivist research are needed and both paradigms produce high-quality credible scholarly evidence.

4.3 Research methods

As discussed above, research methodology describes an approach to the research process as a whole, and to some extent, it provides the direction and guidance for the choices of research methods. Methods define the particular ways of collecting and analysing data in the research process. Typically, research can be conducted using quantitative or qualitative methods or a combination of both. Prior to the discussion of different research methods, it is necessary to understand the purpose of the research, which can affect the selection of research methods.

4.3.1 Purpose of research

In terms of general research purpose, there are three kinds of social research: exploratory, descriptive and explanatory (Singleton and Straits, 2005). Exploratory research relates to topics about which information is insufficient. Thus, the main purpose of exploratory research is to collect as much knowledge about a research issue as possible. Exploratory studies usually tend to be qualitative. Descriptive research is more of a 'fact-finding enterprise, focusing on relatively few dimensions of a well-defined entity' (Singleton and Straits, 2005, p. 68). It presents a picture of the specific details of a situation, social setting, or relationship (Neuman, 2006). Descriptive research can be either qualitative or quantitative in nature. Finally, explanatory research can not only describe phenomena, but also test relationships between elements of the research problem; it is typically designed to 'seek the answers to problems and hypotheses' (Singleton and

Straits, 2005, p. 69). Explanatory studies usually employ quantitative methods. In explanatory studies, multiple strategies are used. For example, in some explanatory studies, a novel explanation is developed and then empirical evidence is provided to support it or refute it (Neuman, 2006). Other explanatory studies may start with an existing explanation derived from theory or prior research and then extend it to explain a new issue or setting to see how well the explanation holds up or whether it needs modification or is limited to certain conditions (Neuman, 2006).

4.3.2 Quantitative and qualitative methods

Quantitative methods are means for testing objective theories by examining the relationship among variables that can be measured and then analysed using statistical procedures (Creswell, 2008). Quantitative research often describes a social phenomenon or explains why that phenomenon takes place and it is often guided by a positivist philosophical perspective. This research method employs 'hard' data in the form of numbers, relies more on positivist principles and uses a language of variables and hypotheses (Neuman, 2006). Quantitative research is associated with a deductive process from theories to observations (Bryman, 2008). In quantitative research, the associate research phrases are experimental, empirical and statistical; the sample may be large, random and even representative; and the data may be collected through inanimate instruments such as scales, surveys, questionnaires and database (Merriam, 1998). The results obtained from quantitative research tend to give a broadly generalisable set of findings.

In contrast, qualitative methods are means for understanding and interpreting the meaning of 'variables' that are harder to classify and quantify within the investigated area (Creswell, 2008). Qualitative research is often conducted to explore a new topic or describe a social phenomenon and it is often guided by an interpretivist philosophical perspective. Different from quantitative research, qualitative research method employs 'soft' data in the form of words, photos or symbols and relies more on interpretive or critical principles and uses a language of cases and contexts (Neuman, 2006). Qualitative research is associated with an inductive process from observations to theories (Bryman, 2008). In this research method, the associated research phrases are naturalistic, grounded and subjective; the sample may be small, non-random and theoretical; and the data may be collected by the researcher using interviews, observations and documents (Merriam, 1998). The results of qualitative research tend to give greater understanding of cases and situations.

4.3.3 Mixed methods

4.3.3.1 Justification for mixed methods

Quantitative and qualitative research methods represent different research strategies in terms of the nature and characteristics of research. This distinction is however, not hard and fast because studies that have a broad set of characteristics of one research strategy may also have a characteristic of the other (Bryman, 2008). From a technical perspective, many scholars argue that quantitative and qualitative methods can be combined within an overall research project (Mingers and Gill, 1997; Tashakkori and Teddlie, 2003; Creswell, 2008). They have complementary strengths: qualitative methods may help to understand the meaning of the results produced by quantitative methods and quantitative methods may help to offer precise expression to qualitative ideas. A mix of quantitative and qualitative methods, a mix of quantitative methods, or a mix of qualitative methods can be referred to as mixed methods research (Brannen, 2005).

Owing to the radical conflict in philosophical assumptions, quantitative/positivist and qualitative/interpretivist are viewed as two incompatible paradigms (Kuhn, 1970). The argument against mixed methods research tends to emphasise this point (Smith, 1983). However, advocates of mixed methods research argue that in practice research is driven by pragmatic assumptions as much as it is driven by philosophical assumptions (Bryman, 1984; Morgan, 2007). Sound methodological practice is to select a method appropriate to research question (Creswell, 2008). It seems that any research is likely to comprise a set of research questions, and different questions may be underpinned by different philosophical assumptions (Brannen, 2005). Therefore, the selection of research methods for research questions can be underpinned by both philosophical and pragmatic assumptions. The pragmatic approach advocated by some methodologists (Brannen, 2005; Morgan, 2007) tends to connect issues at the abstract level of epistemology and the technical level of actual methods with equal attention to both epistemology and methods, differing from the traditional paradigms privileging epistemology over methods. Another justification for mixing quantitative and/or qualitative methods is referred to as triangulation, which means that it is better to observe something from more than one angle. Applied to social research, it focuses on the complementarity and complexity added by mixing quantitative and/or qualitative styles of research and data (Neuman, 2006).

4.3.3.2 Ways of using mixed methods

Mixed methods research can be conducted in different ways. According to Creswell (2008), one way of using mixed methods is sequential. For example, the researcher may start with a qualitative method for exploratory purposes and follow up with a quantitative method for generalisation of results. Another way is to use the two methods concurrently. For example, the researcher collects quantitative and qualitative data at the same time in order to provide a comprehensive analysis of the research question. Bryman (2006) also summarised various ways of combining quantitative and qualitative research in practice. According to Bryman (2006), one way of using mixed methods is in the context of instrument development, where qualitative research is employed to develop questionnaire or scale items so that better wording or more comprehensive closed answers can be generated.

4.4 A summary of methods employed in the social and environmental accounting literature

4.4.1 Overview

According to Parker's (2005) review paper, the research methods employed in social and environmental accounting studies, published in the four leading interdisciplinary research journals (i.e. *Accounting, Auditing and Accountability Journal*, *Accounting Forum*, *Critical Perspectives on Accounting*, and *Accounting, Organizations and Society*) from 1988 to 2003, were classified into content analysis, case/field/interview study, survey, literature/theory/commentary, experimental and combined (see Figure 4.1). During this whole period, the dominant inquiry in published research was literature/theory/commentary; content analysis was second, with the relative weighting of content analysis, case/field/interview and survey being evenly balanced (Parker, 2005). Therefore, it is clear that theorising in social and environmental accounting needs a much closer engagement with practice (Adams, 2002).

O'Connor (2006) reviewed 240 social and environmental accounting empirical studies over the 1974–2006 period and summarised the research methods employed in these studies (see Figure 4.2). Among these studies, content analysis was dominant, over 48 per cent (117 out of 240), and the second most employed method was laboratory/model testing.

4.4.2 Studies on social and environmental disclosure practice

In the social and environmental accounting literature, the most prevalent topic of inquiry is corporate social and environmental disclosure (see Parker, 2005; O'Connor, 2006). Empirical studies in this area employed different research

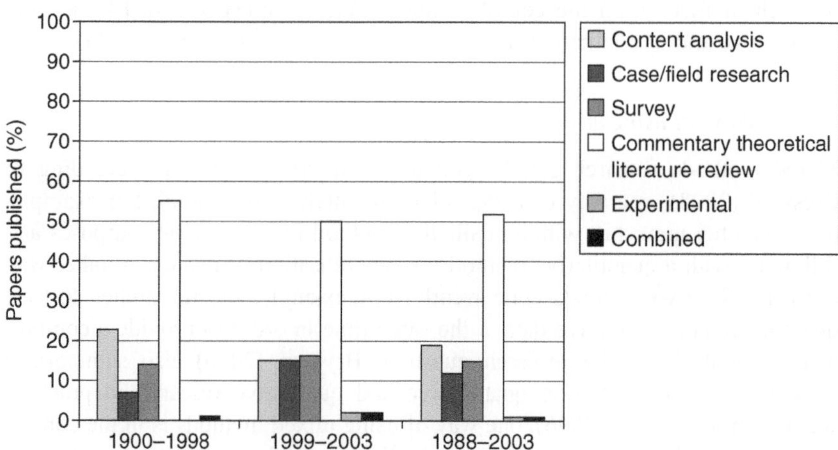

Figure 4.1 Methods in social and environmental accounting research (source: Parker, 2005, p. 854).

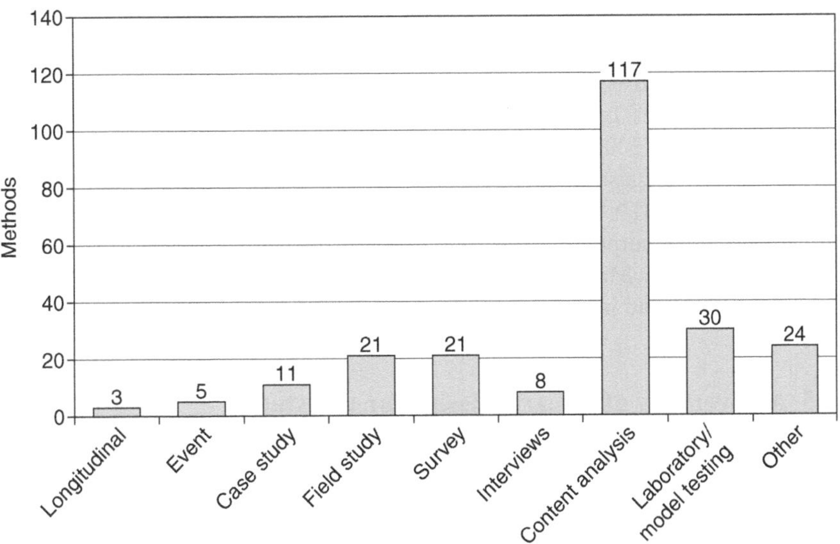

Figure 4.2 Methods in social and environmental accounting empirical research (source: O'Connor, 2006, p. 19).

methods, such as content analysis (Zeghal and Ahmed, 1990; Harte and Owen, 1991; Gray *et al.*, 1995a), survey (Deegan and Gordon, 1996; Wilmshurst and Frost, 2000; Newson and Deegan, 2002), case/interview study (Guthrie and Parker, 1989; Deegan *et al.*, 2002), event (Patten, 1992; Deegan *et al.*, 2000) and longitudinal study (Gray *et al.*, 1996; Campbell, 2004). Of these categories, content analysis was most widely used to assess a firm's social and environmental disclosure (Milne and Adler, 1999).

4.4.3 Studies on determinants of social and environmental disclosure

In the social and environmental accounting literature, the model-testing method was commonly employed to examine the relationship between corporate social and environmental disclosure and hypothesised influencing factors (Roberts, 1992; Hackston and Milne, 1996; Cormier and Magnan, 1999; Choi, 1999; Liu and Anbumozhi, 2009). The related statistical techniques used when testing hypotheses in this area included regression (Roberts, 1992; Hackston and Milne, 1996; Liu and Anbumozhi, 2009), t-test (Hackston and Milne, 1996; Cormier and Magnan, 1999; Choi, 1999), chi-square test (Choi, 1999; Cormier and Gordon, 2001), and ANOVA (Gao *et al.*, 2005). The measure of corporate social and environmental disclosure in these studies usually employed content analysis.

4.4.4 Studies on the relationship between social and environmental disclosure and corporate reputation

There are only a small number of studies that have examined the relationship between social and environmental disclosure and corporate reputation. Among the limited studies on this topic, the model-testing method was commonly employed (Toms, 2002; Hasseldine *et al.*, 2005). Other research methods such as case study were also found in the literature (Bebbington *et al.*, 2008). In addition, among the prior studies that examined the relationship between corporate governance and corporate reputation, various methods were used including model-testing (MacMillan *et al.*, 2004; Musteen *et al.*, 2010), survey (MacMillan *et al.*, 2004), and interviews (Radbourne, 2003; MacMillan *et al.*, 2004).

4.5 An overview of research design for this study

Research design serves as an action plan of a research that shows how the research is to be conducted. It describes how all the major parts of the research (e.g. samples, measures, programmes) work together in order to answer the research questions (Bryman and Bell, 2003). Making decisions about research design gives directions from the underlying philosophical assumptions to method selection and data collection. As discussed in the first chapter, this study attempts to conduct a research into Chinese listed firms' social and environmental disclosure practices. Specifically, the objectives of this study include analysing the current state of Chinese firms' social and environmental disclosure practices, empirically examining what influences the social and environmental disclosure of firms, and empirically testing the link between publishing a separate CSR report and corporate socially responsible reputation. Since this study attempts to describe the problem of social and environmental disclosure practices in China, to test the relationship between such disclosure and hypothesised factors influencing the disclosure, and to investigate the relationship between corporate socially responsible reputation and hypothesised factors, the research objectives of this study are both descriptive and explanatory. A positivistic framework is generally more appropriate for this study as it tests defined theories and hypotheses for answering research questions. Also based on the pragmatic assumption and triangulation purpose, this study uses mixed methods for data collection to approach the research questions from different points of view by using different data sources. For example, to analyse the current state of Chinese listed firms' social and environmental disclosure practices, this study not only collects disclosure data from corporate reports by using content analysis but also collects data about stakeholders' views on the preference of disclosure types by using a questionnaire survey and stakeholders' views on the importance of disclosure items via a stakeholder panel consultation.

This study involved three stages of inquiry. The first stage of the study analysed the current state of Chinese listed firms' social and environmental disclosure practices. In this stage, content analysis was used to collect sample firms' social and environmental disclosure data in their annual reports and CSR reports. The SEDI was constructed as the proxy for a sample firm's social and environmental disclosure. The disclosure index comprised three dimensions: the quantity measure, the quality measure relating to disclosure types and the quality measure relating to the disclosure items. A questionnaire survey method was used to collect stakeholders' perceptions on different disclosure types. This study identified five disclosure types from the literature (Toms, 2002; Clarkson *et al.*, 2008): (1) general narrative, (2) specific endeavours in non-quantitative terms, (3) quantified performance data, (4) quantified performance data relative to benchmarks, and (5) quantified performance data at the disaggregate level. A stakeholder panel consultation method was used to solicit stakeholders' opinions on the relative importance of 121 disclosure items identified from the GRI reporting framework. The SEDI in this study was a product of the three disclosure dimensions: disclosure quantity, disclosure type quality, disclosure item quality.

The second stage of the study examined the determinants influencing the sample firms' social and environmental disclosure. The research method used in this stage was statistical model testing. The SEDI constructed in the first stage was used here as a dependent variable to proxy stakeholder-relevant social and environmental disclosure. Finally, the third stage of the study examined the link between publishing a CSR report (predictor variable) and corporate socially responsible reputation (dependent variable). Similar to the second stage, a model-testing method was also used in this stage.

4.6 Research methods used for the first stage of research

This section describes the research methods used in the first stage of the research, involving content analysis to ascertain disclosure quantity, questionnaire survey to ascertain disclosure quality (based on disclosure types), and stakeholder panel consultation to ascertain disclosure quality (based on disclosure items).

4.6.1 Sample selection and data source

4.6.1.1 Sample selection

According to Gray *et al.* (1995b, p. 87), there are four ways of drawing a sample in the UK CSR literature: 'selection of the largest companies; selection of large, medium and unlisted companies; a broad selection of companies from *The Times 1000*; and a selection of "interesting" or "best practice" examples'. This stage of the study adopted the fourth approach – 'best practice' examples and comprised the 100 socially responsible firms identified by the *2008 Chinese Stock-listed Firms' Social Responsibility Ranking List*. This ranking list is initiated by *Southern Weekend* (one of China's most popular newspapers), and co-investigated by All-China Federation of Trade Unions, All-China Federation of Industry and Commerce, Peking University, Fudan University and Nankai University. It is the first CSR rating system in China and it was developed and is continually being improved by a group of experts and scholars from governments, industries, universities and research institutes. A full list of firms appearing on this ranking list is provided in Appendix 1. Based on prior studies (Roberts, 1992; Hackston and Milne, 1996), the firms from the ranking list, hereafter the sample firms, were further classified into two groups: high-profile industries (i.e. high consumer visibility, high regulatory risk, or concentrated intense competition) and low-profile industries. The sample firms, summarised and grouped according to industry sector, are presented in Table 4.1.

4.6.1.2 Data source

This stage of the study triangulated the data sources of the sample firms' social and environmental disclosure. First, the sample firms' annual reports and separately published CSR reports for the year 2008 were used in identifying corporate social and environmental disclosure. In early studies, the annual report was viewed as the principal means for corporate communication of operations to the public (Wiseman, 1982), and it has been the source for almost all previous social and environmental disclosure studies (Guthrie and Parker, 1989; Harte and Owen,

Table 4.1 Distribution of sample firms

Industry sector	*No. of firms*
High profile	
Metals and non-metallic	28
Banking and insurance	12
Extractive	10
Construction	7
Telecommunication	4
Electricity, gas and water production and supply	3
Transportation and warehousing	3
Oil, chemical and plastic	2
Food and beverage	2
Low profile	
Machinery, equipment and instrumentation	14
Electronics	4
Wholesale and retail trade	4
Information technology	3
Conglomerate	3
Real estate	1
Total	100

Note

The *Regulations of Environmental Inspection on Companies Assessing to or Refinancing on the Stock Market* (SEPA, 2003) stipulates that the following industries are pollution industries: metal, extractive, construction, electricity, oil and chemical, food and beverage. In China, the following industries are viewed with high consumer visibility: banking and insurance, telecommunication and transportation (Roberts, 1992; Hackston and Milne, 1996).

1991; Gray *et al.*, 1995a; Deegan and Gordon, 1996; Campbell, 2004). Further, the use of sources other than annual reports, such as stand-alone social and environmental reports, has also been found in the extant literature (Frost *et al.*, 2005; Clarkson *et al.*, 2008). Both annual reports and CSR reports were used in this study because it is likely that stakeholders consider all publicly available reports in decision-making (Van Staden and Hooks, 2007). Although firms may disclose social and environmental information in other media than annual reports and CSR reports (e.g. corporate websites), as Unerman *et al.* (2007, p. 203) suggested: 'for pragmatic reasons, it was necessary to place limits on the scope of documents analysed – if this were not done then the number of documents to be analysed for any single firm could have been overwhelming'. Therefore, in this study, annual reports and CSR reports were the only types of reporting media examined.

Second, empirical data were collected through a questionnaire survey to ascertain stakeholders' perceptions on the relative importance of different disclosure types. Third, empirical data were collected through a stakeholder panel consultation to ascertain stakeholders' perceptions on the relative importance of disclosure items. By doing so, this study provided insights into the sample firms' social and environmental disclosure, from the stakeholders' points of view rather than only from the researcher's point of view.

4.6.2 Content analysis

4.6.2.1 Overview

Content analysis is a method of codifying the text (or content) of a piece of writing into various groups (or categories) depending on defined criteria (Weber, 1990). Following coding, quantitative scales are derived to facilitate further analysis (Abeysekera, 2007; Milne and Adler, 1999). Content analysis is defined by Krippendorff (2004, p. 18) as 'a research technique for making replicable and valid inferences from texts to the contexts of their use'. According to Krippendorff's definition, the potential contribution of content analysis is that it can empower researchers to work over the text to make valid inferences about hidden or underlying meanings and messages of interest (Weber, 1990). In the social sciences, where meanings and interpretations are crucial to the understanding of social phenomena, content analysis has been commended as possibly one of the most important research techniques (Krippendorff, 2004). Content analysis involves codifying qualitative and quantitative information within the text into pre-defined categories, so the selection and development of analytical categories and units of analysis are essential elements of research design in content analysis.

4.6.2.2 Unit of analysis

When using content analysis, the selection of appropriate units of analysis when gathering data is an important aspect. The meaning of the content is first coded based on pre-defined criteria of disclosure, and then coded disclosure is counted. Hence, when conducting content analysis, two principal kinds of units need to be defined, separated and identified: coding units and measuring/counting units. The selection of units of analysis (i.e. coding units and measuring/counting units) is a matter of judgement. As Gray *et al.* (1995b) reported, there were some debates on this matter in the social and environmental disclosure literature. These debates on the units of analysis confused the issues of what should constitute the basis for coding the text and what should constitute the basis for measuring/counting the amount of disclosure (Milne and Adler, 1999). In other words, some authors failed to distinguish between the unit for coding the text and the unit for measuring/counting the amount of disclosure, but referred only to a single unit of analysis without explicit interpretation.

While the accounting literature's discussion was confused by the lack of clarity in the description of unitising approaches, one point was apparent: many different units were used by accounting researchers when analysing the content of annual reports, and disagreement over the most appropriate unit of analysis persisted (Steenkamp and Northcott, 2007). For example, Gray *et al.* (1995b) reported that pages tended to be the preferred unit of analysis in corporate social disclosure studies. Milne and Adler (1999) claimed that as a basis for coding and measurement, sentences were far more reliable than any other unit of analysis. In contrast, Unerman (2000) concluded that the proportion of a page was the most appropriate unit of analysis. In addition, Guthrie *et al.* (2004) argued that the paragraph method was more appropriate because meaning was commonly established with paragraphs rather than with words or sentences.

In the social and environmental disclosure literature, the use of sentences as the basis for coding is quite common (Wiseman, 1982; Zeghal and Ahmed, 1990; Walden and Schwartz, 1997). However, using sentences as a coding unit has its own weaknesses. First, sentences cannot usually deliver themselves to classification into a single category (Holsti, 1969), i.e. there is a problem of mutual exclusivity. In this situation, a decision needs to be made by the coder regarding in which pre-determined category the sentence is more dominant. Second, choosing sentences as a coding unit may ignore information provided in other forms, such as tables and figures. Alternatively, the use of phrase, clause or theme as a unit of analysis overcomes these problems. A theme is 'a single assertion about some subject' (Holsti, 1969, p. 116). According to Weber (1990, p. 37), 'themes are not bound by grammatical units such as word, sentence or paragraph but rather they refer to a cluster of words with different meaning or connotation that, taken together, refer to some theme or issue'. Using the theme unit enables meanings to be coded from the text of varying length, depending on where narratives of a particular item begin and end. In certain circumstances where sentences may be proved to be large as a unit, the use of theme as a unit enables coders to break down a sentence into its component text unit themes before they are placed in the selected categories (Campbell and Abdul Rahman, 2010). This overcomes the difficulty involved in determining which category is dominant when using sentences as a coding unit. Again, the use of theme as a coding unit facilitates the inclusion of information provided in any tables and figures. Using theme as the unit for coding has been favoured in recent studies (Beattie and Thomson, 2007; Campbell and Abdul Rahman, 2010). This study also used theme as the coding unit to identify social and environmental information with meanings of particular predefined items.

When the text is coded, measuring or counting may be done in many ways. The commonly used measuring/counting units in the social and environmental disclosure literature include word count (Deegan and Rankin, 1996; Deegan and Gordon, 1996), sentence count (Tsang, 1998; Deegan *et al.*, 2000), page count (Cowen *et al.*, 1987; Hackston and Milne, 1996), and page proportion count (Guthrie and Parker, 1989, 1990; Harte and Owen, 1991; Gray *et al.*, 1995a). As discussed, in some methodological studies on social and environmental disclosure content analysis (Milne and Adler, 1999; Unerman, 2000), the debate of what is the most appropriate unit for measuring or counting seems to be unresolved. Each measuring/counting unit (i.e. words, sentences, paragraphs, pages and page proportions) has its own limitations when quantifying the amount of disclosure. For example, pages may include pictures that have no information on social or environmental activities (Al-Tuwaijri *et al.*, 2004), sentences may ignore relevant tables and figures, and page proportions need more subjective judgement on the treatment of blank parts of a page (Unerman, 2000). The consideration of the use of theme for measuring or counting in this study is not only due to these limitations of the above discussed measuring/counting units, but also because different units for coding and counting the information may create further issues that reduce the reliability of content analysis. If the counting unit (e.g. words) is smaller than the coding unit (e.g. theme), it will increase subjectivity as an additional decision needs to be made on which word in the theme belongs to social and environmental information. On the other hand, if the counting unit (e.g. sentences) is larger than the coding unit (e.g. theme) it will lead to the problem of mutual exclusivity. For instance, if more than one theme (using theme as coding unit) is included in one sentence, a decision needs to be made on which theme is dominant. Therefore, using theme as both coding unit and measuring/counting unit is expected to be a better way to ensure that all social and environmental information disclosed is properly coded and counted.

This study used 121 GRI reporting items with operational definitions offered as the coding framework (discussed in the following section). The underlying theme of each reporting item became a coding unit. This study, first coded social and environmental disclosure according to underlying themes of 121 reporting items. The coded information was then measured or counted according to each theme. Since 121 measuring/counting themes were identical to the 121 coding themes, the coding unit and the measuring/counting unit became unitary for this study.

4.6.2.3 Coding framework

The selection and development of a coding framework with predefined categories is another essential element of research design when conducting content analysis. Through a preview of the sample firms' disclosure, it was found that firms do not have to prepare CSR reports, and if they did so voluntarily some of them disclosed social and environmental information based on the GRI sustainability reporting guidelines. The GRI guidelines provide an internationally recognised framework for social and environmental disclosure, which is comprehensive and covers all disclosure aspects such as economic, social and environmental performance (Frost *et al.*, 2005). The use of the GRI guidelines as a coding framework to analyse corporate social and environmental disclosure has been found in previous studies (Clarkson *et al.*, 2008; Adnan *et al.*, 2010). This study therefore, adopted the GRI (G3) guidelines as a coding framework to analyse the sample firms' social and environmental disclosure.

The GRI was initiated in 1997 by the Coalition for Environmentally Responsible Economies (CERES) and the United Nations Environment Programme, whose mission is to develop and disseminate globally accepted sustainability reporting guidelines for assisting firms in reporting on the economic, social and environmental perspectives of their operations (GRI, 2002). The GRI guidelines follow 11 reporting principles (transparency, inclusiveness, auditability, completeness, relevance, sustainability context, accuracy, neutrality, comparability, clarity and timeliness) to ensure that sustainability reports present a balanced and reasonable account of firms' economic, environmental, and social performance and credibly address issues of concern to stakeholders (GRI, 2006). The first version of the GRI guidelines was issued in 2000 and several revisions have followed since then. The latest version, G3, was released in 2006 with improvements including revised indicators, a complete set of technical protocols, a relevance test, report registration, tiered reporting levels, harmonisation with other prominent guidelines, a special section for the financial sector, and a digital interface for communication of reports (GRI, 2006). The GRI (G3) guidelines generally comprise two broad parts: the overall context for understanding organisational performance (i.e. strategy and analysis, organisational profile, report parameters, governance, commitments and engagement), and organisational performance indicators (i.e. economic performance, environmental performance, and social performance (including labour practices, human rights, society, and product responsibility)). In total GRI contains 121 reporting items (GRI, 2006) (Please see Appendix 2 for a detailed description of GRI (G3) reporting items). In this study, these 121 reporting items were used as predefined items to codify corporate social and environmental disclosure.

4.6.2.4 Reliability

When using content analysis, researchers or coders need to demonstrate the reliability of coding instruments and data collected using those instruments and to permit further replicability and valid inferences to be drawn from data derived from the content analysis (Milne and Adler, 1999). According to Krippendorff (2004), the reliability of content analysis covers three distinct types: stability, reproducibility and accuracy. Stability refers to the degree to which a coding process stays the same way over time, which can be assessed through a test–retest procedure, such as the same coder is asked to code a set of annual reports twice at different times (Krippendorff, 2004). If the coding results are the same for each instance, the stability of the content analysis is achieved. The aim of reproducibility is to measure the extent to which coding is the same when multiple coders are involved (Krippendorff, 2004). The assessment of reproducibility is based on inter-observer differences in the interpretation and application of given coding instruments (Weber, 1990). The accuracy measure of reliability involves evaluating coding performance against a predefined standard set by a panel of experts, or known from previous studies (Krippendorff, 2004). However, the accuracy test has not been a popular choice due to the fact that it is hard to determine a standard procedure in conducting content analysis. The extant literature in this area has dealt with matters of reliability for using content analysis. For example, some studies reported the use of multiple coders and the manner in which they constructed their instruments and decision rules in support of meeting reliability (Guthrie and Mathews, 1985; Hackston and Milne, 1996; Tilt and Symes, 1999).

In this study, the author and two other coders (one with coding experience, one familiar with social and environmental disclosure research) were independently involved in the coding of the sample firms' annual reports and CSR reports. To ensure stability, all coders were asked to review their own coding one week later. The final coding arrived at among all coders was cross-checked to ensure a high degree of coding compatibility. Results were compared and any disagreements were thoroughly scrutinised and reconciled by re-evaluation of the disclosure in question. This process assisted the author in meeting stability and reproducibility of the content analysis data.

4.6.3 The SEDI constructed for this study

4.6.3.1 The objective of the SEDI

While the quantity of disclosure is counted, the quality of disclosure is usually assessed by a content analysis disclosure index in social and environmental disclosure studies. An index, which is said to be a variable that correlates with what it claims to indicate, is the most commonly used analytical construct for content analysis (Krippendorff, 2004). It should be sensitive enough to distinguish between different phenomena of interest, and it is constructed to help decide between two phenomena (Krippendorff, 2004), such as whether one firm's social and environmental disclosure level is higher than that of another.

A disclosure index has been defined by Coy *et al.* (1993, p. 122) as: 'A qualitative-based instrument designed to measure a series of items, which when aggregated, gives a surrogate score indicative of the level of disclosure in the specific context for which the index was devised.' Such a disclosure index is commonly used to rate, rank and benchmark corporate reports (Jones and Alabaster, 1999). A disclosure index assigns ratings to the disclosure relating to each of the pre-defined items in a checklist based on their presence or absence and the degree of elaboration of each individual item. Various parties such as the accounting profession and regulatory bodies have provided awards to firms for recognising their excellence in social and environmental disclosure, and the level of excellence is assessed through developing disclosure indices. This effort encourages firms to improve the quality of their social and environmental disclosure.

In this study, the use of a SEDI to rate corporate social and environmental disclosure relating to predetermined GRI items ensures that the research concentrates more on what should be disclosed for stakeholders, rather than what is being disclosed by firms. The greater attention given to what firms should disclose is consistent with the concept of accountability of accounting information. Influential standards and guidelines such as GRI and AccountAbility increasingly inform leading edge disclosure practice and underline the stakeholder accountability of the disclosure process (Cooper and Owen, 2007). For example, according to AccountAbility (1999), a quality disclosure process is governed by the principle of accountability, which is itself underpinned by the principle of inclusivity, i.e. accountability to all stakeholder groups. Similarly, GRI (2002, p. 9) claims that:

> A primary goal of reporting is to contribute to an ongoing stakeholder dialogue. Reports alone provide little value if they fail to inform stakeholders or support a dialogue that influences the decisions and behaviour of both the reporting organisation and its stakeholders.

Therefore, under the accountability principle, one of the concerns for corporate disclosure is the right of all stakeholders to receive all information relating to the firm, including social and environmental information, and the responsibility of the firm to provide it, even though it is not required by the regulatory bodies. This normative view taken by policymakers in constructing reporting frameworks is helpful, but the facets of disclosure captured through reporting frameworks need to be validated from the stakeholder's perspective to establish the stakeholder relevance of disclosure.

4.6.3.2 The measurement of disclosure – quantity versus quality

A summary of social and environmental disclosure measurement in the literature is presented in Appendix 3. In most previous studies, corporate social and environmental disclosure was measured by volume-based content analysis (Gray *et al.*, 1995a; Deegan and Gordon, 1996; Hackston and Milne, 1996; Gao *et al.*, 2005). A key assumption underlying content analysis in social and environmental research is that the quantity of disclosure devoted to an item signifies the relative importance accorded to that item (Unerman, 2000). Nevertheless, there has been recognition that reliance on the mere number of disclosure (i.e. quantity measure) may be misleading or insufficient (Cowen *et al.*, 1987; Toms, 2002; Hasseldine *et al.*, 2005). Further, counting the volume of disclosure does not provide an understanding of the type and importance of information being communicated (van der Laan Smith *et al.*, 2005). The disclosure of more information does not necessarily mean that the disclosure is of high quality. Therefore, some studies investigated corporate social and environmental disclosure by measuring the quality of disclosure (Cormier and Magnan, 1999, 2003; Cormier and Gordon, 2001; Liu and Anbumozhi, 2009). The quality scales of measuring disclosure used in the literature varied as summarised in Table 4.2. They varied from a binary scale to a seven-point scale. As detailed in Appendix 3, the variations in the quality scales were impacted by theoretical underpinning, the measuring unit, the data analysis technique and the data collection method.

There were also some studies that evaluated corporate social and environmental disclosure by using both the quantity measure and the quality measure of disclosure (Wiseman, 1982; Hasseldine *et al.*, 2005; van der Laan Smith *et al.*, 2005; van Staden and Hooks, 2007). Based on these studies, it is found that the quantity measure and the quality measure are not synonymous in assessing corporate social and environmental disclosure. For example, Wiseman (1982) evaluated corporate environmental disclosure by using both the quantity measure (with line count) and the quality measure (with a 1–3 quality scale), and found that the volume of the environmental disclosure is not representative of its quality. Hasseldine *et al.* (2005) tested the impact of environmental disclosure on corporate environmental reputation by using both a quantity variable and a quality variable to measure environmental disclosure and they found that different measures provided different levels of explanations on corporate environmental reputation. Given the difference between the quantity measure and the quality measure of disclosure in conducting the empirical research, consideration should be given as to which one is more meaningful to assess corporate social and environmental disclosure.

Table 4.2 Quality scales of measuring disclosure used in social and environmental accounting literature

Scales	*Literature*
Two-score	Tsang, 1998; King, 2008; Deegan and Gordon, 1996; Frost and Seamer, 2002; Lorraine *et al.*, 2004; Gao *et al.*, 2005; Ahmad *et al.*, 2003; Patten, 2002; Cho and Patten, 2007; Magness, 2006; Cho, 2009; Walden and Schwartz, 1997; Richardson and Welker, 2001
Three-score	Cormier and Gordon, 2001; Choi, 1999; de Villiers and van Staden, 2006; Cormier *et al.*, 2004; Cormier and Magnan, 1999, 2003, 2007; Roberts, 1992; Wiseman, 1982; Robertson and Nicholson, 1996; Aerts and Cormier, 2009
Four-score	Al-Tuwaijri *et al.*, 2004
Five-score	Van Staden and Hooks, 2007; Liu and Anbumozhi, 2009
Six-score	Deegan and Gordon, 1996; Hasseldine *et al.*, 2005; Toms, 2002
Seven-score	Clarkson *et al.*, 2008

Wiseman (1982) suggested that determining the quality of disclosure is especially important if social disclosure is utilised as a surrogate for a firm's social performance in investment decisions and in related research. Hasseldine *et al.* (2005) provided evidence that the significance of the disclosure quality variable in models is much better than that of the disclosure quantity variable in determining the effects on a firm's environmental reputation. However, their study was conducted in the United Kingdom, the quality scales were constructed by surveying investment analysts only rather than stakeholders and their evaluation was centred on examining the relationship between environmental reputation and environment disclosure. The aims of their study, the data for scale construction, and the location specificity, may have influenced their conclusions that a quality measure is better than a quantity measure.

Although the disagreement on the selection of the measuring/counting unit affects the quantification of disclosure, the quantity of disclosure reflecting how much information is disclosed still needs to be considered when attempting to see the whole picture of corporate disclosure. Since theme (a GRI item as a theme) is the measuring/counting unit in this study, the disclosure quantity can be measured by counting the frequency of the item disclosed. By counting the disclosure of an item once only when the item has been disclosed more than once across the report, is a partial capture of disclosure; previous research suggests that if the researcher is trying to compare one firm's level of disclosure with another firm, it is more appropriate to count the number of times each item occurs (Beattie and Thomson, 2007).

4.6.3.3 Quantity measure and quality measure – separate or integrated?

As emerges from the preceding discussion, several previous studies suggest that the disclosure quality is more meaningful than the disclosure quantity in making conclusions about corporate social and environmental disclosure. Unlike disclosure quantity, where each occurrence is treated with equal value or significance, disclosure quality requires assigning weights to each disclosure occurrence on a pre-determined basis. Wiseman (1982) proposed different values for disclosure occurrence as a way of determining disclosure quality, and a disclosure index was developed based on the unequal values of disclosure. Wiseman's approach was subsequently popularised by many researchers (Walden and Schwartz, 1997; Choi, 1999; Cormier and Gordon, 2001). Some studies updated the approach by developing other indices, such as Hackston and Milne's (1996) index and the SustainAbility/UNEP (1997) index.

Most widely used in recent studies are indices constructed based on the GRI framework (Clarkson *et al.*, 2008; Liu and Anbumozhi, 2009; Adnan *et al.*, 2010). Most of these extant disclosure indices only focus on the disclosure quality, except Hasseldine *et al.* (2005), which used a hybrid measure that integrates a quality measure and a quantity measure into a single disclosure index. In such a way, the index captures the joint effect of the quality measure and the quantity measure and shows a more comprehensive picture of corporate social and environmental disclosure.

In this study, a SEDI was constructed by integrating both the quality measure and the quantity measure to evaluate the sample firms' social and environmental disclosure in their annual reports and CSR reports. The disclosure quantity was measured by counting the frequency of the GRI items disclosed. The frequency of disclosure of an item was multiplied by the quality score for disclosure type and the quality score for disclosure item importance. The quality scores in this study were obtained from stakeholders to make the quantity score relevant to stakeholders. This quality–weighted-quantity score captured the combined effect of the quantity measure and the quality measure. The aggregated quality–weighted-quantity scores of all 121 disclosure items became the SEDI for a firm.

A problem may occur if the quality measure of disclosure is disregarded and only the frequency measure used. For example, if a firm disclosed a particular GRI item with a simple sentence twice throughout its annual report, a score of 2 would be recorded in terms of quantity. If a firm disclosed the same item in more detail with two sentences but once, a score of 1 would be recorded. This confusion is overcome by integrating the quality measure on each disclosure. As an example, a quality score of 2 accorded to specific narratives with two sentences once, compared with a quality score of 1 accorded to general narrative with a simple sentence and then doubled for disclosing twice. Therefore, the integration of the frequency measure and the quality measure is more appropriate to reflect the relevance of disclosure to stakeholders.

4.6.3.4 Components of the SEDI

The SEDI constructed in this study comprises the following three dimensions:

1. disclosure quantity based on the frequency of each GRI disclosure item;
2. disclosure quality based on stakeholders' preferences of disclosure types of each GRI disclosure item;
3. disclosure quality based on stakeholders' perceived importance of each GRI disclosure item.

The disclosure quantity was measured as the disclosure frequencies of 121 disclosure items mentioned in the GRI (G3) guidelines. The definitions offered in the GRI framework for each disclosure item were used to guide the development of theme for each GRI disclosure item in the coding process. Using the theme as the coding and measuring/counting unit, social and environmental disclosure was identified by the 'meaning' implied in the text according to the definition of the GRI item and then counted by the number of times that each item was mentioned in the annual report and the CSR report. This enables the capture of the disclosure items more comprehensively than by a manifest content analysis technique such as searching for pre-determined words in annual reports and CSR reports.

In previous studies, the quality of social and environmental disclosure was assessed by assigning an ordinal value to different disclosure types (Wiseman, 1982; Choi, 1999; Toms, 2002; Clarkson *et al.*, 2008). For example, Toms (2002) used a 0–5 rating scale to define the quality of different disclosure types: 0 = no disclosure; 1 = general rhetoric; 2 = specific endeavour, policy not specified; 3 = specific endeavour, policy specified; 4 = implementation and monitoring, use of targets, results not published; and 5 = implementation and monitoring, use of targets, results published. Researchers have exercised their judgement in assigning unequal values to social and environmental disclosure in ascertaining disclosure quality (Wiseman, 1982; Walden and Schwartz, 1997; van Staden and Hooks, 2007; Researchers' judgement may not necessarily align with stakeholders' judgement on the disclosure quality. The unequal values of disclosure can also be ascertained by report preparers (i.e. corporate executives) and report users (i.e. shareholders, creditors and other stakeholders). Toms (2002) conducted a questionnaire survey to ask investment professionals' perceptions on the importance of different types of qualitative environmental disclosure. It is the only study that utilised users' judgement to determine environmental disclosure quality. However, Toms (2002) only considered investment professionals' perceptions and disregarded other stakeholders who may be interested in corporate environmental disclosure.

This study overcomes the above limitation by obtaining various relevant stakeholders' views on the relative importance of different disclosure types identified from the literature. It first identified different GRI disclosure items relevant to different stakeholder groups, and solicited different stakeholder groups' opinions on the perceived importance of disclosure types to them in their decision-making. Further details are provided in the questionnaire survey section.

The motivation for asking relevant stakeholders' opinions on different disclosure types is that the quality measure should have a strong underpinning on the theory. For instance, when using agency theory as the theoretical underpinning, investors become the focal point to measure the quality, and the quality measure should reflect the investors' perspectives. When using stakeholder theory, stakeholders become the focal point, and the quality measure should be relevant to various stakeholders in their decision-making. It is acknowledged that in exploratory studies where there has been less theoretical emphasis, it is easier and less time-consuming to measure the disclosure quality from researchers' perspectives rather than from users' perspectives but it would not reflect the pragmatic reality.

Since the disclosure measure in this study was constructed based on 121 GRI disclosure items, it is necessary to measure the unequal values of disclosure items in relation to stakeholders. However, there appears to be no empirical research that examines the relative importance of GRI disclosure items to stakeholders, but rather has assumed that all disclosure items are of equal value (Clarkson *et al.*, 2011). Reviewing the literature relating to the use of disclosure indices in accounting research, researchers are divided on the issue of whether disclosure items are treated with equal values or unequal values. Those studies assuming an equal importance to disclosure items argued that subjective weights assigned to items can average each other out (Cooke, 1989). In contrast, those proposing unequal values of disclosure items emphasised the fact that certain items are more important than others, and suggested that the importance weighting of the items contributes to enhancing the disclosure relevance as some disclosure items are more informative than others to stakeholders. They noted that an attitude survey among relevant users can provide information about the relative importance of disclosure items (Beattie *et al.*, 2004). For example, Schneider and Samkin (2008) consulted a stakeholder panel to ask their opinions on the relative importance of disclosure items included in their intellectual capital disclosure index.

When considering stakeholders with diverse interests in corporate social and environmental disclosure, disclosure items can have unequal importance to stakeholders. For example, in relation to the items in the GRI framework, employees pay more attention to labour practices disclosure items, and customers pay more attention to product responsibility disclosure items. Even under labour practices disclosure, individual employees can have different concerns regarding different disclosure items, and some items seem to be more important than others. Therefore, to enhance the accuracy of the disclosure measure, this study investigated the stakeholders' perception toward the importance of each disclosure item to them. In doing so, a stakeholder panel consultation was conducted to ask for the importance weighting of GRI disclosure items. Further details are provided in the stakeholder panel consultation section.

In conclusion, when using content analysis to collect the sample firms' social and environmental disclosure data, each disclosure of an item (disclosure frequency) was counted to ascertain the disclosure quantity. And each disclosure was evaluated in terms of the relative importance of disclosure type to ascertain the disclosure quality. In calculating the SEDI of a firm, the quality score of each disclosure type for a given GRI item was multiplied by the disclosure frequency for that disclosure type and then summed for all disclosure types to find the total, this total score multiplied by the importance score of the GRI item resulted in the final disclosure score of the item. The scores of 121 items were totalled to obtain the final score (SEDI) for each sample firm (see Figure 4.3).

4.6.4 Questionnaire survey for the preference of disclosure types

4.6.4.1 Overview

Previous studies suggested a hierarchical importance for different social and environmental disclosure types: from general rhetoric to specific endeavours to implementation and monitoring (Robertson and Nicholson, 1996; Toms, 2002). In this study, a questionnaire survey was conducted to inquire into stakeholders' perceptions on the relative importance placed on social and environmental disclosure types. The questionnaire survey method has been used to investigate stakeholders' perceptions on corporate social and environmental disclosure in

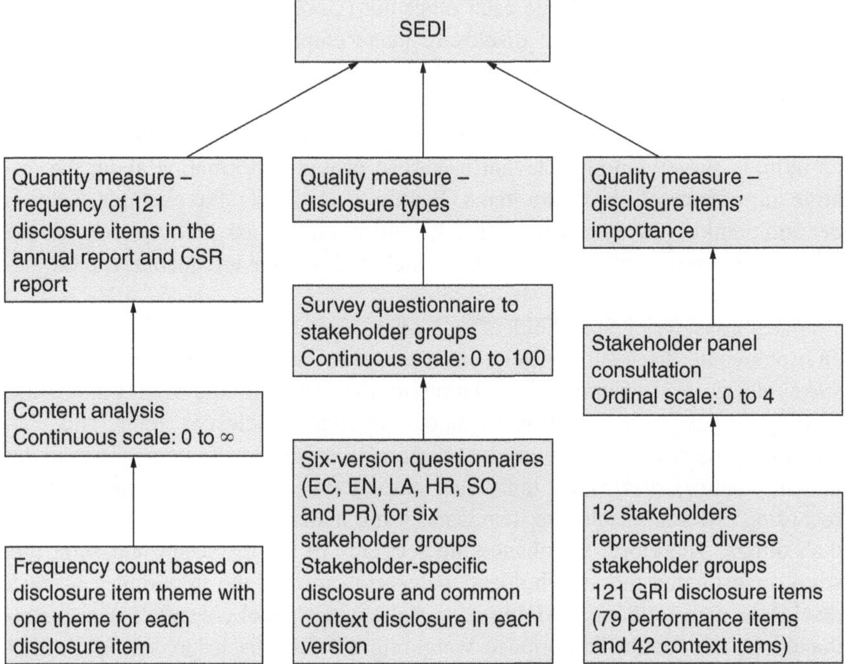

Figure 4.3 SEDI construction.

the accounting literature (Deegan and Gordon, 1996; Deegan and Rankin, 1997, 1999; Newson and Deegan, 2002; Cormier *et al.*, 2004). This study constructed a dual language questionnaire (English and Chinese), along with a cover letter in those languages (please see Appendix 4). The questionnaire comprised two parts: Part one asking each respondent to assign an importance weighting to each disclosure type provided, and Part two asking each respondent to indicate their relationship with the firm. The pilot runs indicated that it took the respondent no more than 15 minutes to complete the questionnaire.

4.6.4.2 Questionnaire design

Based on previous studies (Toms, 2002; Clarkson *et al.*, 2008), this study identified the following disclosure types: (1) general narrative; (2) specific endeavour in non-quantitative terms; (3) quantified performance data; (4) quantified performance data relative to benchmarks (e.g. targets, industry, previous periods); and (5) quantified performance data at a disaggregate level (e.g. plant, business unit, geographic segment). Through a preview of the sample firms' annual reports and CSR reports, it was found that firms reported their performance information (i.e. economic performance, environmental performance, labour practices performance, human rights performance, society performance and product responsibility performance) with all the above disclosure types. In addition to performance information, firms were also found to report their contextual information but with fewer disclosure types: only having general narrative, specific endeavour in non-quantitative terms, and quantified data. Even for GRI context categories – strategy and analysis, and report parameters – sample firms were found to have far fewer disclosure types. Based on the sample firms' annual reports and the CSR reports review undertaken by the author prior to designing the survey questionnaire, this study designed the questionnaire to inquire into the stakeholders' perceptions on the relative importance of different disclosure types occurring for performance items and context items (see Table 4.3).

This survey adopted a continuous rating scale, where respondents were asked to rate the relative importance of the disclosure type by placing a mark at the appropriate position on a continuous line between two fixed points 0 and 100 (Brace, 2004). Although Likert-type scales have been widely used in survey research, this study decided not to adopt them because they have been criticised in the literature for leading to a loss of information due to a limited number of choices offered and allowing the researcher to influence the subjects' responses by determining the labels assigned to the limited number of choices (e.g. very good, good, etc.) (Lodge, 1981; Neibecker, 1984; Zeis *et al.*, 2001). Such operational problems caused by using Likert-type scales can be overcome by using continuous scales (Neibecker, 1984; Brace, 2004). Therefore, continuous scales were adopted as the questionnaire rating scales in this study. Using the continuous rating scale, each progressive '10' was marked on the line to direct the respondents to think in terms of percentage. For instance, if the respondent's preferred score is 75, the respondent makes a mark halfway between 70 and 80.

It is acknowledged that corporate stakeholders include a wide range of various interest groups. Different stakeholder groups focus on different categories of corporate social and environmental disclosure. For example,

Table 4.3 Disclosure types in the questionnaire survey

No.	*Description*
Stakeholder specific disclosure (performance items)	
1	General narrative
2	Specific endeavour in non-quantitative terms
3	Quantified performance data
4	Quantified performance data relative to benchmarks (e.g., targets, industry, previous periods)
5	Quantified performance data at disaggregate level (e.g., plant, business unit, geographic segment)
Context disclosure	
1	General narrative
2	Specific endeavour in non-quantitative terms
3	Quantified data

employees pay more attention to the disclosure of labour practices and shareholders pay more attention to economic performance disclosure. In this regard, corporate annual reports and CSR reports are prepared with different categories of social and environmental disclosure aiming at different stakeholder groups. Therefore, it is important to survey a given stakeholder group about disclosure relevant to their concerns. This study therefore, designed six stakeholder-specific versions of the questionnaire (i.e. economic version, environmental version, labour practices version, human rights version, society version and product responsibility version) for six broad stakeholder groups identified (i.e. economic stakeholders, environmental stakeholders, labour stakeholders, human rights stakeholders, society stakeholders and product stakeholders). Each version had the same question items (i.e. disclosure types) and rating scales (0 to 100), but different examples for each disclosure type. The examples for each disclosure type were stakeholder-relevant and represented disclosure in the performance category relevant to that version. The disclosure type examples were randomly selected from the sample firms' annual reports and CSR reports.

Although the performance disclosure categories in the GRI framework are stakeholder-specific, firms' context disclosure are common to all stakeholder groups. Therefore, each questionnaire version included context categories and the examples chosen for different disclosure types under context categories were the same for all versions of the questionnaire.

4.6.4.3 The selection of stakeholders surveyed and delivery of questionnaire

Although each firm is likely to disclose social and environmental information to diverse stakeholder groups, each firm has its own stakeholder composition. The stakeholder composition varies across firms at a given time and within a firm over time. Unlike shareholders where a registry is maintained by firms as a legal requirement, corporate stakeholder composition cannot be accurately determined. The lack of information about stakeholder composition specific to each firm posed a challenge to determine who would be the actual stakeholders for a given firm surveyed in this study. Although the researcher can choose the stakeholders to complete the questionnaire, those stakeholders may not be specific to a given sample firm.

A firm's management is experientially aware of the stakeholder composition of the firm as they prepare the annual report and the CSR report for corporate stakeholders. Previous stakeholder approach-based studies have provided some surveys of managers' attitudes toward stakeholders (Robertson and Nicholson, 1996; Cormier *et al.*, 2004). Hence, this study contacted corporate executives involved in preparing annual reports and/or CSR reports and requested them to distribute the six questionnaire versions to the relevant stakeholder groups of their firms. Based on the corporate executives' judgements, stakeholders were surveyed for their perceptions on the relative preference of the disclosure types of corporate social and environmental disclosure.

The survey questionnaires with six versions were emailed to the 100 sample firms' executives who were involved in preparing CSR reports and/or annual reports. A written request was made in the initial recruitment email to ask the executives to distribute the questionnaires to the sample firms' stakeholders. In accord with the ethics requirement, the participation information sheet of investigators and the consent form for respondents were also emailed to executives simultaneously. The questionnaire instructions required potential respondents to assign their perceived importance to each disclosure type on a continuous scale from 0 to 100. The respondents were also asked to add any additional disclosure types they thought should appear in the reports and to assign their perceived importance to these additional disclosure types. Deegan and Rankin (1997) noted that who complete the questionnaire need to be carefully monitored in the survey; this study required the respondents to return the questionnaires directly to the researcher, and not to the firm. Although it is typical to report the survey response rate, it is not possible for this survey. Since multiple respondents from one given firm were invited to complete the questionnaire, a response rate cannot be calculated (OCLC, 2009). Additionally, the executives did not report how many questionnaires were distributed to each stakeholder group.

4.6.5 Stakeholder panel consultation for the importance of disclosure items

Since this study assumed that different disclosure items could be perceived as having varying degrees of importance to stakeholders, a stakeholder panel consultation was used to ascertain the relative importance of 121 GRI items. A stakeholder panel serves as a link to information and an approach for better understanding of the business impact on stakeholders. This form of stakeholder engagement offers valuable perspectives through directly engaging with stakeholders (UN Global Compact, 2010). Another reason for using a stakeholder panel consultation is due to the large number (121) of items that needed to be examined for their relative importance. A typical questionnaire survey would take around two hours to complete it, and respondents are unlikely to allocate such a long time period.

The stakeholder panel in this study was a group of stakeholder representatives who were convened by a sample firm to give responses to the relative importance of GRI disclosure items. This panel comprised 12 various stakeholder members: (1) a large individual shareholder, (2) a manager of an institutional shareholder, (3) a banking loan manager, (4) a chief officer of a government authority, (5) an academic, (6) an auditor partner, (7) a human resource manager of the firm, (8) an employee representative, (9) a customer representative, (10) a manager of a major supplier, (11) a representative of local community, and (12) a local media manager. The selection of panel members from a wide range of stakeholder groups is because the disclosure items consulted cover diverse GRI categories (i.e. economic, environmental, labour practices, human rights, society and product responsibility). The size of the panel depends on the objective of the research and such a larger panel may be helpful for exploratory purposes to provide diverse perspectives (UN Global Compact, 2010). The panel members were selected based on their involvement with corporate social and environmental activities, knowledge of what might be included in corporate annual reports and CSR reports, and personal experience. All the panel members selected provided valuable written comments about the annual reports and CSR reports provided to them for review.

The researcher conducted the panel consultation as a moderator. The purpose of the consultation was first introduced to the panel members by the moderator. To ensure the effectiveness of the stakeholder panel, each panel member was asked to review the list of 121 GRI items in a questionnaire. For each item, the panel members were asked for their opinions on whether the item should or should not be disclosed and the varying degrees of importance if it should be disclosed based on rating scales, as used by Schneider and Samkin (2008) (see Table 4.4). The relative importance of each item was determined as the mean (or average) score of the 12 panel members' opinions. Different from the continuous scales used in the questionnaire survey for the preference of disclosure types, a five-point Likert scale was used here to assign the relative importance to the GRI items by the panel members. Upon initial consultations with panel members, it was understood that it is more difficult for panel members (representing stakeholders) to give the relative importance of an item compared with many other items on a continuous scale (as done for disclosure types in the questionnaire survey). Therefore, the panel members required more specific guidance with a limited number of choices to offer their responses on the relative importance of disclosure items. In doing so, this reduced random errors in the panel members' responses.

4.7 Research methods used for the second stage of research

This section describes research methods used in the second stage of the research. An empirical model was employed to examine the effects of stakeholders' power and corporate characteristics on the social and environmental disclosure of socially responsible Chinese listed firms.

Table 4.4 Rating scales used for disclosure items in the stakeholder panel consultation

Score	*Description*
0	Should not be disclosed
1	Should be disclosed but is of minor importance
2	Should be disclosed and is of intermediate importance
3	Should be disclosed and is of great importance
4	It is essential to disclose this item

Source: Schneider and Samkin (2008).

4.7.1 Sample and data

This stage of the research employed the same sample used in the first stage, i.e. the 100 firms listed in the *2008 Chinese Stock-listed Firms' Social Responsibility Ranking List* (see Appendix 1), to examine the relationship between stakeholders' power, corporate characteristics and corporate social and environmental disclosure. For the distribution of the sample firms according to industry sectors, please see Table 4.1. The relevant financial and corporate characteristics data of sample firms for the year 2008 were collected from the China Stock Market and Accounting Research (CSMAR) database and the sample firms' 2008 annual reports.

4.7.2 Empirical model

To test the influences of stakeholders' power and corporate characteristics on the social and environmental disclosure of socially responsible Chinese listed firms, the following empirical model was employed. The SEDI constructed in the first stage of the research was used here as a proxy for corporate social and environmental disclosure. Specifically, the model and the definitions of the variables in the model are presented as follows:

$$\begin{aligned}\text{SEDI} = {} & \beta_0 + \beta_1\text{CSOE} + \beta_2\text{OWN} + \beta_3\text{LEV} + \beta_4\text{AUDIT} + \beta_5\text{SIZE} + \\ & \beta_6\text{FIN} + \beta_7\text{IND} + \beta_8\text{X-LISTED} \qquad (4.1)\end{aligned}$$

The variables in the above model are defined as follows:

DEPENDENT VARIABLE

SEDI: a firm's SEDI for the year 2008, constructed in the first stage of the research (i.e. disclosure quantity, disclosure type quality, disclosure item quality).

INDEPENDENT VARIABLES

CSOE: central SOE, which is a proxy for the government power, indicator that equals 1 for central SOEs, and 0 otherwise.

OWN: concentrated ownership, which is a proxy for the shareholder power, measured by the percentage of shares owned by the largest shareholder at the end of the year 2008.

LEV: financial leverage, which is a proxy for the creditors' power, measured by the total debts/total assets ratio at the end of the year 2008.

AUDIT: auditor, indicator that equals 1 for firms audited by Big-Four auditing firms in the year 2008, and 0 otherwise.

SIZE: firm size, measured by the natural logarithm of total revenues for the year 2008.

FIN: corporate financial performance, measured by the profit margin ratio for the year 2008.
IND: industry membership, indicator that equals 1 for firms belonging to high-profile industries (including metals, banking and insurance, extractive, construction, telecommunications, electricity, transportation, oil and chemical, and food and beverage), and 0 otherwise (see Table 4.1 for the industry classification of the sample firms).
X-LISTED: overseas listing, indicator that equals 1 for firms cross-listed on other developed stock markets in the year 2008 and 0 otherwise.

4.8 Research methods used for the third stage of research

This section describes the research methods used in the third stage of the research. An empirical model was employed to examine the effects of publishing a CSR report on corporate socially responsible reputation in the presence of corporate governance factors (i.e. board characteristics) and corporate characteristics.

4.8.1 Sample and data

Consistent with previous studies on corporate reputation (Toms, 2002; Hasseldine *et al.*, 2005; Musteen *et al.*, 2010), in order to test the effects of publishing a CSR report on corporate socially responsible reputation, the independent variables and control variables were lagged by a year as the effects of these variables would be realised in the following year. In this case, the sample for this stage of the research involved firms in the *Chinese Stock-listed Firms' Social Responsibility Ranking List* published by *Southern Weekend* for both 2008 and 2009. A total of 100 firms were listed in the rankings for each year. CSR, financial and governance data for the year 2008 were obtained from the CSMAR database as well as the sample firms' annual reports. Finally, the sample consisted of 83 firms included in the 2009 ranking list, which also previously appeared on the 2008 ranking list, and for which data were available for all appropriate variables (See Appendix 1 for a contrast between the 2008 and 2009 ranking lists). The categorisation of the final sample firms, summarised and grouped according to sector, is presented in Table 4.5.

4.8.2 Reputation measures

As discussed in the literature chapter, corporate reputation is usually measured via reputation ranking studies (e.g. *Fortune's American Most Admired Companies* (AMAC), *Management Today's UK Most Admired Companies* (MAC), and *Reputex Social Responsibility Ratings*). In this study, corporate reputation particularly refers to socially responsible reputation. To measure corporate reputation, this study used the social responsibility rating score identified by the *Chinese Stock-listed Firms' Social Responsibility Ranking List* for 2009. This

Table 4.5 Distribution of sample firms for examining the relationship between CSR report, governance and reputation

Industry sector	*No. of firms*
High profile	
Metals and non-metallic	21
Banking and insurance	12
Extractive	9
Construction	7
Telecommunication	4
Electricity, gas and water production and supply	3
Transportation and warehousing	3
Oil, chemical and plastic	2
Food and beverage	2
Low profile	
Machinery, equipment and instrumentation	10
Electronics	3
Wholesale and retail trade	3
Information technology	3
Conglomerate	1
Total	83

Note

The *Regulations of Environmental Inspection on Companies Assessing to or Refinancing on the Stock Market* (SEPA, 2003) stipulates that the following industries are pollution industries: metal, extractive, construction, electricity, oil and chemical, food and beverage. In China, following industries are viewed with high consumer visibility: banking and insurance, telecommunication and transportation (Roberts, 1992; Hackston and Milne, 1996).

ranking survey focused on around 200 listed firms having operating revenues above ten billion Chinese yuan. In contrast to some western ranking surveys, such as *Fortune* and *Management Today*, that target only corporate executives and analysts, this ranking survey draws on the perceptions of a broader group of stakeholders, such as governmental officers, academics, executives and analysts, and was conducted through a series of engagements between the research group and listed firms. Respondents were asked to rate the performance of a firm in terms of 11 attributes in four dimensions (see Appendix 5 for specific rating criteria). A limitation of this ranking that should be acknowledged is that it is overly focused on the financial performance of firms (30 per cent weighting).

4.8.3 Empirical model

In light of the above discussion, the influence of publishing a CSR report on corporate socially responsible reputation in the presence of board characteristics and corporate characteristics was tested using the following model:

$$\text{Reputation} = \beta_0 + \beta_1\text{CSR} + \beta_2\text{DUAL} + \beta_3\text{BSIZE} + \beta_4\text{BOWN} + \beta_5\text{BCOMM} + \beta_6\text{FIN} + \beta_7\text{SIZE} + \beta_8\text{IND} \quad (4.2)$$

The variables in the above model are defined as follows:

DEPENDENT VARIABLE

Reputation: corporate reputation, using the social responsibility rating score identified by the *Chinese Stock-listed Firms' Social Responsibility Ranking List* published by *Southern Weekend* for 2009 (see Appendix 1).

INDEPENDENT VARIABLES

CSR: CSR report, coded as 1 if the firm published a CSR report for the year 2008, and 0 otherwise.

CONTROL VARIABLES

DUAL: CEO/chairman duality, coded as 1 if the CEO was also the chairman of the board for the year 2008, and 0 otherwise.
BSIZE: board size, measured by the total number of directors on the board for the year 2008.
BOWN: board ownership, measured by the proportion of ordinary shares owned by all directors at the end of the year 2008.
BCOMM: board committees, measured by the total number of committees on the board for the year 2008.
FIN: financial performance, measured by the profit margin ratio for the year 2008.
SIZE: firm size, measured by the natural logarithm of total revenues for the year 2008.
IND: industry membership, coded as 1 for firms belonging to high-profile industries (including metals, banking and insurance, extractive, construction, telecommunication, electricity, transportation, oil and chemical, and food and beverage), and 0 otherwise (see Table 4.3).

In this stage of the research, the relationships defined in Model (4.2) were tested in four versions of the model. First, Model (4.2.1) examined the effects of corporate characteristics (control variables) on corporate socially responsible reputation. Model (4.2.2) tested the link between publishing a CSR report and corporate socially responsible reputation by controlling for corporate characteristics variables. Model (4.2.3) tested the effects of board characteristics and corporate characteristics (all control variables) on corporate socially responsible reputation. Finally, Model (4.2.4) was the full model, which included all the variables simultaneously.

4.9 Conclusions

This chapter has discussed the research methodology and methods adopted in this study. Mixed methods were used to collect empirical data from different data sources in this study. Content analysis was used to collect the sample firms' social and environmental disclosure quantity from their annual reports and CSR reports. A questionnaire survey was used to collect data on stakeholders' perceptions on the preference of disclosure types, and a stakeholder panel consultation was used to collect empirical data relating to stakeholders' perceptions on the relative importance of GRI items. The three dimensions were combined to construct the Social Environmental Disclosure Index (SEDI) as the proxy for corporate social and environmental disclosure. This study also designed an empirical model to test the relationship between corporate social and environmental disclosure and various influencing factors. Another empirical model was designed to test the effect of publishing a CSR report on corporate socially responsible reputation. The empirical results of each stage research will be presented in the following chapters.

5 Empirical results – the current social and environmental disclosure practices of socially responsible Chinese listed firms

5.1 Introduction

The first stage of this study provided an insight into the current state of the social and environmental disclosure practices of socially responsible Chinese listed firms. A SEDI that involved three dimensions – the quantity measure, the quality measure of disclosure types and the quality measure of disclosure items, was constructed to assess socially responsible firms' social and environmental disclosure in their annual reports and CSR reports. The quality ratings of disclosure types were identified by surveying the relevant stakeholder groups, and the quality ratings of the importance of disclosure items were identified by conducting panel consultation with stakeholders. This chapter first provides a general interpretation of sample firms' social and environmental disclosure practices. The results of the questionnaire survey and stakeholder panel consultation are then discussed and analysed. While the SEDI is used to assess social and environmental disclosure as a whole, the sample firms' disclosure is further evaluated here at both the GRI category level and the performance indicator level.

The remainder of this chapter is organised as follows. Section 5.2 provides a general interpretation of the sample firms' social and environmental disclosure practices. Section 5.3 presents the results and analyses of the questionnaire survey. Section 5.4 presents the results of the stakeholder panel consultation. Section 5.5 then discusses the sample firms' social and environmental disclosure at the overall level. Following this, Sections 5.6 and 5.7 provide analyses of the sample firms' social and environmental disclosure at GRI category level and GRI performance indicator level, respectively. Finally, conclusions are presented in Section 5.8.

5.2 Social and environmental disclosure: communicating legitimacy and stakeholder engagement

The analyses of the sample firms' annual reports and CSR reports indicated that corporate social and environmental information was disclosed in various disclosure types. The most frequently occurring disclosure was in the form of general narrative for most GRI items. For example, concerning corporate environmental performance, PetroChina disclosed in its CSR report that 'the company took energy conservation and emission reduction as important means to change the development modes' (PetroChina, 2008). The disclosure type of specific endeavour in non-quantitative terms was also widely used by sample firms to disclose social and environmental information relating to various GRI items.

In terms of corporate labour practices, Bank of China said in its CSR report, 'we provide employees with benefits that include social security, a housing provident fund, statutory holidays, enterprise annuity, and supplementary medical insurance' (Bank of China, 2008). Compared with the disclosure types of general narrative and specific endeavour in non-quantitative terms, the use of quantified disclosure on social and environmental information was relatively less in firms' annual reports and CSR reports. An example of social and environmental disclosure in quantified performance data was found in Shenhua Energy's CSR report, 'as at 31 December 2008, the company had received a total of state reward on technical reform on energy conservation of approximately RMB12.7 million' (Shenhua Energy, 2008).

Some firms quantified social and environmental information and disclosed them with greater detail, but this occurred less frequently. For instance, quantified performance data were presented relative to benchmarks (e.g. targets, industry and previous periods). 'The education donation (RMB10K) increases year by year, with 1,645 in 2006, 4,549 in 2007 and 12,968 in 2008' (PetroChina, 2008). The sample firms' quantified performance information was also disclosed at a disaggregated level (e.g. plant, business unit and geographic segment). 'Among the employees in domestic institutions, 39,124 are engaged in the corporate banking segment, 149,166 in personal banking segment, 4,522 in treasury operations segment, 87,040 in financial and accounting matters, and 103,060 in other specializations' (ICBC, 2008).

Using these disclosure types, the sample firms communicated their legitimacy to the public and specific stakeholder groups for the purpose of their continuing operations. This study found that different legitimation strategies were used by the sample firms in their disclosure to maintain their strategic positions and to repair their images; for instance, disclosure provided by a firm to inform the public and interested parties about changes in its social and environmental performance for maintaining its legitimacy. 'The number of on-the-job training employees increases year by year, 5,164 in 2006, 6,232 in 2007 and 7,657 in 2008' (Bank of China, 2008). On the other hand, firms also disclosed information to offset negative news about pollution through drawing attention to the firm's strengths for the purpose of repairing the firm's legitimacy. For example, after the Zijin Mining pollution accident[1] was exposed, the firm tended to deflect the public's attention from the pollution accident to the new technologies for environmental protection adopted by the firm and the environmental awards the firm had won.

Further, the sample firms' social and environmental disclosure also dealt with various interests of the different stakeholder groups who can affect or be affected in the process of firms' operations and practices. For instance, the Chinese government needed information to evaluate a firm's implementation of its environmental policies and regulations, and the shareholders needed information to evaluate a firm's financial performance for investment decisions. When providing disclosure, many firms therefore categorised information into different sections, targeting different stakeholder groups. Based on the GRI reporting framework, most sample firms disclosed information relating to their stakeholder composition, approaches to stakeholder engagement or contents of stakeholder engagement in their annual reports or CSR reports. For example, China Mobile said in its CSR report:

> We have seven major stakeholder groups: customers, shareholders and investors, employees, government authorities and regulators, value chain partners, industry peers and the public. Through regular engagement and specific dialogues with our stakeholders, we are able to understand and quickly respond to their needs.
>
> (China Mobile, 2008)

This section presented a general interpretation of the sample firms' social and environmental disclosure practices in their annual reports and CSR reports from the preparers' perspectives. Legitimacy theory posits that the motive for managers and report preparers to make social and environmental disclosure is to communicate the firm's legitimacy to the public and particular stakeholder groups. The specific quantitative results of firms' social and environmental disclosure will be presented and analysed in the following sections.

5.3 Results and analyses of the questionnaire survey

As discussed in Chapter 4, this study conducted a questionnaire survey that inquired into the stakeholders' perceptions on disclosure types in the first stage of research in order to answer the research questions in this study. The results of the questionnaire survey are presented and discussed in this section.

5.3.1 Respondents

In total, 217 completed questionnaire forms were received. A dissection of the number of completed questionnaires received per version in terms of stakeholder classification is presented in Table 5.1. As noted in Chapter 4, the different stakeholder groups received questionnaires with stakeholder-relevant examples of the disclosure types. Of these completed questionnaires, the largest proportion of responses (45 out of 217) was on the labour practices version. All the of the labour practices version questionnaires received were completed by employees. One possible reason is that employees were the stakeholders who were most interested in information relating to corporate labour practices. Chinese employees encountered several issues relating to their employment, which included minimum

Table 5.1 Responses by stakeholder category

Questionnaire version	*Number received*	*Distribution of respondents*	
EC	38	Shareholder	25
		Creditor	7
		Government	2
		Auditor	2
		Supplier	2
EN	31	Government	12
		Creditor	7
		Community	7
		Academic	3
		Auditor	2
LA	45	Employee	45
HR	32	Employee	32
SO	36	Community	17
		Employee	8
		Shareholder	4
		Government	4
		Academic	1
		Auditor	1
		Media	1
PR	35	Customer	22
		Supplier	9
		Government	4
Total	217		

wage, excessive work hours, dangerous working conditions and lack of freedom of association (SustainAbility, 2007). Another possible reason is that it was easier and more convenient for the sample firms' executives who disseminated these survey questionnaires to distribute them to their own employees. The categories of stakeholders giving responses on the economic version of the questionnaire included shareholder, creditor, government, auditor and supplier. Most respondents for this version of the questionnaire were shareholders, followed by creditors. The distribution of respondents of the society version questionnaire was most extensive, which included the community, employee, shareholder, government, academic, auditor and media. However, of these respondents, the community group provided the most number of completed questionnaires. For the product responsibility version, the most number of completed questionnaires came from customers. In comparison, the completed questionnaires received on the environmental version and the human rights version were relatively less. The human rights disclosure is a sensitive aspect for China, as it is often criticised for its labour rights such as 'sweatshop' production where foreign firms subcontract to China (World Bank, 2004). The most number of completed questionnaires on the environmental version were received from the government group.

5.3.2 Responses on context disclosure

Since the GRI framework comprises disclosure items relating to a firm's context and such disclosure is assumed to be stakeholder neutral, in this study, the context disclosure was included in all the questionnaire versions and was rated by all relevant stakeholder groups. The mean values of stakeholders' perceptions on the relative importance of different disclosure types in terms of context categories are indicated in Table 5.2. As shown in the table, the importance of the various disclosure types of context categories that stakeholders assigned was generally low, with the mean of each one being around 20, based on a continuous rating scale from 0 to 100. The context section of the GRI framework has four categories – *strategy and analysis*, *organisational profile*, *report parameters*, and *governance, commitment and engagement*. For the categories *organisational profile* and *governance, commitments and engagement* (which had more than two disclosure types), a nonparametric Kruskal–Wallis test was conducted to determine whether there was a significant difference in the importance responses among various disclosure types (please see Appendix 6 for the results), and it was found that there was no significant statistical difference. Further, Mann–Whitney U-tests were carried out to determine if there was a significant difference between each two of the disclosure types for all categories except for *strategy and analysis* (only having one disclosure type) in the context section, and it was found that there was no significant statistical difference (please also see Appendix 6 for the results). Different disclosure types (i.e. general narrative, specific endeavour and quantified data) did not mean a difference to stakeholders, indicating that there was no quality hierarchy in terms of disclosure type relating to the GRI context related disclosure.

Table 5.2 Stakeholders' perceived importance of different disclosure types – context categories

Category	*Disclosure type*	*Mean*
Strategy and analysis	Specific endeavour in non-quantitative terms	20.00
Corporate profile	General narrative	19.68
	Specific endeavour in non-quantitative terms	20.32
	Quantified data	20.60
Report parameters	General narrative	19.35
	Specific endeavour in non-quantitative terms	20.28
Governance, commitments and engagement	General narrative	19.45
	Specific endeavour in non-quantitative terms	20.28
	Quantified data	20.74

Note
Disclosure types were rated on a continuous scale (0 unimportant to 100 important).

5.3.3 Responses on performance disclosure

As discussed in Chapter 4, each questionnaire version involved one performance category and was sent to the stakeholder group who had direct concern with disclosure in relation to that performance category. The mean values of stakeholders' responses on the relative importance of disclosure types for each performance category are presented in Table 5.3. From the table, it can be seen that for each performance category, different disclosure types had different mean values of importance assigned by stakeholders and there was an increase in the

Table 5.3 Stakeholders' perceived importance of different disclosure types – performance categories

Category	*Disclosure type*	*Mean*
EC	1	20.00
	2	39.47
	3	60.53
	4	80.26
	5	90.00
EN	1	20.00
	2	39.68
	3	60.65
	4	80.00
	5	90.00
LA	1	20.00
	2	39.56
	3	60.67
	4	80.00
	5	90.00
HR	1	20.31
	2	40.00
	3	60.31
	4	80.63
	5	87.81
SO	1	19.72
	2	40.00
	3	59.72
	4	79.44
	5	89.17
PR	1	20.00
	2	40.00
	3	60.57
	4	79.43
	5	90.29

Notes

1 = General narrative, 2 = Specific endeavour in non-quantitative terms, 3 = Quantified performance data, 4 = Quantified performance data relative to benchmarks, and 5 = Quantified performance data at disaggregate level. Disclosure types were rated on a continuous scale (0 unimportant to 100 important).

mean values of importance from general narrative to specific endeavour and to quantified performance data at the disaggregate level. Such results contrast with that of the context section of the GRI framework as stakeholder groups found some disclosure types more relevant to them than others. A Kruskal–Wallis test was performed to determine if there was a significant difference in the importance responses among various disclosure types for each performance category (please see Appendix 7 for the results). The results indicated a significant statistical difference in the importance responses in terms of disclosure types for each performance category. Since the Kruskal–Wallis test only indicates whether disclosure types have differences, but does not identify where the differences occur or how many differences occur, further analysis in the form of Mann–Whitney U-tests was conducted to determine whether differences existed between each pair of disclosure types (please see Appendix 7 for the results). It was found that a significant statistical difference existed between each two disclosure types for each category. Hence, stakeholders placed significantly different responses on the importance to them of different disclosure types, with an evident preference on the quantified and objectified performance disclosure.

This suggested that there was a quality hierarchy in terms of disclosure type for performance categories. The findings provide evidence about the quality hierarchy of disclosure types from a user perspective in a developing country setting, to advance the previous literature in a developed country setting (Robertson and Nicholson, 1996; Toms, 2002).

Although respondents were asked to add any additional disclosure type they thought should be disclosed in the published reports and also to assign a weighting to any disclosure type they added, there were no any additional disclosure types added by respondents. According to the discussion in the method chapter (Chapter 4), this study used the mean values of stakeholders' responses on each disclosure type for each GRI category as the disclosure type quality rating in calculating the sample firms' SEDI.

5.4 Results of stakeholder panel consultation

A stakeholder panel consultation was conducted to collect the data relating to stakeholders' perceptions on the relative importance of 121 GRI disclosure items. The mean values of panel members' responses on the importance of GRI disclosure items are presented in Appendix 8. The mean value was calculated as the average of all scores awarded by panel members to each GRI item. According to the results, the level of importance of most GRI items was located between intermediate importance (score=2) and essential to disclose (score=4).

A minimum mean score of 1.92 was awarded to the *report parameter* item 'state any specific limitations on the scope or boundary of the report', indicating that stakeholders viewed it as the least relevant to them. A maximum mean score of 4 was awarded to the *organisational profile* item 'name of the organisation' and the *report parameter* item 'reporting period for information provided', indicating that stakeholders viewed these two items as essential for disclosure.

As discussed in Chapter 4, the mean values of the panel members' responses on the importance of each GRI item were used as the disclosure item quality to calculate the sample firms' SEDI.

5.5 A general comparison of disclosure between different reporting media at SEDI level

Based on the frequency of each disclosure type reported, the quality rating scores of each disclosure type identified by the stakeholder survey and the relative importance of the GRI items determined by the stakeholder panel, a SEDI for each sample firm was developed to evaluate its social and environmental disclosure practice. The results of the descriptive statistics of SEDI for the two reporting media (i.e. annual report and CSR report) are presented in Table 5.4. The SEDI (total) ranged from a minimum score of 5,172.50 to a maximum score of 33,299.16, with a mean value of 12,783.86 and a standard deviation of 5,253.86, indicating that firms differed widely in making stakeholder-relevant social and environmental disclosure. Comparing the two reporting media, the disclosure variation among firms of CSR report, with SEDI (CSR report) having a mean of 6,288.15 and a standard deviation of 4,741.58, was exceedingly larger than that of annual report, with SEDI (annual report) having a mean of 6,495.71 and a standard deviation of 1,477.62. A minimum score of 0 for SEDI (CSR report) shows that some sample firms did not publish a CSR report for the year 2008 with any information based on GRI guidelines. On the other hand, all annual reports contained some disclosure relating to GRI items.

Table 5.5 presents the distribution of the sample firms that published a CSR report or otherwise in both high-profile industries and low-profile industries. As indicated in the table, 81 (out of 100) sample firms published CSR reports for the year 2008. Among these firms with CSR reports, 74 per cent were from high-profile industries (60 out of 81), higher than high-profile firms as a percentage of

Table 5.4 Descriptive statistics of SEDI for different reporting media

Reporting media	*Obs.*	*Mean*	*Std. Dev.*	*Min.*	*Max.*	*Median*
SEDI (Annual report)	100	6,495.71	1,477.62	4,570.83	14,359.99	6,062.50
SEDI (CSR report)	100	6,288.15	4,741.58	0	20,815	5,716.67
SEDI (Total)	100	12,783.86	5,253.86	5,172.50	33,299.16	12,034.17

Table 5.5 Industrial distribution of sample firms in terms of publishing CSR report

	Number of firms with CSR report	*Number of firms without CSR report*	*Total*
High-profile industries	60	11	71
Low-profile industries	21	8	29
Total	81	19	100

the whole sample (71 out of 100). And also 60 (out of 71) high-profile firms published CSR reports, with the proportion higher than that (21 out of 29) of low-profile industries. This result indicates that more high-profile firms in the sample published CSR reports for 2008 than low-profile firms. Such findings can be explained by legitimacy theory in terms of public visibility. Firms in high-profile industries are usually subject to more regulations and industry standards (e.g. environmentally sensitive industries subject to more environmental regulations) and are more likely to be scrutinised by the public, both domestic and international given that China is the largest emitter of environmentalhouse gases (Guo, 2010). Therefore, high-profile firms were more likely to legitimate their social and environmental performance to the relevant stakeholders by publishing CSR reports.

For the 81 sample firms publishing CSR reports, a paired samples t-test and a Wilcoxon matched-pairs signed-ranks test were used to examine whether social and environmental disclosure varied between the annual report and the CSR report. The results are shown in Table 5.6. As the table indicates, social and environmental disclosure varied significantly between the annual report and the CSR report, with the CSR report having more stakeholder-relevant social and environmental disclosure than the annual report. This finding is consistent with previous studies (see Frost *et al.*, 2005; Adnan *et al.*, 2010). This finding may be due to the explicit purpose of the CSR report being the provision of social and environmental disclosure compared to the annual report and the knowledge that the two reports are directed to different user groups (Rowbottom and Lymer, 2009).

To sum up, there is a large variation in social and environmental disclosure among socially responsible Chinese listed firms. Social and environmental disclosure is still voluntary and encouraged by the Chinese government and most firms on the social responsibility ranking list published CSR reports for the year 2008. Compared to the annual report, the CSR report is a more valuable source of stakeholder-relevant information on firms' social and environmental activities.

5.6 A general comparison of disclosure between different reporting media on GRI categories

This section reports the disclosure scores of each GRI category (i.e. overall context (context), economic performance, environmental performance, labour practices, human rights, society and product responsibility) calculated according

Table 5.6 A comparison of social and environmental disclosure between annual report and CSR report (n = 81)

	Mean	*Std. Dev.*	*Median*	*t-test*		*Wilcoxon test*	
				t-stat.	*Sig.*	*z-stat.*	*Sig.*
Annual report	6,380.81	1,544.17	5,925.83	−3.4279	0.001	−2.507	0.0122
CSR report	7,763.15	4,028.46	6,370				

to the three dimensions (disclosure quantity, disclosure type quality and disclosure item quality). The results of the descriptive statistics of the disclosure scores on GRI categories for the two reporting media are presented in Table 5.7.

As Table 5.7 indicates, all sample firms disclosed information about the overall context for understanding corporate performance (context), economic performance and labour practices in their annual reports. By contrast, 81 per cent of firms disclosed information about context and economic performance, and 80 per cent of firms disclosed information about labour practices in their CSR reports.

As to environmental performance, 81 per cent of sample firms reported this information in their CSR reports and only 63 per cent in their annual reports, indicating that more firms chose to disclose environmental performance information in a report that is dedicated to social and environmental issues (e.g. CSR report) rather than the annual report. Similarly, 76 per cent of the firms disclosed information about human rights in CSR reports, which is significantly higher than the percentage for annual reports (9 per cent).

With reference to the other two GRI categories, society and product responsibility, more sample firms disclosed information on them in their annual reports (94 per cent and 91 per cent respectively) than CSR reports (81 per cent and 80 per cent respectively). Among all categories, human rights was the least disclosed category for both CSR reports and annual reports.

In terms of the mean values of GRI categories, all the categories other than context and economic performance had higher mean values for CSR reports than for annual reports. This result suggests that the sample firms disclosed more stakeholder-relevant information on social and environmental dimensions in their CSR reports than annual reports. Moreover, all GRI categories had higher standard deviation values for CSR reports than for annual reports, indicating that there was a larger variation among sample firms on each disclosure category for CSR reports than for annual reports.

In conclusion, more firms on the social responsibility ranking list disclosed information on environmental performance and human rights in their CSR reports rather than their annual reports. In contrast, more firms disclosed information on the context, economic performance, labour practices, society, and product responsibility in their annual reports rather than CSR reports. However, in terms of the quantity and quality of information, firms disclosed more stakeholder-relevant information relating to environmental performance, labour practices, human rights, society, and product responsibility in their CSR reports rather than annual reports. Hence, in accordance with the previous discussion, the CSR report provides more stakeholder-relevant social and environmental disclosure.

5.7 Disclosure on GRI indicators by media

The sample firms' specific disclosure in accordance with GRI performance indicators in the two reporting media are discussed in this section. The results for the

Table 5.7 Descriptive statistics of disclosure by sample firms on GRI categories for different reporting media (n = 100)

GRI categories	*Discloser as a % of sample*			*Mean*			*Std. Dev.*			*Min.*			*Max.*		
	Annual report	*CSR report*	*Total*	*Annual report*	*CSR report*	*Total*	*Annual report*	*CSR report*	*Total*	*Annual report*	*CSR report*	*Total*	*Annual report*	*CSR report*	*Total*
Context	100	81	100	2,495.07	1,429.17	3,924.23	505.26	1,001.51	1,236.27	1,881.67	0	2,063.33	4,793.33	4,311.67	9,105.00
EC	100	81	100	2,261.43	1,382.16	3,643.58	484.60	1,132.98	1,330.53	1,519.17	0	1,885.83	5,548.33	4,780.00	9,932.50
EN	63	81	96	345.72	1,261.40	1,607.12	407.31	1,237.35	1,397.93	0	0	0	1,781.67	7,003.33	7,975.83
LA	100	80	100	687.93	760.00	1,447.93	173.05	608.40	637.35	340.00	0	340.00	1,680.00	2,766.67	3,511.67
HR	9	76	82	15.53	146.57	162.10	55.71	132.03	136.06	0	0	0	318.33	823.33	823.33
SO	94	81	100	442.83	981.86	1,424.69	328.98	949.28	1,126.17	0	0	60.00	1,910.00	3,793.33	5,703.33
PR	91	80	100	249.67	324.53	574.20	147.86	237.37	257.66	0	0	143.33	830.00	1,111.67	1,600.00

Note
Discloser is a firm that disclosed at least one item of each GRI category.

incidence of disclosure on GRI indicators by the sample firms in the two reporting media are presented below.

The economic performance category comprises nine indicators (EC1–EC9). With the exception of EC5, all the indicators were disclosed by the sample firms in the annual report but with variations in the disclosing percentage of the sample. In contrast to the annual report, firms made disclosure on all economic indicators in the CSR report, with wide variations in the disclosing percentage of the sample. As shown in Table 5.8, EC1 and EC3 were most frequently reported in the annual report (100 per cent of sample firms), but in contrast, EC1 and EC8 were most frequently reported in the CSR report (81 per cent respectively). Across the nine economic performance indicators, more firms disclosed EC1, EC3, EC4 and EC6 in the annual report than in the CSR report. The other five indicators (EC2, EC5, EC7, EC8 and EC9) were more frequently reported in the CSR report than in the annual report. Some economic indicators were frequently disclosed in both the annual report and the CSR report, such as EC1, EC3, EC6 and EC9, suggesting that some information reported in the annual report was replicated in the CSR report.

Compared to the economic performance indicators, firms disclosed environmental performance indicators (EN1–EN30) less frequently. As reported in Table 5.9, there were differences in the level of coverage of indicators between the two reporting media, with the annual report having over half (16/30) of the indicators disclosed, but the CSR report having all the indicators except EN25 disclosed. Moreover, with the exception of EN17, all the indicators were more frequently disclosed in the CSR report than in the annual report. Across the 30 environmental performance indicators, the two most frequently disclosed in both the CSR report and the annual report were EN6 and EN26, which reported the sample firms' initiatives to save energy and mitigate the environmental impacts of products and services. Indicators showing a significantly negative influence on the environment and resources, such as EN9, EN24 and EN25, were scantily disclosed by the sample firms. Such a case provides evidence that firms prefer to disclose their positive environmental efforts and steer away from disclosing their negative environmental impacts, which supports previous studies (Guthrie and Parker, 1990; Deegan and Gordon, 1996). For the energy-related indicators (EN3–EN7), more firms provided information to stakeholders on issues relating to initiatives to save energy and energy saved rather than issues relating to actual energy consumption. For the water-related indicators (EN8–EN10), the most frequently disclosed in both the CSR report and the annual report was EN10, which related to water recycling and reusing. In relation to the carbon emission related indicators (EN16–EN19), information concerning initiatives to reduce carbon emissions (EN18) was most frequently disclosed by the sample firms. Indicators relating to pollutant discharge including emissions, effluents and wastes, such as EN20, EN21 and EN22, were addressed by the sample firms with similar disclosing percentages of the sample in the same reporting medium. Finally, information on environmental protection expenditure and investment (EN30) was also frequently disclosed by 25 per cent of the sample firms in the annual report and 42 per cent of the sample firms in the CSR report, respectively.

Table 5.8 Social and environmental disclosure by sample firms on GRI economic performance indicators

GRI indicators		*Disclosing firms as % of sample* (n = *100)*	
Code	*Description*	*Annual report*	*CSR report*
EC1	Direct economic value generated and distributed, including revenues, operating costs, employee compensation, donations and other community investments, retained earnings and payments to capital providers and governments.	100	81
EC2	Financial implications and other risks and opportunities for the organisation's activities due to climate change.	16	24
EC3	Coverage of the organisation's defined benefit plan obligations.	100	77
EC4	Significant financial assistance received from government.	79	5
EC5	Range of ratios of standard entry level wage compared to local minimum wage at significant locations of operation.	0	8
EC6	Policy, practices and proportion of spending on locally-based suppliers at significant locations of operation.	61	49
EC7	Procedures for local hiring and proportion of senior management hired from the local community at significant locations of operation.	6	32
EC8	Development and impact of infrastructure investments and services provided primarily for public benefit through commercial, in-kind, or pro bono engagement.	24	81
EC9	Understanding and describing significant indirect economic impacts, including the extent of impacts.	44	75

As to social performance indicators, the first aspect being discussed in the GRI framework concerns labour practices. As indicated in Table 5.10, within 14 labour practices indicators (LA1–LA14), there are three indicators, LA3, LA5 and LA6, without any disclosure in either the annual report or the CSR report. For the indicators disclosed, LA1 and LA13, which reported about total workforce and breakdown of employees, were more frequently disclosed in the annual report than in the CSR report. In contrast, firms disclosed other indicators more frequently in the CSR report. Similar to the economic performance indicators, some information reported in the annual report concerning employment, for example LA1 and LA13, was often replicated in the CSR report. The most frequently disclosed information in the CSR report was about employee training and education, such as LA10 and LA11. Another indicator frequently disclosed in the CSR report was LA8, which covered education, training, counselling, prevention and risk-control programmes in terms of OHS.

The second aspect of social performance being discussed is human rights (HR1–HR9). As shown in Table 5.10, for human rights indicators, the level of coverage of indicators varied between the two reporting media, with the annual report having four indicators (HR4–HR7) being disclosed, but the CSR report having eight indicators (all except HR3) being disclosed. Also, all the indicators were more frequently disclosed in the CSR report than in the annual report. Across the nine indicators, the most frequently disclosed in both the annual report and the CSR report was HR5, which was related to freedom of association and collective bargaining. The other two indicators frequently disclosed in both reporting media were HR7 and HR4, which reported actions taken to eliminate forced and compulsory labour and against discrimination, respectively.

In relation to society indicators (SO1–SO8), similar to economic performance indicators, the level of coverage of indicators was relatively high, with only SO7 not being disclosed in the annual report. With the exception of SO6 and SO8, all the indicators were more frequently disclosed in the CSR report than in the annual report. Within the eight society indicators, the most frequently disclosed in the annual report was SO6, which was about the financial and in-kind contributions to political parties. In contrast, the most frequently disclosed indicator in the CSR report was SO1, which covered programmes and practices that assess and manage the impacts of operations on communities. Another indicator frequently disclosed in both reporting media was SO5, which concerned public policy. However, the indicators that required disclosing negative information, such as significant fines and sanctions for non-compliance with laws and regulations (SO8), were less disclosed by firms in both reporting media.

The last aspect of social performance being discussed is on product responsibility (PR1–PR9). The level of coverage of indicators varied between the two reporting media, with the annual report having less than half (4/9) being disclosed, but the CSR report having all the indicators being disclosed. With the exception of PR6, all the indicators were more frequently disclosed in the CSR report than in the annual report. As shown in Table 5.10, the most frequently disclosed indicator in both reporting media was PR6, which reported programmes

Table 5.9 Social and environmental disclosure by sample firms on GRI environmental performance indicators

GRI indicators		*Disclosing firms as % of sample* (n = *100)*	
Code	*Description*	*Annual report*	*CSR report*
EN1	Materials used by weight or volume.	0	3
EN2	Percentage of materials used that are recycled input materials.	7	15
EN3	Direct energy consumption by primary energy source.	10	35
EN4	Indirect energy consumption by primary source.	0	5
EN5	Energy saved due to conservation and efficiency improvements.	12	43
EN6	Initiatives to provide energy-efficient or renewable energy based products and services and reductions in energy requirements as a result of these initiatives.	37	65
EN7	Initiatives to reduce indirect energy consumption and reductions achieved.	2	31
EN8	Total water withdrawal by source.	8	24
EN9	Water sources significantly affected by withdrawal of water.	0	1
EN10	Percentage and total volume of water recycled and reused.	12	34
EN11	Location and size of land owned, leased, managed in, or adjacent to, protected areas and areas of high biodiversity value outside protected areas.	0	1
EN12	Description of significant impacts of activities, products and services on biodiversity in protected areas and areas of high biodiversity value outside protected areas.	0	4
EN13	Habitats protected or restored.	2	11
EN14	Strategies, current actions and future plans for managing impacts on biodiversity.	1	24
EN15	Number of IUCN Red List species and national conservation list species with habitats in areas affected by operations, by level of extinction risk.	0	2

EN16	Total direct and indirect environmentalhouse gas emissions by weight.	0	5
EN17	Other relevant indirect environmentalhouse gas emissions by weight.	1	1
EN18	Initiatives to reduce environmentalhouse gas emissions and reductions achieved.	6	42
EN19	Emissions of ozone-depleting substances by weight.	0	1
EN20	NO, SO and other significant air emissions by type and weight.	11	42
EN21	Total water discharge by quality and destination.	10	45
EN22	Total weight of waste by type and disposal method.	10	46
EN23	Total number and volume of significant spills.	0	1
EN24	Weight of transported, imported, exported, or treated waste deemed hazardous under the terms of the Basel Convention Annex I, II, III and VIII and percentage of transported waste shipped internationally.	0	1
EN25	Identity, size, protected status and biodiversity value of water bodies and related habitats significantly affected by the reporting organisation's discharges of water and runoff.	0	0
EN26	Initiatives to mitigate environmental impacts of products and services and extent of impact mitigation.	24	73
EN27	Percentage of products sold and their packaging materials that are reclaimed, by category.	0	2
EN28	Monetary value of significant fines and total number of non-monetary sanctions for noncompliance with environmental laws and regulations.	0	4
EN29	Significant environmental impacts of transporting products and other goods and materials used for the organisation's operations and transporting members of the workforce.	0	2
EN30	Total environmental protection expenditures and investments by type.	25	42

Table 5.10 Social and environmental disclosure by sample firms on GRI social performance indicators

GRI indicators		*Disclosing firms as % of sample* (n = *100)*	
Code	*Description*	*Annual report*	*CSR report*
Labour practices and decent work performance indicators			
LA1	Total workforce by employment type, employment contract and region.	100	34
LA2	Total number and rate of employee turnover by age group, gender and region.	1	5
LA3	Benefits provided to full-time employees that are not provided to temporary or part-time employees, by major operations.	0	0
LA4	Percentage of employees covered by collective bargaining agreements.	8	62
LA5	Minimum notice period(s) regarding operational changes, including whether it is specified in collective agreements.	0	0
LA6	Percentage of total workforce represented in formal joint management–worker health and safety committees that help monitor and advise on occupational health and safety programmes.	0	0
LA7	Rates of injury, occupational diseases, lost days and absenteeism and number of work-related fatalities by region.	10	25
LA8	Education, training, counseling, prevention and risk-control programmes in place to assist workforce members, their families, or community members regarding serious diseases.	4	72
LA9	Health and safety topics covered in formal agreements with trade unions.	1	27
LA10	Average hours of training per year per employee by employee category.	13	78
LA11	Programmes for skills management and lifelong learning that support the continued employability of employees and assist them in managing career endings.	18	79
LA12	Percentage of employees receiving regular performance and career development reviews.	29	53

LA13	Composition of governance bodies and breakdown of employees per category according to gender, age group, minority group membership and other indicators of diversity.	95	23
LA14	Ratio of basic salary of men to women by employee category.	2	13
Human rights performance indicators			
HR1	Percentage and total number of significant investment agreements that include human rights clauses or that have undergone human rights screening.	0	1
HR2	Percentage of significant suppliers and contractors that have undergone screening on human rights and actions taken.	0	4
HR3	Total hours of employee training on policies and procedures concerning aspects of human rights that are relevant to operations, including the percentage of employees trained.	0	0
HR4	Total number of incidents of discrimination and actions taken.	2	14
HR5	Operations identified in which the right to exercise freedom of association and collective bargaining may be at significant risk and actions taken to support these rights.	8	72
HR6	Operations identified as having significant risk for incidents of child labour and measures taken to contribute to the elimination of child labour.	1	9
HR7	Operations identified as having significant risk for incidents of forced or compulsory labour and measures to contribute to the elimination of forced or compulsory labour.	2	28
HR8	Percentage of security personnel trained in the organisation's policies or procedures concerning aspects of human rights that are relevant to operations.	0	2
HR9	Total number of incidents of violations involving rights of indigenous people and actions taken.	0	2
Society performance indicators			
SO1	Nature, scope and effectiveness of any programmes and practices that assess and manage the impacts of operations on communities, including entering, operating and exiting.	32	81
SO2	Percentage and total number of business units analysed for risks related to corruption.	17	40

continued

Table 5.10 Continued

GRI indicators		*Disclosing firms as % of sample* (n = *100)*	
Code	*Description*	*Annual report*	*CSR report*
SO3	Percentage of employees trained in organisation's anti-corruption policies and procedures.	6	25
SO4	Actions taken in response to incidents of corruption.	7	19
SO5	Public policy positions and participation in public policy development and lobbying.	36	59
SO6	Total value of financial and in-kind contributions to political parties, politicians and related institutions by country.	87	80
SO7	Total number of legal actions for anti-competitive behavior, anti-trust and monopoly practices and their outcomes.	0	2
SO8	Monetary value of significant fines and total number of non-monetary sanctions for noncompliance with laws and regulations.	1	1
Product responsibility performance indicators			
PR1	Life cycle stages in which health and safety impacts of products and services are assessed for improvement and percentage of significant products and services categories subject to such procedures.	6	31
PR2	Total number of incidents of non-compliance with regulations and voluntary codes concerning health and safety impacts of products and services during their life cycle, by type of outcomes.	0	1

PR3	Type of product and service information required by procedures and percentage of significant products and services subject to such information requirements.	7	12
PR4	Total number of incidents of non-compliance with regulations and voluntary codes concerning product and service information and labeling, by type of outcomes.	0	1
PR5	Practices related to customer satisfaction, including results of surveys measuring customer satisfaction.	28	72
PR6	Programmes for adherence to laws, standards and voluntary codes related to marketing communications, including advertising, promotion and sponsorship.	89	75
PR7	Total number of incidents of non-compliance with regulations and voluntary codes concerning marketing communications, including advertising, promotion and sponsorship by type of outcomes.	0	1
PR8	Total number of substantiated complaints regarding breaches of customer privacy and losses of customer data.	0	4
PR9	Monetary value of significant fines for noncompliance with laws and regulations concerning the provision and use of products and services.	0	1

related to marketing communications. PR5 was also frequently disclosed in both reporting media, which reported practices related to customer satisfaction. Indicators reflecting non-compliance in terms of product responsibility and significant fines, such as PR2, PR4, PR7 and PR9, were least disclosed in both reporting media.

Altogether, the level of coverage of GRI indicators disclosed for each performance category varied between the annual report and the CSR report, with the CSR report covering more indicators. Also, most indicators were more frequently disclosed in the CSR report than in the annual report. Such findings suggest that firms viewed the CSR report as a preferred medium for social and environmental disclosure.

5.8 Conclusions

This stage of the study makes an incremental contribution to the social and environmental accounting literature by providing an insight into the social and environmental disclosure practices of socially responsible listed firms in the context of a developing country, China. The results reported in this chapter show that most socially responsible Chinese firms (identified by the social responsibility ranking list) published separate CSR reports for the year 2008, but social and environmental disclosure varied among firms. Firms made more social and environmental disclosure in the CSR report than in the annual report.

From the report preparers' perspectives, legitimacy theory posits that firms used social and environmental disclosure to communicate their legitimacy as a response to the concerns and expectations of general public and particular stakeholder groups within the society. It is evident from the analyses of disclosure types and contents that firms preferred to disclose positive news and were reluctant to disclose negative news, as disclosing negative news required to repair legitimacy later. On the other hand, positive news could help firms to build corporate images and to maintain legitimacy, and it was a less costly strategy to make firms' social and environmental activities more understandable to stakeholders. From the users' perspectives, CSR reports provided more stakeholder-relevant social and environmental disclosure than annual reports. According to stakeholder theory, the different reporting media were directed by the sample firms to different stakeholder groups. For instance, annual reports were prepared for stakeholders who are interested in the economic performance of a firm and therefore contained less social and environmental disclosure, CSR reports however, were prepared for stakeholders who are interested in the social and environmental activities of a firm and therefore contained more social and environmental disclosure.

This chapter has analysed the current state of the social and environmental disclosure practices of socially responsible Chinese listed firms. The next stage of the research (Chapter 6) will empirically examine the factors influencing the social and environmental disclosure of these firms.

Note

1 Zijin Mining, as the largest gold producer in China, was exposed by the poisonous wastewater spill that poisoned tons of fish and polluted two reservoirs in 2007 and was listed as one of the firms that failed to get approval of 'Environmental Credit' by the state in 2008.

6 Empirical results – stakeholders' power, corporate characteristics, and social and environmental disclosure

6.1 Introduction

The previous chapter presented the empirical results of the first stage of this study. The second stage of this study examined the influence of stakeholders' power and corporate characteristics on the social and environmental disclosure practices of socially responsible Chinese listed firms. The results of testing the relationship between stakeholders' power, corporate characteristics, and corporate social and environmental disclosure are presented in this chapter. The empirical results are analysed, with disclosure being examined first at the SEDI level and then at four broad GRI categories level (i.e. context, economic performance, environmental performance, and social performance). This chapter also provides additional analyses of empirical results in terms of using different proxies for corporate social and environmental disclosure by making appropriate modifications to the construction of the SEDI.

The remainder of this chapter is organised as follows. Section 6.2 presents the descriptive statistical analyses for the variables tested in this chapter. Section 6.3 provides the analyses of empirical results with disclosure being examined at the SEDI level. Section 6.4 presents the analyses of empirical results with disclosure being examined at the GRI categories level. Following this, Section 6.5 provides additional analyses of empirical results by constructing the SEDI in different ways. Finally, conclusions are presented in Section 6.6.

6.2 Descriptive analysis for the variables

In this stage of the research, an empirical model was employed to examine the effects of stakeholders' power and corporate characteristics on the social and environmental disclosure of socially responsible Chinese listed firms. The disclosure index, SEDI, constructed in the first stage was used here as a dependent variable.

The results of the descriptive statistics for the SEDI, various disclosure categories based on GRI (G3 version) guidelines and other continuous variables are presented in Table 6.1. The dependent variable SEDI ranged from a minimum score of 5,172.50 to a maximum score of 33,299.16, with a mean of 12,783.86

and a standard deviation of 5,253.86, indicating that there was a large variation in social and environmental disclosure among sample firms.

For different disclosure categories, information related to context items and economic performance items were the most disclosed, with a mean value of 3,924.23 for context and a mean value of 3,643.58 for economic performance. The variation in disclosure among sample firms for both environmental performance items and social performance items was relatively large, with a standard deviation of 1,397.93 and 1,868.07, respectively. A minimum score of 0 for environmental performance and human rights suggests that some firms did not disclose any information about their environmental performance and human rights.

The variable that represents shareholder power in this study, concentrated ownership (OWN), had a minimum of 0.068 and a maximum of 0.864, with a mean of 0.487 and a standard deviation of 0.188, indicating that firms had varying degrees of shareholder concentration. The variable that represents creditor power in this study, financial leverage (LEV), had a high mean value of 0.619, indicating that on average firms were highly geared.

The corporate characteristic variable, corporate profitability (FIN), had a low mean value of 0.079 and this might be due to the fact that many firms may have been influenced by the global economic crisis of 2008 as these firms earn a high proportion of revenue from international trade.

6.3 Analysis – disclosure at the SEDI level

The results of Pearson correlation for the SEDI and all continuous variables tested in Model (4.1) are reported in Table 6.2. These correlations indicate that collinearity is not present as the highest correlation coefficient is 0.4732 between

Table 6.1 Descriptive statistics for SEDI, GRI categories and other continuous variables

Variable	*Obs.*	*Mean*	*Std. dev.*	*Min.*	*Max.*	*Median*
SEDI	100	12,783.86	5,253.86	5,172.50	3,3299.16	12,034.17
Context	100	3,924.23	1,236.27	2,063.33	9,105.00	3,675.00
Economic performance	100	3,643.58	1,330.53	1,885.83	9,932.50	3,369.17
Environmental performance	100	1,607.12	1,397.93	0	7,975.83	1,317.50
Social performance	100	3,608.92	1,868.07	758.33	9,405.00	3,020.42
Labour	100	1,447.93	637.35	340.00	3,511.67	1,278.33
Human rights	100	162.10	136.06	0	823.33	125.00
Society	100	1,424.69	1,126.17	60.00	5,703.33	1,048.33
Product responsibility	100	574.20	257.66	143.33	1,600.00	552.50
OWN	100	0.487	0.188	0.068	0.864	0.504
LEV	100	0.619	0.193	0.177	0.968	0.626
SIZE	100	24.417	1.043	22.512	28.004	24.171
FIN	100	0.079	0.138	−0.120	0.566	0.030

OWN and SIZE. Also, the variance inflation factors on these two variables are low (1.63 and 2.12, respectively), which further supports the absence of collinearity. This supports the fact that each predictor represents a unique characteristic and no two variables are statistically very similar.

From Table 6.2, it is clear that SIZE is positively associated with the dependent variable SEDI. Consistent with previous studies (Hackston and Milne, 1996; Cormier and Gordon, 2001), the results of this study indicate that the larger firms made more social and environmental disclosure. As hypothesised, FIN is positively associated with the SEDI. This is consistent with Roberts (1992), indicating that firms with better financial performance made more social and environmental disclosure. As to the stakeholder variables, this study found that shareholder concentration and creditor power had no positive correlations with corporate social and environmental disclosure.

To avoid the problem of heteroscedasticity (where the variances of errors are different across observation points), ordinary least squares (OLS) regression with heteroscedasticity robust standard errors (White, 1980), was used to test the relationships implicit in Model (4.1). The results for regression are shown in Table 6.3.

As indicated in Table 6.3, hypothesis 1.5 (H1.5) is strongly supported in the multivariate results with a significantly positive association between SIZE and SEDI at $p=0.000$. This is consistent with the bi-variable result in the correlation matrix (shown in Table 6.2). Consistent with legitimacy theory, the larger listed Chinese firms disclosed more social and environmental information to demonstrate their legitimacy to the public and relevant stakeholders as a means of ensuring their continued operations. Also, consistent with the bi-variable result in the correlation matrix, there is a significantly positive association between FIN and SEDI at $p=0.000$. Therefore, hypothesis 1.6 (H1.6) is also strongly supported. Chinese firms with high profitability have sufficient financial capability to undertake costly social responsibility disclosure as argued by Ullman (1985) and need to legitimate firms' activities to stakeholders due to greater organisational visibility among stakeholders. Another corporate characteristic variable, industry classification was found to be significantly ($p=0.005$) and positively associated with SEDI, thus supporting hypothesis

Table 6.2 Pearson correlation coefficients of SEDI and other continuous variables

	SEDI	*OWN*	*LEV*	*SIZE*	*FIN*
SEDI	1.000				
OWN	0.1803	1.000			
LEV	0.0026	−0.1650	1.000		
SIZE	0.6857[a]	0.4732[a]	0.0758	1.000	
FIN	0.4286[a]	−0.2155[b]	0.0810	0.1240	1.000

Notes
a Significance is at the 0.01 level.
b Significance is at the 0.05 level.

Table 6.3 Regression results for SEDI

	β_0	*CSOE*	*OWN*	*LEV*	*AUDIT*	*SIZE*	*FIN*	*IND*	*X-LISTED*
Coefficient	−62,355.32	259.27	−3,593.02	−2,746.15	594.28	3,108.05	11,881.71	1,810.99	242.26
t-Statistics	−4.76	0.38	−1.74	−1.21	0.73	5.36	3.99	2.91	0.22
p-value	0.000	0.705	0.085	0.229	0.470	0.000	0.000	0.005	0.823
Hypothesis		H1.1	H1.2	H1.3	H1.4	H1.5	H1.6	H1.7	H1.8
Expected sign		+	−	+/−	+	+	+	+	+
Actual sign and significance		+	−*	−	+	+***	+***	+***	+

Notes
$R^2=0.6285$, $F=12.96$ and $N=100$.
*significant at $p<0.1$; **significant at $p<0.05$; ***significant at $p<0.01$.

1.7 (H1.7). The significant relationship between industry classification and SEDI provides evidence to support the public pressure perspective of legitimacy theory. Chinese listed firms in high-profile industries disclosed more social and environmental information as a response to high consumer visibility and regulatory risk. For instance, specific regulatory documents directed towards polluting industries, such as the *Regulations of Environmental Inspection on Companies Accessing to or Refinance on the Stock Market* (SEPA, 2003), appeared to have prompted firms in polluting industries to disclose more environmental information than other firms. Similar to firm size and corporate profitability, therefore, industry classification is also a statistically significant determinant of corporate social and environmental disclosure in China. However, the positive association predicted between the variable X-LISTED and SEDI was found to be insignificant in the multivariate results. One possible explanation for this result is that when this research was conducted corporate social and environmental disclosure was still voluntary in most countries where listing rules had no requirement for listed firms to disclose social and environmental information.

As reported in Table 6.3, stakeholder power variables (i.e. government (CSOE), creditor (LEV) and auditor (AUDIT)) were not found to have a statistically significant relationship ($p<0.1$) with corporate social and environmental disclosure. The shareholder power (OWN) was found to be negatively associated with SEDI at $p<0.1$ level, suggesting that, controlling for other variables in the regression, shareholder concentration negatively influenced firms' social and environmental disclosure. An explanation for the insignificant result between CSOE and SEDI might be that some central state-owned enterprises have not made a substantially positive response to government recommendations of making social and environmental disclosure in published reports. It is implied that the Chinese government and its agencies should prescribe detailed corporate social and environmental disclosure guidelines and make them mandatory for listed firms because the soft approach of encouraging voluntary disclosure has not been effective (Taylor and Shan, 2007). A possible reason for the insignificant relationship between AUDIT and SEDI might be the fact that auditors paid little attention to corporate social and environmental disclosure practices, especially because these were not required to be audited in most jurisdictions, including China.

6.4 Further analysis – disclosure at the GRI categories level

To provide additional insights, this section further analyses the relationships between stakeholders' power, corporate characteristics and corporate social and environmental disclosure across the four broad GRI categories: context, economic performance, environmental performance, and social performance. The regression was repeated by replacing the SEDI in Model (4.1) with the score of each GRI category as the dependent variable. Similarly, heteroscedasticity robust standard errors (White, 1980) were used in all regressions to ensure that the variances of errors across observations did not follow a consistent pattern. The results for a series of regressions are reported in Table 6.4.

As shown in Table 6.4, similar to SEDI, the results for the context category indicate that SIZE, FIN and IND are all significantly and positively associated with context related disclosure. Further, OWN was found to be significantly and negatively associated with context related disclosure. This result suggests that less concentrated ownership encouraged management to disclose the overall context information for understanding corporate performance, such as corporate strategy, profile and governance.

Similar to context, the results for the economic performance category also indicate a significantly negative association between shareholder concentration and economic performance, suggesting that shareholder dispersion was likely to motivate management to disclose information about corporate economic performance. However, the positive association between industry and economic performance is insignificant in this regression.

The results for the environmental performance category are substantially different from the results obtained from the main model. A significantly negative association was found between LEV and environmental performance, which suggests that firms with low leverage disclosed more environmental information as a proactive measure to present the firm as a responsible corporate citizen and to receive a favourable assessment of their financial risk by creditors. This result may also be related to the environmental credit policy[1] implemented by many Chinese banks at present (SEPA, PBC and CBRC, 2007). Firms in demand of credit proactively disclosed environmental information so as to gain environmental loans for their operations. The relationship between corporate profitability and environmental disclosure was found to be insignificant, which means that firms with higher profitability failed to disclose more environmental information.

Finally, the results for the social performance category are similar to the results for SEDI in the main model, indicating a statistically significant and positive association with social performance disclosure found for firm size, profitability and industry, respectively; and a significantly negative association between social performance disclosure and concentrated ownership.

6.5 Additional analysis

In this study, the disclosure index – SEDI was constructed with three dimensions involving the quantity measure, the quality measure of disclosure types and the quality measure of the importance of disclosure items. In this section, additional analyses are conducted with some changes to the construction of SEDI. First, the SEDI is reconstructed without the dimension concerning the importance of disclosure items, supposing that all disclosure items are viewed as equally important to stakeholders. Second, the quality ratings of disclosure types in the index are determined from the researcher's perspective, as in previous studies, rather than stakeholders' perspectives (using stakeholder survey responses conducted in this

Table 6.4 Regression results for GRI categories

Panel A: context

	β_0	*CSOE*	*OWN*	*LEV*	*AUDIT*	*SIZE*	*FIN*	*IND*	*X-LISTED*
Coefficient	−13,357.84	138.62	−978.04	35.90	82.52	700.03	2,963.90	330.84	215.32
t-Statistics	−3.57	0.89	−2.11	0.07	0.45	4.21	4.79	2.31	1.02
p-value	0.001	0.376	0.038	0.945	0.650	0.000	0.000	0.023	0.312

Note
$R^2=0.6412$, $F=12.52$ and $N=100$.

Panel B: economic performance

	β_0	*CSOE*	*OWN*	*LEV*	*AUDIT*	*SIZE*	*FIN*	*IND*	*X-LISTED*
Coefficient	−15,785.37	−103.22	−1,307.47	−746.98	178.67	821.38	2,995.64	220	92.08
t-Statistics	−3.63	−0.53	−2.48	−1.13	0.79	4.28	4.02	1.30	0.37
p-value	0.000	0.594	0.015	0.262	0.430	0.000	0.000	0.198	0.709

Note
$R^2=0.5948$, $F=9.99$ and $N=100$.

Panel C: environmental performance

	β_0	*CSOE*	*OWN*	*LEV*	*AUDIT*	*SIZE*	*FIN*	*IND*	*X-LISTED*
Coefficient	−12,326.13	152.31	86.68	−2,486.69	11.70	608.65	449.39	782.46	−229.99
t-Statistics	−3.52	0.67	0.12	−3.42	0.05	3.89	0.41	4.33	−0.68
p-value	0.001	0.506	0.902	0.001	0.960	0.000	0.679	0.000	0.50

Note
$R^2=0.4107$, $F=6.82$ and $N=100$.

Panel D: social performance

	β_0	*CSOE*	*OWN*	*LEV*	*AUDIT*	*SIZE*	*FIN*	*IND*	*X-LISTED*
Coefficient	−20,885.98	71.56	−1,394.20	451.62	321.40	977.99	5,472.79	477.68	164.85
t-Statistics	−5.42	0.29	−1.95	0.62	1.07	5.74	5.51	2.05	0.43
p-value	0.000	0.771	0.054	0.535	0.289	0.000	0.000	0.044	0.668

Note
$R^2=0.6603$, $F=18.83$ and $N=100$.

study).[2] It was anticipated that when these changes (i.e. the quality measure from the stakeholder perspective is removed from the SEDI) occurred, there would be no significant changes in the patterns of statistical results revealed by the SEDI. The results of regressions with the above changes in the SEDI dependent variable are discussed and analysed as follows.

6.5.1 SEDI without disclosure item quality dimension

As discussed in Chapter 4, there was a debate in the literature on whether each disclosure item should be assigned a weighting in constructing a disclosure index. Previous social and environmental disclosure studies weighted all disclosure items equally (i.e. each disclosure item is equally relevant to all stakeholders) when constructing disclosure indices (Clarkson *et al.*, 2011). This determination was made by researchers rather than by stakeholders, as previous studies did not conduct an extensive survey that solicited stakeholders' perceptions about GRI disclosure items.

This additional analysis also calculated sample firms' SEDI by assuming that all disclosure items are equally important to stakeholders. The results of the descriptive statistics for the SEDI that treated all disclosure items as equally weighted are compared with that of the normal SEDI constructed in this study in Table 6.5. The Pearson correlation between the normal SEDI and the SEDI without disclosure item quality is positive and significant ($r=0.99$, $p<0.0001$). The results of regression for using the SEDI dependent variable with equally weighted items as in Model (4.1) are presented in Table 6.6.

From Table 6.6, it can be seen that the results of using the SEDI as the dependent variable with equally weighted items appear in a pattern very similar to the original regression results shown in Table 6.3, with SIZE, FIN and IND indicating significantly positive relationships with the SEDI (without disclosure item quality) (at $p<0.01$ level), and OWN indicating a negative relationship with the SEDI (without disclosure item quality) (at $p<0.1$ level). Previous studies indicated that item importance weighted and unweighted disclosure scores tend to give the similar results where there are a large number of items (Chow and Wong-Boren, 1987; Marston and Shrives, 1991; Beattie *et al.*, 2004). For instance, Chow and Wong-Boren (1987) conducted an attitude survey toward loan officers of banks to ask for their opinions on the importance of items and compared importance weighted disclosure scores with unweighted disclosure

Table 6.5 Descriptive statistics for SEDI with different constructions

Variable	*Obs.*	*Mean*	*Std. Dev.*	*Min.*	*Max.*	*Median*
SEDI (normal)	100	12,783.86	5,253.86	5,172.50	33,299.16	12,034.17
SEDI (without disclosure item quality)	100	3,983	1,632.48	1,610	10,370	3,755
SEDI (researcher driven)	100	201.28	82.12	82	522	189

Table 6.6 Regression results for SEDI (without disclosure item quality)

	β_0	*CSOE*	*OWN*	*LEV*	*AUDIT*	*SIZE*	*FIN*	*IND*	*X-LISTED*
Coefficient	−19,452.98	98.27	−1,091.34	−828.61	157.63	968.54	3,681.66	559.81	79.68
t-Statistics	−4.76	0.46	−1.69	−1.18	0.62	5.35	3.97	2.90	0.24
p-value	0.000	0.645	0.095	0.240	0.535	0.000	0.000	0.005	0.813

Note
R^2=0.6268, F=12.63 and N=100.

scores. They found that almost identical results were obtained in the subsequent regression analyses of using weighted scores and unweighted scores alternatively as the dependent variable. The findings of this study provide evidence to support the previous studies.

6.5.2 SEDI with researcher driven quality measure

In this study, the quality ratings in the SEDI were determined by stakeholders' responses on the preference of various disclosure types. As discussed in Chapter 4, researchers in previous social and environmental disclosure studies assumed the role of stakeholders and determined the quality ratings of disclosure types themselves in constructing social and environmental disclosure indices (Wiseman, 1982; Walden and Schwartz, 1997; van Staden and Hooks, 2007). This study also tested the SEDI given that the quality ratings of disclosure types were identified by the researcher's knowledge rather than by stakeholders' responses.

Specifically, to reflect the spirit of the GRI guidelines, and with the assumption that stakeholders prefer credible disclosure that is hard to mimic, when constructing the SEDI a heavy emphasis was placed on firms' disclosure related to objective measures of their social and environmental performance. As Clarkson *et al.* (2008) argued, a firm with good social and environmental performance will voluntarily disclose objective measures of its social and environmental impact such as quantitative performance indicators, but a firm with poor performance will not. Stakeholders also demand hard and objective measures of firms' social and environmental performance so that poor performers cannot mimic good performers by presenting soft and unverifiable claims (e.g. a statement of corporate environmental policy). Therefore, similar to Clarkson *et al.* (2008), this study used different rating scales for GRI context items and performance indicator items. For 42 context items, which were easy to mimic, a score of 1 or 0 was assigned to each item based on disclosure or no disclosure. For 79 performance indicator items, which were hard to mimic, a score from 0 to 5 was assigned to various disclosure types of each individual item.

According to the various disclosure types in the extant literature where researchers determined the stakeholder preference of disclosure types, specific definitions of quality rating scales adopted for disclosure types are indicated as follows: score = 0, no disclosure; score = 1, general narrative; score = 2, specific endeavour in non-quantitative terms; score = 3, performance data is presented with quantified results; score = 4, performance data is presented with quantified results relative to benchmark (e.g. targets/industry/previous periods); and score = 5, performance data is presented with quantified results at disaggregate level (e.g. plant, business unit, geographic segment). Using the above quality rating scales, the SEDI was recalculated, and the descriptive statistical results are shown in Table 6.5. The Pearson correlation between the normal SEDI and the researcher driven SEDI is positive and significant ($r = 0.99$, $p < 0.0001$). The results of regression for using the researcher driven SEDI as a dependent variable in Model (4.1) are provided in Table 6.7.

Table 6.7 Regression results for SEDI (researcher driven)

	β_0	*CSOE*	*OWN*	*LEV*	*AUDIT*	*SIZE*	*FIN*	*IND*	*X-LISTED*
Coefficient	−971.92	5.08	−54.84	−40.69	8.71	48.44	187.02	28.18	3.56
t-Statistics	−4.73	0.47	−1.69	−1.16	0.68	5.33	4.01	2.90	0.21
p-value	0.000	0.637	0.095	0.251	0.496	0.000	0.000	0.005	0.834

Note
$R^2=0.6270$, $F=12.74$ and $N=100$.

As indicated in Table 6.7, the regression results of using the SEDI driven by the researcher as a dependent variable appear in a pattern similar to the original regression results shown in Table 6.3. Again, corporate characteristic variables SIZE, FIN and IND have statistically significant positive relationships with the SEDI (researcher driven) (at $p<0.01$ level), and shareholder variable OWN has a negative relationship with the SEDI (researcher driven) (at $p<0.1$ level). These findings suggest that the quality ratings of disclosure types in constructing the disclosure index determined by stakeholders' responses were not statistically different from those determined by the researcher in the subsequent regression analyses.

In summary, using different proxies for corporate social and environmental disclosure by constructing the SEDI in different ways gave rise to similar results being obtained from subsequent regressions of using those proxies of the SEDI as the dependent variable. The SEDI with the quality measures from stakeholders' perceptions provided insights into corporate social and environmental disclosure from the users' perspectives. The SEDI not weighted for stakeholders' perceptions had no significant changes in the statistical results, which provided sufficient justification to use such SEDI as a valid measure to proxy for corporate disclosure from the preparers' perspectives and thus enabled the use of it in testing and commenting on legitimacy.

6.6 Conclusions

This chapter makes a contribution to the social and environmental accounting literature by examining the determinants of corporate social and environmental disclosure within the legitimacy and stakeholder framework in the context of a developing nation, China. The empirical results provide important insights into the influence of stakeholders' power and corporate characteristics on corporate social and environmental disclosure in China. Corporate characteristics, such as firm size, profitability and industry classification are all significant factors influencing corporate social and environmental disclosure. Consistent with the public pressure perspective of legitimacy theory, those firms that are more likely to be subject to public scrutiny, such as larger firms and firms in high-profile industries, disclosed more social and environmental information to meet the expectations of the public. The pressures from various stakeholders, such as government, creditors and auditors tested in this study, generally appear to be weak in China at present. However, along with the increase in the stakeholders' concerns about CSR behaviours, shareholders have influenced firms' social and environmental disclosure; and creditors have influenced firms' disclosure related to their environmental performance. According to stakeholder theory, those firms that seek to gain or maintain the support of powerful stakeholders have started to adopt a disclosure strategy. This chapter also conducted additional analyses of empirical results by reconstructing the SEDI in different ways. Similar regression results obtained from using different SEDI constructions provide further evidence to support the findings of this stage of the research.

This stage of the research also provides us with several unexpected but insightful results. For instance, Chinese listed firms with central state ownership were encouraged to make social and environmental disclosure as per the SASAC recommendations, but these firms have not made a substantial difference in the social and environmental disclosure compared with other Chinese listed firms. The involvement of the Big Four in the financial audit has also made no substantial difference in corporate social and environmental disclosure.

This stage of the research has investigated some influencing factors of social and environmental disclosure practices of socially responsible Chinese listed firms. The next stage of the study (Chapter 7) will consider another related research question – whether publishing a separate CSR report has a positive effect on the socially responsible reputation of Chinese listed firms.

Notes

1 A policy requires commercial banks, when reviewing businesses' applications for bank credits, to consider whether the applying business has followed environmental laws and regulations. The firms that violate the environmental laws and regulations will not gain approval, while the environmentally sensitive businesses will receive favourable treatment in this regard.

2 The importance weighting of items was not considered in this way of reconstructing the SEDI.

7 Empirical results – CSR report, corporate governance and corporate reputation

7.1 Introduction

The previous chapter presented the empirical results of the second stage of this study, which examined the determinants of the social and environmental disclosure practices of socially responsible Chinese listed firms. The third stage of this study investigates the link between a firm's publication of a CSR report and the socially responsible reputations of the firms in the presence of corporate governance factors and corporate characteristics. The empirical results of testing the relationship between the CSR report, board characteristics (as proxies of corporate governance), corporate characteristics and corporate socially responsible reputation are presented in this chapter. The results are first discussed in terms of descriptive statistics for the variables tested in this chapter, followed by the correlation analyses, regression analyses, and additional analyses that evaluate the link between the quality of the CSR report and corporate socially responsible reputation.

The remainder of this chapter is organised as follows. Section 7.2 presents the descriptive statistical analyses for the variables tested in this chapter. Section 7.3 presents the correlation analyses of continuous variables. Section 7.4 discusses the regression results for socially responsible reputation. Section 7.5 presents additional analyses in terms of testing the link between the quality of the CSR report and socially responsible reputation. Finally, Section 7.6 provides conclusions.

7.2 Descriptive analysis for the variables

In this stage of the research, an empirical model was employed to examine the relationship between publishing a CSR report, governance factors, corporate characteristics in the current period and socially responsible reputation of the sample firms in the future period. The results of descriptive statistics for all the variables are shown in Table 7.1. Panel A contains the dependent variable – socially responsible reputation (reputation) and other continuous variables – board size (BSIZE), board ownership (BOWN), board committees (BCOMM), profitability (FIN), and firm size (SIZE). Panel B contains dummy variables – CSR report (CSR), CEO duality (DUAL), and industry classification (IND).

Table 7.1 Descriptive statistics for reputation, CSR and control variables

Panel A: continuous variables

Variable name	*Obs.*	*Mean*	*Std. dev.*	*Min.*	*Max.*	*Median*
Reputation	83	33.997	7.954	25.338	74.877	32.397
BSIZE	83	11.205	2.874	7	19	11
BOWN	83	0.00076	0.00392	0	0.03062	0
BCOMM	83	4	1	1	7	4
FIN	83	0.082	0.138	−0.113	0.552	0.031
SIZE	83	24.551	1.060	23.088	28.004	24.341

Panel B: dummy variables

Variable name	*Obs.*	*No. of samples with 1*	*%*	*No. of samples with 0*	*%*
CSR	83	74	89	9	11
DUAL	83	12	14	71	86
IND	83	63	76	20	24

As shown in Panel A of Table 7.1, the mean reputation score for firms in this study is 33.997 with a minimum score of 25.338 and a maximum score of 74.877. The range of board size (BSIZE) is from a minimum score of 7 to a maximum score of 19 with a mean value of 11.205, consistent with findings reported in prior studies (Musteen *et al.*, 2010). A mean value of 0.00076 for board ownership (BOWN) shows a low percentage of shareholdings by directors in firms. A mean value of 4 for board committees (BCOMM) meets the requirement of CSRC.[1] In terms of financial performance (FIN), a low mean value of 0.082 shows that many sample firms may have been influenced by the global economic crisis of 2008. As shown in Panel B of Table 7.1, 89 per cent of sample firms published a CSR report (CSR) for the year 2008. The CEO was also the chairman on the board of directors (DUAL) in 14 per cent of sample firms.

7.3 Correlation matrix and bivariate analysis

The results of Pearson correlation for socially responsible reputation and other continuous variables are reported in Table 7.2. These correlations indicate that collinearity is not present, as the highest correlation coefficient is 0.432 between BSIZE and FIN. Also, the variance inflation factors on these two variables are low (1.34 and 1.43 respectively), indicating the absence of collinearity. The absence of collinearity suggests that each variable represents a unique characteristic in relation to the socially responsible reputation. As shown in Table 7.2, all the continuous variables have significant correlations with the dependent variable (reputation) except board ownership (BOWN). As hypothesised, the board characteristics variables – board size (BSIZE) and board committees (BCOMM) – are positively associated with reputation. The corporate characteristics variables – profitability (FIN) and firm size (SIZE) – are positively associated with reputation.

Table 7.2 Pearson correlation coefficients of reputation and other continuous variables

	Reputation	*BSIZE*	*BOWN*	*BCOMM*	*FIN*	*SIZE*
Reputation	1.000					
BSIZE	0.244**	1.000				
BOWN	−0.084	0.069	1.000			
BCOMM	0.203*	0.365***	−0.136	1.000		
FIN	0.327***	0.432***	0.091	0.402***	1.000	
SIZE	0.719***	0.171	−0.121	0.044	0.167	1.000

Notes
* significant at $p < 0.1$.
** significant at $p < 0.05$.
*** significant at $p < 0.01$.

7.4 Regression and multivariate analysis

OLS regression, with heteroscedasticity robust standard errors (White, 1980), was used to test the relationships implicit in Model (4.2). As discussed in Chapter 4, the relationships implicit in Model (4.2) were tested with four versions of the model. The results for regressions of all versions of the model are shown in Table 7.3.

As indicated in Table 7.3, Model (4.2.2) tested for the relationship between publishing a CSR report and corporate socially responsible reputation only by controlling for corporate characteristics variables. The full model, Model (4.2.4), tested for the relationship between publishing a CSR report and socially responsible reputation by controlling for board characteristics and corporate characteristics variables. It was found that CSR had a significant and positive association with reputation in both Model (4.2.2) and Model (4.2.4). Thus, hypothesis 2.1 (H2.1) is strongly supported. As hypothesised, a firm's publication of a CSR report has a positive influence on its socially responsible reputation. Since reputation is derived from the external collective perceptions of a firm's fulfilment of its social responsibilities (Fombrun and Van Riel, 1997), a published CSR report as a source of such information signals a socially responsible image of the firm in the minds of the external stakeholders, and then such an image being held by the stakeholders contributes to the formation of the firm's reputation. Publishing a CSR report as a tool of impression management can increase a firm's positive, future visibility and distinctiveness in the eyes of the stakeholders (Fombrun, 1996).

As shown in Table 7.3, Model (4.2.3) tested for the relationship between board characteristics, corporate characteristics and corporate socially responsible reputation, and the full model, Model (4.2.4), examined the link between publishing a CSR report and socially responsible reputation while controlling for board characteristics and corporate characteristics variables simultaneously. It was found that CEO/chairman duality (DUAL) was significantly and negatively associated with reputation in both Model (4.2.3) and Model (4.2.4). Hypothesis 2.2 (H2.2), therefore, is also strongly supported. This significant, negative association suggests that CEO duality influences the effectiveness of the corporate

Table 7.3 Regression results for reputation

	Hypothesis	*Expected sign*	*Actual sign*	*Model (4.2.1) Control variables*[a]	*Model (4.2.2)*[b] *CSR*	*Model (4.2.3)*[c] *Board characteristics*	*Model (4.2.4)*[d] *Full model*
constant				−94.440***	−93.816***	−97.340***	−96.836***
CSR	H2.1	+	+		2.332**		2.566**
DUAL	H2.2	−	−			−4.626***	−4.636***
BSIZE	H2.3	+	+			0.077	0.076
BOWN	H2.4	+	+			109.726	102.353
BCOMM	H2.5	+	+			0.594	0.650
FIN	H2.6	+	+	12.461***	11.732**	10.896**	9.966**
SIZE	H2.7	+	+	5.214***	5.107***	5.243***	5.126***
IND	H2.8	+	−	−0.771	−0.795	−1.225	−1.273

Notes

a F: 11.31, R^2: 0.562, N: 83.

b F: 11.76, R^2: 0.570, N: 83.

c F: 6.99, R^2: 0.609, N: 83.

d F: 7.16, R^2: 0.619, N: 83.

* significant at $p < 0.1$.

** significant at $p < 0.05$.

*** significant at $p < 0.01$.

board in performing the governance function through the concentration of decision making and control power, which has an adverse impact on the quality of management and thereby corporate reputation. Contrary to expectations, there were no significant relationships between reputation and other board characteristics variables, i.e. board size (BSIZE), board ownership (BOWN) and board committees (BCOMM). A possible reason for these insignificant relationships is that these board characteristics as proxies for governance have been less visible to stakeholders involved in the assessment of socially responsible reputation. The findings suggest that CEO/chairman duality is a more appropriate measure of governance in assessing corporate socially responsible reputation in China than the other measures used in this study.

The control variables, financial performance (FIN) and firm size (SIZE) were found to be significantly and positively associated with reputation in all models. This is consistent with the bivariate results in the correlation matrix (see Table 7.2). Therefore, hypotheses H2.6 and H2.7 are strongly supported. A significant and positive association between financial performance and socially responsible reputation shows that reputation has a financial 'halo effect' (Toms, 2002, p. 257). A significant and positive association between firm size and socially responsible reputation provides evidence that larger firms are more positively viewed by various stakeholders when assessing the corporate socially responsible reputation. However, the impact of industry (IND) on corporate socially responsible reputation was found to be insignificant. The findings of financial performance, firm size and industry are consistent with previous studies (Fombrun and Shanley, 1990; Musteen *et al.*, 2010).

To sum up, the empirical results show that publishing a CSR report has a positive effect on a firm's socially responsible reputation. Impression management theory could explain this finding. Those firms publishing a CSR report as an impression management tool demonstrate their social responsibility fulfilments to powerful stakeholders, who provide the financial resources necessary to firms' operations or are involved in the assessment of firms' socially responsible reputations. The positive impressions that firms impart on stakeholders by publishing a CSR report might assist them in increasing the firm's financial wealth in terms of higher revenues and profits, and lower costs of funds. The empirical results of this stage of the research also indicate that CEO/chairman duality as a measure of corporate governance has a negative effect on corporate socially responsible reputation. In the eyes of the stakeholders, CEO/chairman duality can adversely influence the effectiveness of corporate board in performing the governance function and thereby the quality of management and corporate socially responsible reputation. Corporate characteristics of financial performance and firm size are positively associated with corporate socially responsible reputation, which is achieved through visible firms' legitimating to social norms and practices.

7.5 Additional analysis

Previous studies that examined the relationship between environmental disclosure and corporate reputation considered the effects of the quality of environmental disclosure on corporate environmental reputation (Toms, 2002; Hasseldine *et al.*, 2005). The findings of these studies indicated that the quality of environmental disclosure was positively associated with corporate environmental reputation. Based on the previous studies, this study also examined the link between the quality of the CSR report in the year 2008 and corporate socially responsible reputation in the year 2009, which will be discussed in this section. The relationships implicit in Model (4.2) were retested by replacing the independent variable CSR with the quality of CSR report (CSRquality).

The variable CSRquality was measured by considering the quality of social and environmental disclosure in firms' CSR reports. Consistent with the construction of the SEDI in previous chapters, this study used stakeholders' perceptions on disclosure types (obtained from the questionnaire survey) and GRI items (obtained from the panel consultation) to measure the quality of social and environmental disclosure in CSR reports. In this study, consistent with previous studies (Toms, 2002; Hasseldine *et al.*, 2005), the highest perceived quality rating of disclosure type for a given GRI item was used as the disclosure type quality score of that GRI item disclosure. This is because the lower level narrative type disclosure can be imitated without equivalent commitment, but the higher level quantified type disclosure is more likely to represent actual social and environmental activities, and imitation by competitors is difficult (Toms, 2002). The stakeholders' perceptions on the relative importance of disclosure items were used as the disclosure item quality score of the GRI item disclosure. As a result, the quality of the CSR report (CSRquality) was evaluated by the combined measures of the highest quality rating of disclosure type for a GRI item and the quality rating on the importance of that item disclosed in firms' CSR reports.

Using CSRquality as the proxy for the quality of CSR report, this study reexamined the relationship between CSR report and socially responsible reputation by repeating the regressions of both Model (4.2.2), which tested the relationship between the quality of the CSR report and corporate reputation only by controlling for corporate characteristics variables, and Model (4.2.4), which tested the relationship between the quality of the CSR report and corporate reputation while controlling for both board characteristics and corporate characteristics variables. The results of regressions are indicated in Table 7.4.

Panel A of Table 7.4 presents the results of the relationship between the quality of the CSR report (CSRquality) and corporate reputation. CSRquality has a significantly positive association with the dependent variable reputation, which suggests that the quality of the CSR report has a significantly positive effect on corporate socially responsible reputation. Control variables FIN and SIZE are also significantly associated with reputation, which confirms that financial performance and firm size positively influence corporate socially responsible reputation.

Table 7.4 Regression results for reputation – additional test

Panel A: Model (4.2.2) CSRquality

	Constant	*CSRquality*	*FIN*	*SIZE*	*IND*
Coefficient	−83.045	0.001	10.018	4.638	−1.012
t-Statistics	−3.35	2.65	2.14	4.48	−0.87
p-value	0.001	0.010	0.036	0.000	0.385

Note
F: 12.71, R^2: 0.5868, N: 83.

Panel B: Model (4.2.4) full model

	Constant	*CSRquality*	*DUAL*	*BSIZE*	*BOWN*	*BCOMM*	*FIN*	*SIZE*	*IND*
Coefficient	−87.446	0.001	−4.046	0.101	71.730	0.702	8.153	4.711	−1.469
t-Statistics	−3.51	2.60	−2.78	0.51	0.93	1.11	1.63	4.64	−1.42
p-value	0.001	0.011	0.007	0.615	0.356	0.271	0.107	0.000	0.159

Note
F: 7.03, R^2: 0.6285, N: 83.

Panel B of Table 7.4 presents the results of the relationship between the quality of the CSR report, corporate governance factors, corporate characteristics, and corporate socially responsible reputation. The results indicate a significantly positive relationship between CSRquality and reputation, which confirms that the quality of the CSR report has a positive influence on corporate socially responsible reputation. The significantly positive relationship between the quality of the CSR report and socially responsible reputation suggests that a good quality CSR report is a powerful signal in managing the stakeholders' impressions of a firm as being socially responsible. Again, similar to the results shown in Table 7.3, the board characteristics variable DUAL has a significantly negative association with reputation, indicating the negative effect of CEO/chairman duality on a firm's socially responsible reputation.

7.6 Conclusions

This chapter examined the link between the CSR report (the publication of a CSR report and the quality of that CSR report) and corporate socially responsible reputation in the context of China. The empirical results provided meaningful insights into the relationship between the CSR report, corporate governance, corporate characteristics and the socially responsible reputation of socially responsible Chinese listed firms. For those socially responsible Chinese listed firms, the publication of a CSR report and the quality of that CSR report have positive impacts on that firm's corporate socially responsible reputation. A firm's CSR report and the quality of that report can be viewed as impression management signals that positively influence the stakeholders' perceptions on corporate socially responsible reputation. On the other hand, CEO/chairman duality adversely influences corporate socially responsible reputation. Therefore, firms with good governance practices publish CSR reports and then enhance their socially responsible reputation in the eyes of stakeholders. This stage of the research also provided evidence that sound financial performance and larger firm size favourably influence corporate socially responsible reputation.

This stage of the research contributes to the literature by incorporating three domains – CSR report, corporate governance and corporate socially responsible reputation. It fills a void in the current research by investigating the link between CSR report and corporate socially responsible reputation in the context of a developing country, China. This chapter also adds to the research on board attributes as important governance signals of influencing corporate reputation by investigating this issue in the context of China.

Note

1 According to CSRC (2002), the board of a listed firm may establish four basic committees: corporate strategy committee, audit committee, nomination committee, and remuneration and appraisal committee; and other special committees in accordance with the resolutions of the shareholders' meetings.

8 Conclusions

8.1 Introduction

This chapter presents conclusions to this study by summarising the research findings of each stage of this study and discussing the research limitations and opportunities for further research.

The remainder of this chapter is organised as follows. Section 8.2 presents an overview of this study. Section 8.3 provides the conclusions of the research findings. Section 8.4 presents the practical implications. Section 8.5 then discusses the research limitations. Following this, Section 8.6 provides suggestions for future research.

8.2 Research overview

With increasing academic concerns in the phenomenon of social and environmental disclosure, this study investigated the corporate social and environmental disclosure practices in the context of the largest developing country – China. The study inquired into three research issues related to this topic: the current state of the social and environmental disclosure practices of socially responsible Chinese listed firms, the determinants influencing these firms' social and environmental disclosure in their annual reports and CSR reports, and the link between firms' CSR reporting (i.e. publishing a CSR report and the quality of the CSR report) and their socially responsible reputation. Acknowledging the nomological relations among theories used in the social and environmental accounting literature, this study adopted legitimacy theory and stakeholder theory to aid the understanding of Chinese listed firms' social and environmental disclosure practices. Impression management theory, stakeholder theory and legitimacy theory were employed to understand the effects of CSR report publication and the quality of the CSR report on firms' socially responsible reputation. Based on the pragmatic assumption, this study used mixed methods to approach the research issues from different points of view by triangulating data sources (content analysis data, questionnaire survey data and panel consultation data). To measure firms' social and environmental disclosure, content analysis was used to collect empirical data about the disclosure quantity from corporate annual reports and CSR reports. A questionnaire survey was used to collect the data about disclosure quality relating to disclosure types through investigating stakeholders' perceptions on the preference of different disclosure types. A stakeholder panel consultation was used to collect the data about disclosure quality relating to disclosure items through investigating stakeholders' perceptions on the relative importance of disclosure items. The disclosure quantity, disclosure type quality and disclosure item quality were combined to form the stakeholder-driven, three-dimensional SEDI as the proxy for corporate social and environmental disclosure. Two empirical models were designed respectively to examine the determinants influencing firms' social and environmental disclosure and the link between firms' publication of a CSR report (and the quality of the disclosure in the CSR report) and their socially responsible reputation.

8.3 Findings

The first stage of the study involved observing the current state of social and environmental disclosure practices of Chinese listed firms. Through analysing both the annual reports and the CSR reports of socially responsible Chinese listed firms, it was found that firms disclosed social and environmental information in various disclosure types to communicate their legitimacy to the public and to meet the demands of different stakeholder groups, but social and environmental disclosure varied across firms with a wide disparity. The results of this stage also indicated that firms' social and environmental disclosure varied across the two reporting media, i.e. annual report versus CSR report. The CSR report was found to be a more valuable source of information on the social and environmental dimension than the annual report. These initial findings contribute to the social and environmental disclosure literature by providing a current empirical observation of corporate social and environmental disclosure in the context of China. This stage of the research also makes a methodological contribution to the literature in terms of instrument development by constructing a SEDI with three dimensions (disclosure quantity, disclosure type quality, disclosure item quality) and measuring the quality dimensions from the stakeholders' perspectives. By applying legitimacy theory from the preparers' perspectives, the results revealed that socially responsible Chinese listed firms have used social and environmental disclosure to communicate their legitimacy as a response to the concerns and expectations of the general public and particular stakeholder groups within society. By considering stakeholder theory from the users' perspectives, it was shown that the variation of social and environmental disclosure between the annual report and the CSR report may be due to the fact that the two reporting media are oriented to different stakeholder groups, for example, annual reports are prepared for shareholders who are interested in the economic performance of a firm but CSR reports are prepared for stakeholders who are interested in the CSR activities of a firm. In this manner, a joint consideration of legitimacy theory and stakeholder theory is applicable to the context of China.

The second stage of the study examined factors influencing the social and environmental disclosure of socially responsible Chinese listed firms. The results of this stage indicated that corporate characteristics – size, profitability and industry classification – were all significant factors influencing the social and environmental disclosure of these firms. It was also found that despite a weak influence from various stakeholders on the whole, shareholders have influenced firms' social and environmental disclosure and creditors have influenced firms' disclosure related to their environmental performance. A joint framework of legitimacy theory and stakeholder theory partially explains the influence of those factors tested in this stage on corporate social and environmental disclosure. Consistent with the public pressure perspective of legitimacy theory, those firms that are more likely to be subject to public scrutiny disclosed more social and environmental information to communicate their legitimacy. According to stakeholder theory, socially responsible firms have adopted a disclosure strategy to meet the expectations of powerful stakeholders (i.e. financial stakeholders). This part of the study makes a contribution to the social and environmental disclosure literature of developing countries by examining the determinants of firms' disclosure and employing theories to explain the disclosure phenomenon.

The third stage of the research investigated the link between CSR reporting and the socially responsible reputation of sample firms in the presence of corporate governance factors and corporate characteristics. This stage of the study found that for those socially responsible firms, publishing a CSR report and the quality of disclosure in the CSR report had positive effects on their socially responsible reputation, but CEO/chairman duality had a negative effect on their socially responsible reputation. As a tool of impression management, firms' CSR reports signalled socially responsible images of those firms to their stakeholders and such images influenced the stakeholders' perceptions on the firms' socially responsible reputations. From the stakeholder perspective, CEO/chairman duality was viewed as unfavourable in performing the governance function when stakeholders engaged in an assessment of the firms' reputations. Overall, impression management theory and stakeholder theory support that firms with good governance practices published CSR reports and then enhanced their socially responsible reputation in the eyes of stakeholders in the context of China. The results of this stage also indicated that good financial performance and large firm size were favourable to the socially responsible reputation of a firm. According to legitimacy theory, firms with good financial performance and large size are more likely to seek legitimacy and then reputation. This stage of the study fills a void in the current social and environmental disclosure literature by investigating the link between CSR reporting (i.e. publishing a CSR report and the quality of the CSR report) and a firm's socially responsible reputation in the context of China.

8.4 Practical implications

In the current Chinese context, there is a large variation in the social and environmental disclosure practice among Chinese firms. The Chinese government, as both regulator and facilitator, has issued regulations and guidelines in promoting firms' CSR behaviours and social and environmental disclosure practices. However, ambiguity and uncertainty within governmental regulations and guidelines has led to noncomparable disclosure practices among firms. Therefore, the Chinese government needs to make continuous efforts by providing more detailed guidance regarding the content and extent of social and environmental disclosure to assist firms to communicate their CSR activities effectively to regulatory bodies and other stakeholders.

To improve the quality and credibility of social and environmental disclosure, external assurance should be provided as part of the accountability process (Adams, 2004). However, in the current Chinese context, verification of CSR reports through independent third parties is still in its infancy. Professional auditors, such as the 'Big Four' have not been involved in providing assurance for Chinese firms' social and environmental performance. Therefore, in the future, audit firms can be encouraged to provide reasonable assurance for firms' social and environmental disclosure in annual reports and CSR reports.

8.5 Research limitations

This study is subject to the following limitations. First, owing to the manual collection of disclosure data and a labour-intensive latent content analysis process, a relatively small sample was used, which may limit the application of the findings to firms outside the social responsibility ranking list. Also, there might be a best practice bias in the studied sample as only the 100 most socially responsible Chinese listed firms were analysed.

Second, when adopting questionnaire survey and panel consultation as the primary methods of inquiry to gain insights into the relevant stakeholders' perceptions on corporate social and environmental disclosure, the stakeholders' responses might be influenced by various factors (e.g. cognitive, cultural and political). Hence, as with most research that relies on survey as a source of information, the results need to be interpreted acknowledging potential bias and inaccuracy in the responses.

Third, despite extensive efforts made regarding the choice and construction of accurate proxies for the variables tested in the study, an element of subjectivity was unavoidable. It was acknowledged that the industry classification of sample firms can be made in alternative ways. The choice of proxies for variables was also limited by data availability. Likewise, there might be an element of subjectivity involved in the coding process when using content analysis to collect the social and environmental disclosure data.

8.6 Future research

The findings of this study provide a springboard for the following further research endeavours. First, the first stage of this study analysed the corporate social and environmental disclosure practices based on standard disclosure specified by the GRI (G3) guidelines. As the GRI has now published specific sector supplements for some sectors, future research may take these sector supplements into account for data collection and results interpretation.

Second, whilst the second stage of the study examined the effects of several corporate characteristics and stakeholders' power on corporate social and environmental disclosure, future studies may consider including other potential influencing factors derived from alternative theoretical positions. Likewise, further research may consider other potential influencing factors derived from alternative theoretical positions when testing the effect of the CSR report on corporate socially responsible reputation.

Third, this study focused on the 100 socially responsible firms identified by a social responsibility ranking list. Another proposition for future research is to investigate the social and environmental disclosure practices of firms outside the social responsibility ranking list and to compare the findings between firms on the list and those outside the list.

Finally, this study examined the social and environmental disclosure data on one-year basis, and a longitudinal study on issues relating to corporate social and environmental disclosure practices in developing countries would be a valuable addition to the extant literature.

Appendix 1

2008 and 2009 Chinese listed firms' social responsibility ranking list

2008 list

Rank	*Firm name*	*Score*
1	Petro China Company Limited	79.572
2	China Petroleum and Chemical Corporation	64.873
3	Industrial and Commercial Bank of China	59.284
4	China Mobile Communications Corporation	54.997
5	China Construction Bank	54.759
6	Bank of China	53.399
7	China Shenhua Energy Company Limited	44.730
8	Baoshan Iron and Steel Company Limited	44.533
9	China life Insurance Group Company	44.172
10	China Railway Construction Corporation Limited	43.564
11	Aluminum Corporation of China Limited	42.709
12	Zijin Mining Group Company Limited	42.630
13	China COSCO Holdings Company Limited	42.156
14	China Railway Group Limited	41.709
15	Angang Steel Company Limited	41.665
16	Wuhan Iron and Steel Company Limited	41.125
17	China Merchants Bank	41.085
18	Huaneng Power International, Incorporated	41.047
19	Bank of Communications	40.487
20	Anhui Jianghuai Automobile Company Limited	39.959
21	China Telecommunications Corporation	39.751
22	Yunnan Copper Company Limited	39.440
23	Hua Xia Bank	39.324
24	Laiwu Steel Company Limited	39.324
25	Qingdao Haier Company Limited	39.134
26	Gree Electric Appliances, Incorporated of Zhuhai	39.034
27	Sichuan Changhong Electric Company Limited	39.024
28	Xiamen International Trade Group Company Limited	38.959
29	Xinxing Ductile Iron Pipes Company Limited	38.893
30	China Pacific Insurance Group Company Limited	38.644
31	SAIC Motor Corporation Limited	38.264
32	PICC Property and Casualty Company Limited	38.262
33	Industrial Bank Company Limited	38.115

continued

Rank	*Firm name*	*Score*
34	China Citic Bank	38.071
35	Shanghai Pudong Development Bank	37.426
36	Maanshan Iron and Steel Company Limited	37.168
37	Konka Group Company Limited	36.979
38	Faw Car Company Limited	36.749
39	China International Marine Containers Group Company Limited	36.662
40	Beiqi Foton Motor Company Limited	36.638
41	Tsingdao Brewery Company Limited	36.635
42	Haitong Securities Company Limited	36.531
43	China National Offshore Oil Corporation	36.513
44	Shanxi Taigang Stainless Steel Company Limited	36.349
45	China CSSC Holdings Limited	36.344
46	China Coal Energy Company Limited	36.328
47	China Unicom Company Limited	36.195
48	Shenzhen Energy Group Company Limited	36.072
49	Shanxi Guoyang New Energy Company Limited	35.987
50	China Gezhouba Group Company Limited	35.924
51	Sinopec Shanghai Petrochemical Company Limited	35.830
52	China Railway Erju Company Limited	35.624
53	Sinoma International Engineering Company Limited	35.552
54	Baotou Iron and Steel Union Company Limited	35.279
55	China Southern Airlines Company Limited	35.244
56	Liuzhou Iron and Steel Company Limited	35.208
57	CITIC Securities Company Limited	34.933
58	Beijing Shougang Company Limited	34.897
59	Great Wall Technology Company Limited	34.881
60	Sinochem International Company Limited	34.817
61	Lianyungang Ideal Group Company Limited	34.716
62	Shenzhen Kaifa Technology Company Limited	34.676
63	Dongfeng Motor Group Company Limited	34.447
64	China Communications Construction Company Limited	34.377
65	China Vanke Company Limited	33.887
66	Hisense Electric Company Limited	33.408
67	Shanghai Electric Group Company Limited	33.261
68	Hunan Valin Steel Company Limited	32.879
69	China Communications Services Corporation	32.877
70	Yanzhou Coal Mining Company Limited	32.841
71	Tangshan Iron and Steel Company Limited	32.742
72	Chongqing Changan Automobile Company Limited	32.676
73	Henan Shuanghui Investment and Development Company Limited	32.594
74	Minmetals Development Company Limited	32.547
75	Weichai Power Company Limited	32.425
76	China National Materials Company Limited	32.129
77	Hunan Nonferrous Metals Corporation Limited	32.045
78	Zhuzhou Smelter Group Company Limited	31.951
79	SGIS Songshan Company Limited	31.924
80	Sinopec Yizheng Chemical Fibre Company Limited	31.779
81	BOE Technology Group Company Limited	31.702
82	Jinan Iron and Steel Company Limited	31.644
83	Panzhihua New Steel and Vanadium Company Limited	31.239

Rank	*Firm name*	*Score*
84	Handan Iron and Steel Company Limited	31.201
85	Hangzhou Iron and Steel Company Limited	30.627
86	Xiamen C and D Incorporated	30.527
87	Jiangxi Copper Company Limited	29.151
88	GD Power Development Company Limited	29.012
89	Shanghai International Port Group Company Limited	28.724
90	Xiamen King Long Motor Group Company Limited	28.692
91	Tsinghua Tongfang Company Limited	28.431
92	Tongling Nonferrous Metals Group Company Limited	28.317
93	Bengang Steel Plates Company Limited	28.256
94	Shanghai Zhenhua Port Machinery Company Limited	28.189
95	Chongqing Iron and Steel Company Limited	28.166
96	Sansteel Min Guang Company Limited, Fujian	28.142
97	CNHTC Jinan Truck Company Limited	28.130
98	Nanchang Changli Iron and Steel Company Limited	27.913
99	Xinjiang Ba Yi Iron and Steel Company Limited	27.735
100	Chengde Xinxin Vanadium and Titanium Company Limited	27.629

Source: *Southern Weekend*, 2008a.

2009 list

Rank	*2008 Rank*	*Firm name*	*Score*
1	1	Petro China Company Limited	74.877
2	3	Industrial and Commercial Bank of China	56.489
3	2	China Petroleum and Chemical Corporation	56.162
4	5	China Construction Bank	54.794
5	6	Bank of China	51.566
6	4	China Mobile Communications Corporation	48.074
7	7	China Shenhua Energy Company Limited	45.102
8	10	China Railway Construction Corporation Limited	39.866
9	8	Baoshan Iron and Steel Company Limited	39.714
10	9	China life Insurance Group Company	38.347
11	13	China COSCO Holdings Company Limited	38.491
12	11	Aluminum Corporation of China Limited	37.732
13	35	Shanghai Pudong Development Bank	37.380
14	16	Wuhan Iron and Steel Company Limited	37.308
15	33	Industrial Bank Company Limited	37.179
16	15	Angang Steel Company Limited	37.112
17	26	Gree Electric Appliances, Incorporated. of Zhuhai	37.000
18	74	Minmetals Development Company Limited	36.957
19	36	Maanshan Iron and Steel Company Limited	36.651
20	–	China South Locomotive and Rolling Corporation Limited	36.598
21	31	SAIC Motor Corporation Limited	36.489
22	53	Sinoma International Engineering Company Limited	36.424
23	18	Huaneng Power International, Incorporated	36.422
24	23	Hua Xia Bank	36.098
25	–	China Oilfield Services Limited	36.094

continued

Rank	*2008 Rank*	*Firm name*	*Score*
26	17	China Merchants Bank	35.910
27	29	Xinxing Ductile Iron Pipes Company Limited	35.893
28	24	Laiwu Steel Company Limited	35.612
29	22	Yunnan Copper Company Limited	35.479
30	20	Anhui Jianghuai Automobile Company Limited	35.461
31	70	Yanzhou Coal Mining Company Limited	34.987
32	14	China Railway Group Limited	34.890
33	47	China Unicom Company Limited	34.618
34	19	Bank of Communications	33.999
35	57	CITIC Securities Company Limited	33.864
36	32	PICC Property and Casualty Company Limited	33.840
37	46	China Coal Energy Company Limited	33.680
38	40	Beiqi Foton Motor Company Limited	33.390
39	64	China Communications Construction Company Limited	33.375
40	–	Bank of Beijing	33.107
41	27	Sichuan Changhong Electric Company Limited	33.045
42	28	Xiamen International Trade Group Company Limited	32.998
43	–	Shanghai Airlines Company Limited	32.499
44	38	Faw Car Company Limited	32.468
45	48	Shenzhen Energy Group Company Limited	32.464
46	–	Tianjin Port (Group) Company Limited	32.425
47	44	Shanxi Taigang Stainless Steel Company Limited	32.397
48	39	China International Marine Containers Group Company Limited	32.385
49	71	Tangshan Iron and Steel Company Limited	32.307
50	34	China Citic Bank	32.143
51	72	Chongqing Changan Automobile Company Limited	31.652
52	21	China Telecommunications Corporation	31.536
53	79	SGIS Songshan Company Limited	31.498
54	41	Tsingdao Brewery Company Limited	31.467
55	58	Beijing Shougang Company Limited	31.454
56	76	China National Materials Company Limited	31.416
57	63	Dongfeng Motor Group Company Limited	31.382
58	51	Sinopec Shanghai Petrochemical Company Limited	31.377
59	80	Sinopec Yizheng Chemical Fibre Company Limited	31.245
60	30	China Pacific Insurance Group Company Limited	31.192
61	25	Qingdao Haier Company Limited	31.118
62	–	Shandong Chenming Paper Group Company Limited	29.770
63	12	Zijin Mining Group Company Limited	29.314
64	–	Shanxi Lu'an Environmental Energy Development Company Limited	29.042
65	37	Konka Group Company Limited	28.860
66	–	Shenzhen Development Bank	28.782
67	–	Poly Real Estate Group Company Limited	28.777
68	–	China State Construction Engineering Corporation Limited	28.743
69	66	Hisense Electric Company Limited	28.734
70	56	Liuzhou Iron and Steel Company Limited	28.666
71	–	Henan Shenhuo Coal and Electricity Power Company Limited	28.644
72	60	Sinochem International Company Limited	28.611

Rank	*2008 Rank*	*Firm name*	*Score*
73	59	Great Wall Technology Company Limited	28.605
74	75	Weichai Power Company Limited	28.552
75	89	Shanghai International Port Group Company Limited	28.393
76	82	Jinan Iron and Steel Company Limited	28.144
77	–	Sinotrans Limited	28.139
78	88	GD Power Development Company Limited	28.114
79	84	Handan Iron and Steel Company Limited	28.106
80	–	Anhui Conch Cement Company Limited	28.081
81	73	Henan Shuanghui Investment and Development Company Limited	27.994
82	92	Tongling Nonferrous Metals Group Company Limited	27.960
83	83	Panzhihua New Steel and Vanadium Company Limited	27.842
84	98	Nanchang Changli Iron and Steel Company Limited	27.592
85	55	China Southern Airlines Company Limited	27.579
86	–	Zoomlion Heavy Industry Science and Technology Development Company Limited	27.443
87	100	Chengde Xinxin Vanadium and Titanium Company Limited	27.349
88	96	Sansteel Min Guang Company Limited Fujian	27.271
89	–	Zhong Chu Development Stock Company Limited	27.225
90	43	China National Offshore Oil Corporation	27.108
91	91	Tsinghua Tongfang Company Limited	27.010
92	69	China Communications Services Corporation	26.676
93	50	China Gezhouba Group Company Limited	26.648
94	67	Shanghai Electric Group Company Limited	26.587
95	77	Hunan Nonferrous Metals Corporation Limited	26.316
96	54	Baotou Iron and Steel Union Company Limited	26.021
97	52	China Railway Erju Company Limited	25.570
98	62	Shenzhen Kaifa Technology Company Limited	25.338
99	–	Shanghai Material Trading Company Limited	25.060
100	–	Shanxi Xishan Coal and Electricity Power Company Limited	24.986

Source: *Southern Weekend*, 2009.

Appendix 2

Standard disclosure items of the GRI (G3) sustainability reporting guidelines

No.	*Item description*	*Code*
	Strategy and analysis	
1	Statement from the most senior decision maker of the organisation (e.g. CEO, chair, or equivalent senior position) about the relevance of sustainability to the organisation and its strategy.	1.1
2	Description of key impacts, risks and opportunities.	1.2
	Organisational profile	
3	Name of the organisation.	2.1
4	Primary brands, products and/or services.	2.2
5	Operational structure of the organisation, including main divisions, operating companies, subsidiaries and joint ventures.	2.3
6	Location of organisation's headquarters.	2.4
7	Number of countries where the organisation operates, and names of countries with either major operations or that are specifically relevant to the sustainability issues covered in the report.	2.5
8	Nature of ownership and legal form.	2.6
9	Markets served (including geographic breakdown, sectors served and types of customers/beneficiaries).	2.7
10	Scale of the reporting organisation.	2.8
11	Significant changes during the reporting period regarding size, structure, or ownership.	2.9
12	Awards received in the reporting period.	2.10
	Report parameters	
13	Reporting period (e.g. fiscal/calendar year) for information provided.	3.1
14	Date of most recent previous report (if any).	3.2
15	Reporting cycle (annual, biennial, etc.)	3.3
16	Contact point for questions regarding the report or its contents.	3.4
17	Process for defining report content.	3.5
18	Boundary of the report (e.g. countries, divisions, subsidiaries, leased facilities, joint ventures, suppliers).	3.6
19	State any specific limitations on the scope or boundary of the report.	3.7
20	Basis for reporting on joint ventures, subsidiaries, leased facilities, outsourced operations and other entities that can significantly affect comparability from period to period and/or between organisations.	3.8

No.	*Item description*	*Code*
21	Data measurement techniques and the bases of calculations, including assumptions and techniques underlying estimations applied to the compilation of the indicators and other information in the report.	3.9
22	Explanation of the effect of any re-statements of information provided in earlier reports, the reasons for such re-statement (e.g. mergers/ acquisitions, change of base years/periods, of business, measurement methods).	3.10
23	Significant changes from previous reporting periods in the scope, boundary, or measurement methods applied in the report.	3.11
24	Table identifying the location of the standard disclosures in the report.	3.12
25	Policy and current practice with regard to seeking external assurance for the report.	3.13
Governance, commitments and engagement		
26	Governance structure of the organisation, including committees under the highest governance body responsible for specific tasks, such as setting strategy or organisational oversight.	4.1
27	Indicate whether the chair of the highest governance body is also an executive officer.	4.2
28	For organisations that have a unitary board structure, state the number of members of the highest governance body that are independent and/or non-executive members.	4.3
29	Mechanisms for shareholders and employees to provide recommendations or direction to the highest governance body.	4.4
30	Linkage between compensation for members of the highest governance body, senior managers and executives (including departure arrangements), and the organisation's performance (including social and environmental performance).	4.5
31	Processes in place for the highest governance body to ensure conflicts of interest are avoided.	4.6
32	Process for determining the qualifications and expertise of the members of the highest governance body for guiding the organisation's strategy on economic, environmental and social topics.	4.7
33	Internally developed statements of mission or values, codes of conduct, and principles relevant to economic, environmental and social performance and the status of their implementation.	4.8
34	Procedures of the highest governance body for overseeing the organisation's identification and management of economic, environmental and social performance, including relevant risks and opportunities, and adherence or compliance with internationally agreed standards, codes of conduct and principles.	4.9
35	Processes for evaluating the highest governance body's own performance, particularly with respect to economic, environmental and social performance.	4.10
36	Explanation of whether and how the precautionary approach or principle is addressed by the organisation.	4.11
37	Externally developed economic, environmental and social charters, principles, or other initiatives to which the organisation subscribes or endorses.	4.12

continued

No.	*Item description*	*Code*
38	Memberships in associations (such as industry associations) and/or national/international advocacy organisations.	4.13
39	List of stakeholder groups engaged by the organisation.	4.14
40	Basis for identification and selection of stakeholders with whom to engage.	4.15
41	Approaches to stakeholder engagement, including frequency of engagement by type and by stakeholder group.	4.16
42	Key topics and concerns that have been raised through stakeholder engagement, and how the organisation has responded to those key topics and concerns, including through its reporting.	4.17
Economic performance indicators		
43	Direct economic value generated and distributed, including revenues, operating costs, employee compensation, donations and other community investments, retained earnings, and payments to capital providers and governments.	EC1
44	Financial implications and other risks and opportunities for the organisation's activities due to climate change.	EC2
45	Coverage of the organisation's defined benefit plan obligations.	EC3
46	Significant financial assistance received from government.	EC4
47	Range of ratios of standard entry level wage compared to local minimum wage at significant locations of operation.	EC5
48	Policy, practices and proportion of spending on locally-based suppliers at significant locations of operation.	EC6
49	Procedures for local hiring and proportion of senior management hired from the local community at locations of significant operation.	EC7
50	Development and impact of infrastructure investments and services provided primarily for public benefit through commercial, in-kind, or pro bono engagement.	EC8
51	Understanding and describing significant indirect economic impacts, including the extent of impacts.	EC9
Environmental performance indicators		
52	Materials used by weight or volume.	EN1
53	Percentage of materials used that are recycled input materials.	EN2
54	Direct energy consumption by primary energy source.	EN3
55	Indirect energy consumption by primary source.	EN4
56	Energy saved due to conservation and efficiency improvements.	EN5
57	Initiatives to provide energy-efficient or renewable energy based products and services, and reductions in energy requirements as a result of these initiatives.	EN6
58	Initiatives to reduce indirect energy consumption and reductions achieved.	EN7
59	Total water withdrawal by source.	EN8
60	Water sources significantly affected by withdrawal of water.	EN9
61	Percentage and total volume of water recycled and reused.	EN10
62	Location and size of land owned, leased, managed in, or adjacent to, protected areas and areas of high biodiversity value outside protected areas.	EN11
63	Description of significant impacts of activities, products, and services on biodiversity in protected areas and areas of high biodiversity value outside protected areas.	EN12
64	Habitats protected or restored.	EN13

No.	*Item description*	*Code*
65	Strategies, current actions and future plans for managing impacts on biodiversity.	EN14
66	Number of IUCN Red List species and national conservation list species with habitats in areas affected by operations, by level of extinction risk.	EN15
67	Total direct and indirect environmentalhouse gas emissions by weight.	EN16
68	Other relevant indirect environmentalhouse gas emissions by weight.	EN17
69	Initiatives to reduce environmentalhouse gas emissions and reductions achieved.	EN18
70	Emissions of ozone-depleting substances by weight.	EN19
71	NO, SO and other significant air emissions by type and weight.	EN20
72	Total water discharge by quality and destination.	EN21
73	Total weight of waste by type and disposal method.	EN22
74	Total number and volume of significant spills.	EN23
75	Weight of transported, imported, exported, or treated waste deemed hazardous under the terms of the Basel Convention Annex I, II, III, and VIII, and percentage of transported waste shipped internationally.	EN24
76	Identity, size, protected status and biodiversity value of water bodies and related habitats significantly affected by the reporting organisation's discharges of water and runoff.	EN25
77	Initiatives to mitigate environmental impacts of products and services, and extent of impact mitigation.	EN26
78	Percentage of products sold and their packaging materials that are reclaimed by category.	EN27
79	Monetary value of significant fines and total number of non-monetary sanctions for noncompliance with environmental laws and regulations.	EN28
80	Significant environmental impacts of transporting products and other goods and materials used for the organisation's operations and transporting members of the workforce.	EN29
81	Total environmental protection expenditures and investments by type.	EN30
Social performance indicators		
Labour practices and decent work performance indicators		
82	Total workforce by employment type, employment contract and region.	LA1
83	Total number and rate of employee turnover by age group, gender and region.	LA2
84	Benefits provided to full-time employees that are not provided to temporary or part-time employees, by major operations.	LA3
85	Percentage of employees covered by collective bargaining agreements.	LA4
86	Minimum notice period(s) regarding operational changes, including whether it is specified in collective agreements.	LA5
87	Percentage of total workforce represented in formal joint management–worker health and safety committees that help monitor and advise on occupational health and safety programmes.	LA6
88	Rates of injury, occupational diseases, lost days and absenteeism, and number of work-related fatalities by region.	LA7
89	Education, training, counselling, prevention, and risk-control programmes in place to assist workforce members, their families, or community members regarding serious diseases.	LA8
90	Health and safety topics covered in formal agreements with trade unions.	LA9
91	Average hours of training per year per employee by employee category.	LA10

continued

No.	*Item description*	*Code*
92	Programmes for skills management and lifelong learning that support the continued employability of employees and assist them in managing career endings.	LA11
93	Percentage of employees receiving regular performance and career development reviews.	LA12
94	Composition of governance bodies and breakdown of employees per category according to gender, age group, minority group membership and other indicators of diversity.	LA13
95	Ratio of basic salary of men to women by employee category.	LA14
Human rights performance indicators		
96	Percentage and total number of significant investment agreements that include human rights clauses or that have undergone human rights screening.	HR1
97	Percentage of significant suppliers and contractors that have undergone screening on human rights and actions taken.	HR2
98	Total hours of employee training on policies and procedures concerning aspects of human rights that are relevant to operations, including the percentage of employees trained.	HR3
99	Total number of incidents of discrimination and actions taken.	HR4
100	Operations identified in which the right to exercise freedom of association and collective bargaining may be at significant risk, and actions taken to support these rights.	HR5
101	Operations identified as having significant risk for incidents of child labour, and measures taken to contribute to the elimination of child labour.	HR6
102	Operations identified as having significant risk for incidents of forced or compulsory labour, and measures to contribute to the elimination of forced or compulsory labour.	HR7
103	Percentage of security personnel trained in the organisation's policies or procedures concerning aspects of human rights that are relevant to operations.	HR8
104	Total number of incidents of violations involving rights of indigenous people and actions taken.	HR9
Society performance indicators		
105	Nature, scope and effectiveness of any programmes and practices that assess and manage the impacts of operations on communities, including entering, operating and exiting.	SO1
106	Percentage and total number of business units analysed for risks related to corruption.	SO2
107	Percentage of employees trained in organisation's anti-corruption policies and procedures.	SO3
108	Actions taken in response to incidents of corruption.	SO4
109	Public policy positions and participation in public policy development and lobbying.	SO5
110	Total value of financial and in-kind contributions to political parties, politicians and related institutions by country.	SO6
111	Total number of legal actions for anti-competitive behaviour, anti-trust and monopoly practices and their outcomes.	SO7
112	Monetary value of significant fines and total number of non-monetary sanctions for noncompliance with laws and regulations.	SO8

No.	*Item description*	*Code*
	Product responsibility performance indicators	
113	Life cycle stages in which health and safety impacts of products and services are assessed for improvement, and percentage of significant products and services categories subject to such procedures.	PR1
114	Total number of incidents of non-compliance with regulations and voluntary codes concerning health and safety impacts of products and services during their life cycle, by type of outcomes.	PR2
115	Type of product and service information required by procedures, and percentage of significant products and services subject to such information requirements.	PR3
116	Total number of incidents of non-compliance with regulations and voluntary codes concerning product and service information and labelling, by type of outcomes.	PR4
117	Practices related to customer satisfaction, including results of surveys measuring customer satisfaction.	PR5
118	Programmes for adherence to laws, standards and voluntary codes related to marketing communications, including advertising, promotion and sponsorship.	PR6
119	Total number of incidents of non-compliance with regulations and voluntary codes concerning marketing communications, including advertising, promotion and sponsorship by type of outcomes.	PR7
120	Total number of substantiated complaints regarding breaches of customer privacy and losses of customer data.	PR8
121	Monetary value of significant fines for noncompliance with laws and regulations concerning the provision and use of products and services.	PR9

Source: online, available at: www.globalreporting.org.

Appendix 3

Social and environmental disclosure measurement in the literature

	Authors	*Year*	*Variable*	*Variable type*	*Data source*	*Data collection method*	*Analysis technique*	*Disclosure measurement*	*Scale*	*Score*	*Scale description*	*Theory*
1	Van Staden and Hooks	2007	Environmental disclosure	IV	Annual reports, environmental reports, websites, other	Content analysis	Multiple regression	Number of sentences	Ordinal	0 to 4	0: Not disclosed, no discussion of the issue 1: Minimum coverage, little detail – general terms. Anecdotal or briefly mentioned 2: Descriptive: the impact of the company or its policies was clearly evident 3: Quantitative: the environmental impact was clearly defined in monetary terms or actual physical quantities 4: Truly extraordinary. Benchmarking against best practice	Legitimacy (proof) – disclosure legitimises firms' environmental responsiveness

2	Tsang	1998	Social disclosure	V	Annual reports	Content analysis	Descriptive analysis (means)	Percentage of sentences	Nominal	1 or 0	1: Disclosed 0: Not disclosed	Legitimacy (proof) – disclosure to become a good corporate citizen
3	King	2008	Corporate response to social movement to activism	DV	(Five national newspapers) Factiva database	Content analysis	Probit regression	Presence of word 'boycott'	Nominal	1 or 0	1: Recognition by firm the boycotters' demands and a public expression of conformity to demands 0: Not disclosed	Political economy (proof) – safeguarding firm reputation (challenging the legitimacy of firms' practices)
4	Deegan and Gordon	1996	Environmental disclosure and environmental sensitivity	V	a) Annual reports b) survey of executives	Content analysis	Correlation	a) Number of words 'environment' b) Industry sensitivity index	Nominal Ordinal	1 or 0 0 to 5	1: Disclosed 0: Not disclosed 0: lowest environmental sensitivity to 5: highest environmental sensitivity	Legitimacy (lack of proof)
5	Frost and Seamer	2002	Environmental disclosure	DV	Annual reports	Content analysis	Multiple regression	Number of words	Nominal	0 or 1	Environment was defined as relationship between firm and its physical environment, including energy usage, waste, and actual physical impact	Legitimacy (proof)

continued

	Authors	Year	Variable	Variable type	Data source	Data collection method	Analysis technique	Disclosure measurement	Scale	Score	Scale description	Theory
6	Lorraine, Collison and Power	2004	Environmental disclosure	IV	Annual reports	Content analysis	Multiple regression	Incidents reported by environmental agency	Nominal	1 or −1	1: good news firm −1: bad news firm	Impression management (share price) (lack of proof)
7	Cormier and Gordon	2001	Environmental disclosure Social disclosure	DV DV	Annual reports Annual reports	Content analysis Content analysis	Multiple regression	About environmental responsibility About social responsibility	Ordinal Ratio	1 to 3%	1: discussed in general terms 2: item described specifically 3: item described in monetary or quantitative terms Average instances of disclosure over 12 years (1985 to 1996)	Legitimacy (return on equity) (lack of proof) Legitimacy (return on equity) (proof)
8	Choi	1999	Environmental disclosure	DV	Annual reports	Content analysis	Multiple regression	About environmental responsibility	Ordinal	1 to 3	1: discussed in general terms 2: item described specifically 3: item described in monetary or quantitative terms Disclosure then analysed as to the decision to disclose or not based on corporate characteristics	Stakeholder theory (auditors have a negative effect on disclosure) (lack of proof)

9	De Villiers and van Staden	2006	Environmental disclosure	V	Annual reports	Content analysis	Trend analysis	Environmental responsibility	Ordinal	1 to 3	1: discussed in general terms 2: item described specifically 3: item described in monetary or quantitative terms But items in instruments identified first as general or specific to assign weights prior to coding	Legitimacy (proof)
10	Cormier, Gordon and Magnan	2004	Environmental disclosure	DV	Annual report and environmental report	Content analysis and survey	Multiple regression	Meaning of items	Ordinal	1 to 3	1: described in general 2: described specifically 3: described in monetary or quantitative terms	Legitimacy and stakeholder theories
11	Moore	2001	Social performance	V	Annual reports, and various other sources	Survey framework	Correlation	Social accountability	Ordinal	1 to 10	1 (lowest) to 10 (highest) on a continuous scale	
12	Cormier and Magnan	1999	Environmental disclosure	DV	Annual reports	Content analysis	Multiple regression	Meaning of items	Ordinal	1 to 3	1: discussed in general terms 2: item described specifically 3: item described in monetary or quantitative terms	Stakeholder theory (interpreted as cost–benefit with stakeholders) (proof)

continued

	Authors	*Year*	*Variable*	*Variable type*	*Data source*	*Data collection method*	*Analysis technique*	*Disclosure measurement*	*Scale*	*Score*	*Scale description*	*Theory*
13	Liu and Anburnozhi	2009	Environmental disclosure	DV	Annual reports	Content analysis	Multiple regression	Meaning of items	ordinal	1 to 5	1: no information 3: item that is descriptive or incomplete quantitative data 5: item that is descriptive and quantitative data in detail Convert the total into percentage score based on maximum score of 30	Stakeholder theory (firms respond to stakeholder concerns) (proof)
14	Gao *et al.*	2005	Environmental disclosure	DV	Annual reports	Content analysis	ANOVA	Number of words based on content themes	Binary	1or 0	1: Disclosed 0: Not disclosed	No theory noted
15	Roberts	1992	Social responsibility disclosure	DV	Council on Economic priorities (CEP)	CEP rating for firm	Multiple regression	Ranking based on CEP rating	Ordinal	0 to 2	0: poor disclosure – CEP rating for firm 'f' 1: good disclosure – CEP rating for firm 'c' 2: excellent disclosure – CEP rating for firm 'a'	Stakeholder theory (shareholder power, strategic posture, and economic performance) (proof)

16	Ahmad, Hassan and Mohammad	2003	Environmental disclosure	DV	Annual report		Logistic regression	Environmental information operationalised as any sentence that mentions any aspect of the natural environment and/or its relationship with the firm	Binary	1or 0	1: Disclosed 0: Not disclosed	Political costs perspective (proof)
17	Murray, Sinclair, Power and Gray	2006	Social and environmental disclosure	IV	CSEAR database	Content analysis	Multiple regression	Number of pages allotted to social and environmental issues	Interval	0 to ∞	Quantity measure	No single theoretical explanation
18	Tilt and Symes	1999	Environmental disclosure	DV	Annual report	Content analysis	Kruskal–Wallis test and Mann–Whitney U test	Number of sentences about environment operationally defined – any sentence that mentions/ discusses any aspect of the natural environment and/or its relationship with the firm	Interval	0 to ∞	Quantity measure	Political costs or visibility hypothesis (proof)

continued

	Authors	*Year*	*Variable*	*Variable type*	*Data source*	*Data collection method*	*Analysis technique*	*Disclosure measurement*	*Scale*	*Score*	*Scale description*	*Theory*
19	Walden and Schwartz	1997	Environmental disclosure	DV	Annual report	Content analysis	(one-tailed) Wilcoxon test	Number of words based on keywords list	Interval Ordinal	0 to ∞ 0 to 1 for 4 facets	Interval for quantity measure effect – significant or not; quantification – monetary or not; specificity – place, person, event, etc. or not; time frame – past, present, or future	Political economy perspective
20	Cormier and Magnan	2003	Environmental disclosure	DV	Annual report and environmental report	Content analysis	Multiple regression	39-item instrument for meaning	Ordinal	1 to 3	1: discussed in general terms 2: item described specifically 3: item described in monetary or quantitative terms	Cost–benefit framework (proof)
21	Van der laan Smith, Adhikari and Tondkar	2005	Social disclosure	IV	Annual report	Content analysis	Logistic regression (for each unit of analysis)	Words, sentences, proportion of page	binary	Not known	Proactive and future disclosure more valuable than reactive, historical, and promotional disclosure Numeric information higher quality than other	Stakeholder theory (proof)

22	Wiseman	1982	Environmental disclosure	V	Annual report	Content analysis	Spearman correlation	Sentences	Ordinal	1 to 3	1: discussed in general terms 2: item described specifically 3: item described in monetary or quantitative terms	No theory
23	Hasseldine, Salama and Toms	2005	Environmental disclosure	IV	Annual report	Content analysis	Multiple regression	A qualitative indicator, a quantitative indicator, and a hybrid indicator	Interval Ordinal	0 to ∞ 0 to 5	Interval for quantity measure 0: no disclosure 1: general rhetoric 2: specific endeavour, policy only 3: specific endeavour or intent, policy specified 4: implementation and monitoring, use of targets references to outcomes, but quantified results not published 5: implementation and monitoring, use of targets, quantified results published	Quality-signalling theory, resource based view

continued

	Authors	*Year*	*Variable*	*Variable type*	*Data source*	*Data collection method*	*Analysis technique*	*Disclosure measurement*	*Scale*	*Score*	*Scale description*	*Theory*
24	Toms	2002	Environmental disclosure	IV	Annual report	Content analysis	Multiple regression	The quality of disclosure	Ordinal	0 to 5	0: no disclosure 1: general rhetoric 2: specific endeavour, policy only 3: specific endeavour or intent, policy specified 4: implementation and monitoring, use of targets references to outcomes, but quantified results not published 5: implementation and monitoring, use of targets, quantified results published	Quality-signalling theory, resource based view

25	Clarkson, Li, Richardson and Vasvari	2008	Environmental disclosure	DV	Environmental reports, websites	Content analysis	Multiple regression	Meaning of items	Ordinal	0 to 1 for soft, 0 to 6 for hard	0: not disclosed 1: disclosed 0: not disclosed 1: performance data is presented 2: performance data is presented relative to peers/rivals or industry 3: performance data is presented relative to previous periods 4: performance data is presented relative to targets 5: performance data is presented both in absolute and normalised form 6: performance data is presented at disaggregate level	Economics based voluntary disclosure theories and socio-political theories
26	Robertson and Nicholson	1996	Social disclosure	V	Annual report	Survey	Ratio	Social responsibility	Ordinal	1 to 3	1: general rhetoric level 2: specific endeavour level 3: implementation and monitoring level	Social responsibility framework
27	Campbell	2004	Environmental disclosure	V	Annual report	Content analysis	Trend analysis	Number of words	Interval	0 to ∞	Interval for quantity measure	Legitimacy theory (proof)

continued

	Authors	*Year*	*Variable*	*Variable type*	*Data source*	*Data collection method*	*Analysis technique*	*Disclosure measurement*	*Scale*	*Score*	*Scale description*	*Theory*
28	Hackston and Milne	1996	Social and environmental disclosure	DV	Annual report	Content analysis	Multiple regression	Number of sentences and pages	Interval	0 to ∞	Interval for quantity measure	No theory
29	Al-Tuwaijri, Christensen and Hughes	2004	Environmental disclosure	DV and IV	Annual report	Content analysis	3SLS regression	Meaning of items	Ordinal	0 to 3	0: no 1: qualitative non-specific 2: qualitative specific 3: quantitative	No theory
30	Patten	2002	Environmental disclosure	DV	Annual report	Content analysis	Multiple regression	Number of lines	Interval Binary	0 to ∞ 0 or 1	quantity measure 0: not disclosed 1: disclosed	Legitimacy theory (proof) – negative relation between environmental performance and disclosure
31	Cho and Patten	2007	Environmental disclosure	DV	Annual report	Content analysis	t-test ANOVA Mann–Whitney test	Meaning of items	Binary	0 or 1	0: not disclosed 1: disclosed	Legitimacy theory (proof)
32	Deegan and Rankin	1996	Environmental disclosure	V	Annual report	Content analysis	t-test Kruskal–Wallis test Mann–Whitney test	Number of words	Interval	0 to ∞	Quantity measure	Legitimacy theory (proof)

33	Magness	2006	Environmental disclosure	DV	Annual report	Content analysis	Multiple regression	Meaning of items (7 items)	Binary	0 or 1	0: not disclosed 1: disclosed	Legitimacy theory (proof)
34	Cho	2009	Environmental disclosure	V	Annual report	Content analysis and interview	Trend analysis	Number of instances	Binary	0 or 1	0: not disclosed 1: disclosed	Legitimacy theory (proof)
35	Wilmshurst and Frost	2000	Environmental disclosure	DV	Annual report and survey of executives	Content analysis	Multiple regression, correlation	Number of words	Interval	0 to ∞	Quantity measure	Legitimacy theory (limited support)
36	Neu, Warsame and Pedwell	1998	Environmental disclosure	DV	Annual report	Content analysis	Multiple regression	Number of words	Interval	0 to ∞	Quantity measure	Legitimacy theory (proof) – public impression perspective
37	Brown and Deegan	1998	Environmental disclosure	DV	Annual report	Content analysis	Trend analysis	Number of words	Interval	0 to ∞	Quantity measure	Media agenda setting theory and legitimacy theory
38	Aerts and Cormier	2009	Environmental disclosure	DV	Annual report	Content analysis	3SLS regression	Meaning of items (39 items)	Ordinal	1 to 3	1: described in general 2: described specifically 3: described in monetary or quantitative terms	Media agenda setting theory and legitimacy theory
39	Richardson and Welker	2001	Social disclosure	DV	Annual report	Content analysis	Multiple regression	Meaning of items	Binary	0 or 1	0: not disclosed 1: disclosed	Not mentioned

continued

	Authors	*Year*	*Variable*	*Variable type*	*Data source*	*Data collection method*	*Analysis technique*	*Disclosure measurement*	*Scale*	*Score*	*Scale description*	*Theory*
40	Cormier and Magnan	2007	Environmental disclosure	DV and IV	Annual report and environmental report	Content analysis	3SLS regression	Meaning of items (37 items)	Ordinal	1 to 3	1: described in general 2: described specifically 3: described in monetary or quantitative terms	Not mentioned

Notes
IV = independent variable, V = variable and DV = dependant variable.

Appendix 4

Questionnaire

Economic (EC) version

Part 1

Instructions: Please indicate your response to each of the following disclosure types by circling the scale number that best describes your feeling.

Context information for understanding corporate performance

Disclosure type	*Typical example*	*Rating scale*
Strategy and analysis		
1. Specific endeavour in non-quantitative terms	'CSEC stuck to the goal of building an enterprise incorporating the Five-Model of "intrinsic safety, quality and efficiency, technological innovation, resource saving and harmonious development" and incorporated social responsibilities into the whole process of corporate strategic, cultural, production and operation activities' (Shenhua Energy, 2008, p. 6).	**Unimportant** **Important** 0 10 20 30 40 50 60 70 80 90 100
Corporate profile		
1. General narrative information	'Address: No. 55 Fuxingmennei Avenue, Xicheng District, Beijing, PRC' (ICBC, 2008, p. 2).	**Unimportant** **Important** 0 10 20 30 40 50 60 70 80 90 100
2. Specific endeavour in non-quantitative terms	'The businesses of CSEC mainly cover production and sales of coal, railway and port transportation of coal-related material as well as the power generation and sales' (Shenhua Energy, 2008, preface).	**Unimportant** **Important** 0 10 20 30 40 50 60 70 80 90 100

continued

Disclosure type	*Typical example*	*Rating scale*
3. Quantified data	'The Group has a total number of 138,368 employees' (China Mobile, 2008, p. 5).	**Unimportant** **Important** 0 10 20 30 40 50 60 70 80 90 100
Report parameters		
1. General narrative information	'The issues highlighted in the report are mainly related to our performances on the economic, environmental and social responsibilities fronts in 2008' (PetroChina, 2008, preface).	**Unimportant** **Important** 0 10 20 30 40 50 60 70 80 90 100
2. Specific endeavour in non-quantitative terms	'We are committed to observing and supporting the ten Principles advocated by the Global Compact in the fields of human rights, labour rights, environment protection and anti-corruption, using the ten Principles to guide our practices in fulfilling social responsibilities. Starting from this year, we will disclose our progress in keeping with the ten Principles in the Global Compact in our annual report. Please see the following table…' (PetroChina, 2008, p. 48).	**Unimportant** **Important** 0 10 20 30 40 50 60 70 80 90 100
Governance, commitments and engagement		
1. General narrative information	'The positions of chairman and president of the Bank are separate' (ICBC, 2008, p. 22).	**Unimportant** **Important** 0 10 20 30 40 50 60 70 80 90 100
2. Specific endeavour in non-quantitative terms	'The Board of Directors has four board committees, namely the Audit Committee, the Investment and Development Committee, the Evaluation and Remuneration Committee, and the Health, Safety and Environment Committee. The Audit Committee is mainly responsible for…' (PetroChina, 2008, p. 9).	**Unimportant** **Important** 0 10 20 30 40 50 60 70 80 90 100
3. Quantified data	'The Board of Directors is composed of 15 members, including the Chairman, 3 executive directors, 7 nonexecutive directors and 4 independent directors' (Bank of China, 2008, p. 38).	**Unimportant** **Important** 0 10 20 30 40 50 60 70 80 90 100

Performance information (economic)		
1. General narrative information	'The Company employs local residents first for selected post, a way to provide more jobs for local residents and to perform social responsibility for local economic development' (BaoSteel, 2008, p. 23).	**Unimportant** **Important** 0 10 20 30 40 50 60 70 80 90 100
2. Specific endeavour in non-quantitative terms	'Cost cutting measures have been introduced, which focus on reducing administrative expenditures. The resources saved have been applied to managing crises, supporting key state projects and assisting customers' (Bank of China, 2008, p. 25).	**Unimportant** **Important** 0 10 20 30 40 50 60 70 80 90 100
3. Quantified performance data	'As at 31 December 2008, the Company had received a total of State reward on technical reform on energy conservation of approximately RMB12.7 million' (Shenhua Energy, 2008, p. 39).	**Unimportant** **Important** 0 10 20 30 40 50 60 70 80 90 100
4. Quantified performance data relative to benchmarks	'The Company's taxation payments (billion yuan) are 30.1 in 2006, 42.1 in 2007 and 36.8 in 2008' (China Mobile, 2008, p. 60).	**Unimportant** **Important** 0 10 20 30 40 50 60 70 80 90 100
5. Quantified performance data at the disaggregate level (e.g. plant, business unit, geographic segment)	'Within the huge investment of the West–East Gas Pipeline project, about RMB34 billion went to the Western provinces, of which over RMB20 billion went to Xinjiang, creating a huge consumption market and a large number of job opportunities. Meanwhile, the project has brought the economic structure adjustment of the East into a new level' (PetroChina, 2008, p. 41).	**Unimportant** **Important** 0 10 20 30 40 50 60 70 80 90 100

Please indicate any additional disclosure type that you feel should be included in the list and assign a weighting to it:

Disclosure type	*Typical example*	*Rating scale*
		Unimportant **Important** 0 10 20 30 40 50 60 70 80 90 100

Part 2 (respondent's profile)

Instructions: Please complete the following question. Your information will be kept strictly confidential.
What is your relationship with the firm that sends you this survey?
Shareholder Creditor Government/Regulator Employee
Customer Supplier Community Media Audit firm
Academic Other (Please specify)

Environmental (EN) version

Part 1

Instructions: Please indicate your response to each of the following disclosure types by circling the scale number that best describes your feelings.

Context information for understanding corporate performance

Disclosure type	*Typical example*	*Rating scale*
Strategy and analysis		
1. Specific endeavour in non-quantitative terms	'CSEC stuck to the goal of building an enterprise incorporating the Five-Model of "intrinsic safety, quality and efficiency, technological innovation, resource saving and harmonious development" and incorporated social responsibilities into the whole process of corporate strategic, cultural, production and operation activities' (Shenhua Energy, 2008, p. 6).	**Unimportant** **Important** 0 10 20 30 40 50 60 70 80 90 100
Corporate profile		
1. General narrative information	'Address: No. 55 Fuxingmennei Avenue, Xicheng District, Beijing, PRC' (ICBC, 2008, p. 2).	**Unimportant** **Important** 0 10 20 30 40 50 60 70 80 90 100

2. Specific endeavour in non-quantitative terms	'The businesses of CSEC mainly cover production and sales of coal, railway and port transportation of coal-related material as well as the power generation and sales' (Shenhua Energy, 2008, preface).	**Unimportant** **Important** 0 10 20 30 40 50 60 70 80 90 100
3. Quantified data	'The Group has a total number of 138,368 employees' (China Mobile, 2008, p. 5).	**Unimportant** **Important** 0 10 20 30 40 50 60 70 80 90 100
Report parameters		
1. General narrative information	'The issues highlighted in the report are mainly related to our performances on the economic, environmental and social responsibilities fronts in 2008' (PetroChina, 2008, preface).	**Unimportant** **Important** 0 10 20 30 40 50 60 70 80 90 100
2. Specific endeavour in non-quantitative terms	'We are committed to observing and supporting the ten Principles advocated by the Global Compact in the fields of human rights, labour rights, environment protection and anti-corruption, using the ten Principles to guide our practices in fulfilling social responsibilities. Starting from this year, we will disclose our progress in keeping with the ten Principles in the Global Compact in our annual report. Please see the following table…' (PetroChina, 2008, p. 48).	**Unimportant** **Important** 0 10 20 30 40 50 60 70 80 90 100
Governance, commitments and engagement		
1. General narrative information	'The positions of chairman and president of the Bank are separate' (ICBC, 2008, p. 22).	**Unimportant** **Important** 0 10 20 30 40 50 60 70 80 90 100
2. Specific endeavour in non-quantitative terms	'The Board of Directors has four board committees, namely the Audit Committee, the Investment and Development Committee, the Evaluation and Remuneration Committee, and the Health, Safety and Environment Committee. The Audit Committee is mainly responsible for…' (PetroChina, 2008, p. 9).	**Unimportant** **Important** 0 10 20 30 40 50 60 70 80 90 100
3. Quantified data	'The Board of Directors is composed of 15 members, including the Chairman, 3 executive directors, 7 nonexecutive directors and 4 independent directors' (Bank of China, 2008, p. 38).	**Unimportant** **Important** 0 10 20 30 40 50 60 70 80 90 100

continued

Disclosure type	Typical example	Rating scale
Performance information (environmental)		
1. General narrative information	'The company took energy conservation and emission reduction as important means to change the development modes' (PetroChina, 2008, p. 30).	**Unimportant** **Important** 0 10 20 30 40 50 60 70 80 90 100
2. Specific endeavour in non-quantitative terms	'Baosteel focused on controlling the sulphur content of raw fuel and installing flue gas desulphurization facilities in the sintering factory and power plants for SO_2 emission reduction' (BaoSteel, 2008, p. 45).	**Unimportant** **Important** 0 10 20 30 40 50 60 70 80 90 100
3. Quantified performance data	'In terms of energy conservation and emission reduction, the company has set up an energy conservation and emission reduction fund, and the investment in energy conservation and emission reduction projects in 2008 amounted to a total of RMB1.39 billion' (Shenhua Energy, 2008, p. 39).	**Unimportant** **Important** 0 10 20 30 40 50 60 70 80 90 100
4. Quantified performance data relative to benchmarks	'Our total Carbon Dioxide emissions (million tonnes) are 5.4 in 2006, 6.9 in 2007 and 7.9 in 2008' (China Mobile, 2008, p. 40).	**Unimportant** **Important** 0 10 20 30 40 50 60 70 80 90 100
5. Quantified performance data at disaggregate level (e.g. plant, business unit, geographic segment)	'In Chengdu branch, energy consumption was reduced and operating costs were saved by strengthening micro-management. For example, standardized control was applied to the on/off time of central air-conditioning while allowing timely notices to be made to the property management for adjustments based on the temperature of the day. In Beijing branch, the lighting source for the front access light box was changed from ordinary fluorescent tubes to energy saving tubes, saving approximately 30% power consumption' (Merchants Bank, 2008, p. 21).	**Unimportant** **Important** 0 10 20 30 40 50 60 70 80 90 100

Please indicate any additional disclosure type that you feel should be included in the list and assign a weighting to it:

Disclosure type	*Typical example*	*Rating scale*
		Unimportant **Important** 0 10 20 30 40 50 60 70 80 90 100

Part 2 (respondent's profile)

Instructions: Please complete the following question. Your information will be kept strictly confidential.

What is your relationship with the firm that sends you this survey?

Shareholder Creditor Government/Regulator Employee
Customer Supplier Community Media Audit firm
Academic Other (Please specify)

Labour practices (LA) version

Part 1

Instructions: Please indicate your response to each of the following disclosure types by circling the scale number that best describes your feelings.

Context information for understanding corporate performance

Disclosure type	*Typical example*	*Rating scale*
Strategy and analysis		
1. Specific endeavour in non-quantitative terms	'CSEC stuck to the goal of building an enterprise incorporating the Five-Model of "intrinsic safety, quality and efficiency, technological innovation, resource saving and harmonious development" and incorporated social responsibilities into the whole process of corporate strategic, cultural, production and operation activities' (Shenhua Energy, 2008, p. 6).	**Unimportant** **Important** 0 10 20 30 40 50 60 70 80 90 100
Corporate profile		
1. General narrative information	'Address: No. 55 Fuxingmennei Avenue, Xicheng District, Beijing, PRC' (ICBC, 2008, p. 2).	**Unimportant** **Important** 0 10 20 30 40 50 60 70 80 90 100
2. Specific endeavour in non-quantitative terms	'The businesses of CSEC mainly cover production and sales of coal, railway and port transportation of coal-related material as well as the power generation and sales' (Shenhua Energy, 2008, preface).	**Unimportant** **Important** 0 10 20 30 40 50 60 70 80 90 100
3. Quantified data	'The Group has a total number of 138,368 employees' (China Mobile, 2008, p. 5).	**Unimportant** **Important** 0 10 20 30 40 50 60 70 80 90 100

Report parameters		
1. General narrative information	'The issues highlighted in the report are mainly related to our performances on the economic, environmental and social responsibilities fronts in 2008' (PetroChina, 2008, preface).	**Unimportant** **Important** 0 10 20 30 40 50 60 70 80 90 100
2. Specific endeavour in non-quantitative terms	'We are committed to observing and supporting the ten Principles advocated by the Global Compact in the fields of human rights, labour rights, environment protection and anti-corruption, using the ten Principles to guide our practices in fulfilling social responsibilities. Starting from this year, we will disclose our progress in keeping with the ten Principles in the Global Compact in our annual report. Please see the following table…' (PetroChina, 2008, p. 48).	**Unimportant** **Important** 0 10 20 30 40 50 60 70 80 90 100
Governance, commitments and engagement		
1. General narrative information	'The positions of chairman and president of the Bank are separate' (ICBC, 2008, p. 22).	**Unimportant** **Important** 0 10 20 30 40 50 60 70 80 90 100
2. Specific endeavour in non-quantitative terms	'The Board of Directors has four board committees, namely the Audit Committee, the Investment and Development Committee, the Evaluation and Remuneration Committee, and the Health, Safety and Environment Committee. The Audit Committee is mainly responsible for…' (PetroChina, 2008, p. 9).	**Unimportant** **Important** 0 10 20 30 40 50 60 70 80 90 100
3. Quantified data	'The Board of Directors is composed of 15 members, including the Chairman, 3 executive directors, 7 nonexecutive directors and 4 independent directors' (Bank of China, 2008, p. 38).	**Unimportant** **Important** 0 10 20 30 40 50 60 70 80 90 100
Performance information (labour practices)		
1. General narrative information	'With respect to employee health and safety, we strictly implement national laws and regulations related to labour protection and safety production' (China Mobile, 2008, p. 19).	**Unimportant** **Important** 0 10 20 30 40 50 60 70 80 90 100

continued

Disclosure type	*Typical example*	*Rating scale*
2. Specific endeavour in non-quantitative terms	'BOC provides employees with benefits that include social security, a housing provident fund, statutory holidays, enterprise annuity, and supplementary medical insurance' (Bank of China, 2008, p. 47).	**Unimportant** **Important** 0 10 20 30 40 50 60 70 80 90 100
3. Quantified performance data	'The capital investment in prevention of occupational diseases was approximately 78 million in 2008' (Shenhua Energy, 2008, p. 66).	**Unimportant** **Important** 0 10 20 30 40 50 60 70 80 90 100
4. Quantified performance data relative to benchmarks	'The number of on-the-job training employees increases year by year, 5,164 in 2006, 6,232 in 2007 and 7,657 in 2008' (Bank of China, 2008, p. 48).	**Unimportant** **Important** 0 10 20 30 40 50 60 70 80 90 100
5. Quantified performance data at disaggregate level (e.g. plant, business unit, geographic segment)	'As at the end of 2008, the Bank had 385,609 employees, an increase of 3,896 persons compared with the end of prior year, of whom 221 are employees in major domestic holding companies and 2,697 are local employees in overseas institutions. Among the employees in domestic institutions, 39,124 are engaged in the corporate banking segment, 149,166 in personal banking segment, 4,522 in treasury operations segment, 87,040 in financial and accounting matters, and 103,060 in other specializations' (ICBC, 2008, p. 80).	**Unimportant** **Important** 0 10 20 30 40 50 60 70 80 90 100

Please indicate any additional disclosure type that you feel should be included in the list and assign a weighting to it:

Disclosure type	*Typical example*	*Rating scale*
		Unimportant **Important** 0 10 20 30 40 50 60 70 80 90 100

Part 2 (respondent's profile)

Instructions: Please complete the following question. Your information will be kept strictly confidential.
What is your relationship with the firm that sends you this survey?
Shareholder Creditor Government/Regulator Employee
Customer Supplier Community Media Audit firm
Academic Other (Please specify)

Human rights (HR) version

Part 1

Instructions: Please indicate your response to each of the following disclosure types by circling the scale number that best describes your feelings.

Context information for understanding corporate performance

Disclosure type	*Typical example*	*Rating scale*
Strategy and analysis		
1. Specific endeavour in non-quantitative terms	'CSEC stuck to the goal of building an enterprise incorporating the Five-Model of "intrinsic safety, quality and efficiency, technological innovation, resource saving and harmonious development" and incorporated social responsibilities into the whole process of corporate strategic, cultural, production and operation activities' (Shenhua Energy, 2008, p. 6).	**Unimportant** **Important** 0 10 20 30 40 50 60 70 80 90 100
Corporate profile		
1. General narrative information	'Address: No. 55 Fuxingmennei Avenue, Xicheng District, Beijing, PRC' (ICBC, 2008, p. 2).	**Unimportant** **Important** 0 10 20 30 40 50 60 70 80 90 100
2. Specific endeavour in non-quantitative terms	'The businesses of CSEC mainly cover production and sales of coal, railway and port transportation of coal-related material as well as the power generation and sales' (Shenhua Energy, 2008, preface).	**Unimportant** **Important** 0 10 20 30 40 50 60 70 80 90 100
3. Quantified data	'The Group has a total number of 138,368 employees' (China Mobile, 2008, p. 5).	**Unimportant** **Important** 0 10 20 30 40 50 60 70 80 90 100
Report parameters		
1. General narrative information	'The issues highlighted in the report are mainly related to our performances on the economic, environmental and social responsibilities fronts in 2008' (PetroChina, 2008, preface).	**Unimportant** **Important** 0 10 20 30 40 50 60 70 80 90 100

2. Specific endeavour in non-quantitative terms	'We are committed to observing and supporting the ten Principles advocated by the Global Compact in the fields of human rights, labour rights, environment protection and anti-corruption, using the ten Principles to guide our practices in fulfilling social responsibilities. Starting from this year, we will disclose our progress in keeping with the ten Principles in the Global Compact in our annual report. Please see the following table…' (PetroChina, 2008, p. 48).	**Unimportant** **Important** 0 10 20 30 40 50 60 70 80 90 100
Governance, commitments and engagement		
1. General narrative information	'The positions of chairman and president of the Bank are separate' (ICBC, 2008, p. 22).	**Unimportant** **Important** 0 10 20 30 40 50 60 70 80 90 100
2. Specific endeavour in non-quantitative terms	'The Board of Directors has four board committees, namely the Audit Committee, the Investment and Development Committee, the Evaluation and Remuneration Committee, and the Health, Safety and Environment Committee. The Audit Committee is mainly responsible for…' (PetroChina, 2008, p. 9).	**Unimportant** **Important** 0 10 20 30 40 50 60 70 80 90 100
3. Quantified data	'The Board of Directors is composed of 15 members, including the Chairman, 3 executive directors, 7 nonexecutive directors and 4 independent directors' (Bank of China, 2008, p. 38).	**Unimportant** **Important** 0 10 20 30 40 50 60 70 80 90 100
Performance information (human rights)		
1. General narrative information	'We are committed to the principles of equal pay for equal work and gender and racial equality' (China Mobile, 2008, p. 19).	**Unimportant** **Important** 0 10 20 30 40 50 60 70 80 90 100
2. Specific endeavour in non-quantitative terms	'The Company pays due attention to employees from ethnic minorities. Minority allowances are paid and Moslem restaurants are provided for these employees. Attention has been paid to appoint employees from ethnic minorities to some important management posts of the Company' (BaoSteel, 2008, p. 24).	**Unimportant** **Important** 0 10 20 30 40 50 60 70 80 90 100

continued

Disclosure type	Typical example	Rating scale
3. Quantified performance data	'The system of "4 shifts with 6 hours for each shift" is implemented in power plants and certain coal mines, which helped to substantially ease the labour intensity of front-line staff' (Shenhua Energy, 2008, p. 33).	**Unimportant** **Important** 0 10 20 30 40 50 60 70 80 90 100
4. Quantified performance data relative to benchmarks	'The second session of our Staff Representative Assembly was held in November 2008. Over 360 staff representatives and nearly 60 non-voting representatives attended the meeting, the number of representatives being higher than that of last session' (Construction Bank, 2008, p. 112).	**Unimportant** **Important** 0 10 20 30 40 50 60 70 80 90 100
5. Quantified performance data at disaggregate level (e.g. plant, business unit, geographic segment)	'During the reporting period, the Bank held 4,089 employees' representative meetings in total, with 40,430 proposals from the employees' representatives, and of which 32,961 (of which 824 from Beijing branch and 798 from Shanghai branch) were fulfilled at the rate of 81.5%' (ICBC, 2008, p. 82).	**Unimportant** **Important** 0 10 20 30 40 50 60 70 80 90 100

Please indicate any additional disclosure type that you feel should be included in the list and assign a weighting to it:

Disclosure type	Typical example	Rating scale
		Unimportant **Important** 0 10 20 30 40 50 60 70 80 90 100

Part 2 (respondent's profile)

Instructions: Please complete the following question. Your information will be kept strictly confidential.
What is your relationship with the firm that sends you this survey?
Shareholder Creditor Government/Regulator Employee
Customer Supplier Community Media Audit firm
Academic Other (Please specify)

Society (SO) version

Part 1

Instructions: Please indicate your response to each of the following disclosure types by circling the scale number that best describes your feelings.

Context information for understanding corporate performance

Disclosure type	*Typical example*	*Rating scale*
Strategy and analysis		
1. Specific endeavour in non-quantitative terms	'CSEC stuck to the goal of building an enterprise incorporating the Five-Model of "intrinsic safety, quality and efficiency, technological innovation, resource saving and harmonious development" and incorporated social responsibilities into the whole process of corporate strategic, cultural, production and operation activities' (Shenhua Energy, 2008, p. 6).	**Unimportant** **Important** 0 10 20 30 40 50 60 70 80 90 100
Corporate profile		
1. General narrative information	'Address: No. 55 Fuxingmennei Avenue, Xicheng District, Beijing, PRC' (ICBC, 2008, p. 2).	**Unimportant** **Important** 0 10 20 30 40 50 60 70 80 90 100
2. Specific endeavour in non-quantitative terms	'The businesses of CSEC mainly cover production and sales of coal, railway and port transportation of coal-related material as well as the power generation and sales' (Shenhua Energy, 2008, preface).	**Unimportant** **Important** 0 10 20 30 40 50 60 70 80 90 100
3. Quantified data	'The Group has a total number of 138,368 employees' (China Mobile, 2008, p. 5).	**Unimportant** **Important** 0 10 20 30 40 50 60 70 80 90 100

continued

Disclosure type	*Typical example*	*Rating scale*
Report parameters		
1. General narrative information	'The issues highlighted in the report are mainly related to our performances on the economic, environmental and social responsibilities fronts in 2008' (PetroChina, 2008, preface).	**Unimportant** **Important** 0 10 20 30 40 50 60 70 80 90 100
2. Specific endeavour in non-quantitative terms	'We are committed to observing and supporting the ten Principles advocated by the Global Compact in the fields of human rights, labour rights, environment protection and anti-corruption, using the ten Principles to guide our practices in fulfilling social responsibilities. Starting from this year, we will disclose our progress in keeping with the ten Principles in the Global Compact in our annual report. Please see the following table…' (PetroChina, 2008, p. 48).	**Unimportant** **Important** 0 10 20 30 40 50 60 70 80 90 100
Governance, commitments and engagement		
1. General narrative information	'The positions of chairman and president of the Bank are separate' (ICBC, 2008, p. 22).	**Unimportant** **Important** 0 10 20 30 40 50 60 70 80 90 100
2. Specific endeavour in non-quantitative terms	'The Board of Directors has four board committees, namely the Audit Committee, the Investment and Development Committee, the Evaluation and Remuneration Committee, and the Health, Safety and Environment Committee. The Audit Committee is mainly responsible for…' (PetroChina, 2008, p. 9).	**Unimportant** **Important** 0 10 20 30 40 50 60 70 80 90 100
3. Quantified data	'The Board of Directors is composed of 15 members, including the Chairman, 3 executive directors, 7 nonexecutive directors and 4 independent directors' (Bank of China, 2008, p. 38).	**Unimportant** **Important** 0 10 20 30 40 50 60 70 80 90 100
Performance information (society)		
1. General narrative information	'The Company strengthens anti-corruption education to improve the ability to fight against corruption' (Shenhua Energy, 2008, p. 24).	**Unimportant** **Important** 0 10 20 30 40 50 60 70 80 90 100

2. Specific endeavour in non-quantitative terms	'In 2008, we continued to implement the Rural Program and meet the commitment to rural development. By extending the reach of our "three networks", we benefited the rural residents, rural businesses and rural governments and supported the development of Chinese rural areas' (China Mobile, 2008, p. 22).	**Unimportant** **Important** 0 10 20 30 40 50 60 70 80 90 100
3. Quantified performance data	'Each year, the Company spends more than RMB150 billion on purchasing materials, thus directly promoting the industries of steel, construction materials, machinery, and electronics' (PetroChina, 2008, p. 41).	**Unimportant** **Important** 0 10 20 30 40 50 60 70 80 90 100
4. Quantified performance data relative to benchmarks	'The education donation (RMB10K) increases year by year, with 1,645 in 2006, 4,549 in 2007 and 12,968 in 2008' (PetroChina, 2008, p. 49).	**Unimportant** **Important** 0 10 20 30 40 50 60 70 80 90 100
5. Quantified performance data at disaggregate level (e.g. plant, business unit, geographic segment)	'After the quake, all the overseas institutions of the bank supported the affected population by various means. ICBC Indonesia opened a free-charge donation remittance channel to the whole country, and transmitted more than US$500,000 of donation to the Ministry of Civil Affairs, the Red Cross Society of China and the China Charity Federation; New York Branch donated to the 150 undergraduates in State University of New York at Stony Brook, who came from Sichuan under the "China 150 Program"' (ICBC, 2008, p. 35).	**Unimportant** **Important** 0 10 20 30 40 50 60 70 80 90 100

Please indicate any additional disclosure type that you feel should be included in the list and assign a weighting to it:

Disclosure type	*Typical example*	*Rating scale*
		Unimportant **Important** 0 10 20 30 40 50 60 70 80 90 100

Part 2 (respondent's profile)

Instructions: Please complete the following question. Your information will be kept strictly confidential.
What is your relationship with the firm that sends you this survey?
Shareholder Creditor Government/Regulator Employee
Customer Supplier Community Media Audit firm
Academic Other (Please specify)

Product responsibility (PR) version

Part 1

Instructions: Please indicate your response to each of the following disclosure types by circling the scale number that best describes your feeling.

Context information for understanding corporate performance

Disclosure type	*Typical example*	*Rating scale*
Strategy and analysis		
1. Specific endeavour in non-quantitative terms	'CSEC stuck to the goal of building an enterprise incorporating the Five-Model of "intrinsic safety, quality and efficiency, technological innovation, resource saving and harmonious development" and incorporated social responsibilities into the whole process of corporate strategic, cultural, production and operation activities' (Shenhua Energy, 2008, p. 6).	**Unimportant** **Important** 0 10 20 30 40 50 60 70 80 90 100
Corporate profile		
1. General narrative information	'Address: No. 55 Fuxingmennei Avenue, Xicheng District, Beijing, PRC' (ICBC, 2008, p. 2).	**Unimportant** **Important** 0 10 20 30 40 50 60 70 80 90 100

2. Specific endeavour in non-quantitative terms	'The businesses of CSEC mainly cover production and sales of coal, railway and port transportation of coal-related material as well as the power generation and sales' (Shenhua Energy, 2008, preface).	**Unimportant** **Important** 0 10 20 30 40 50 60 70 80 90 100
3. Quantified data	'The Group has a total number of 138,368 employees' (China Mobile, 2008, p. 5).	**Unimportant** **Important** 0 10 20 30 40 50 60 70 80 90 100
Report parameters		
1. General narrative information	'The issues highlighted in the report are mainly related to our performances on the economic, environmental and social responsibilities fronts in 2008' (PetroChina, 2008, preface).	**Unimportant** **Important** 0 10 20 30 40 50 60 70 80 90 100
2. Specific endeavour in non-quantitative terms	'We are committed to observing and supporting the ten Principles advocated by the Global Compact in the fields of human rights, labour rights, environment protection and anti-corruption, using the ten Principles to guide our practices in fulfilling social responsibilities. Starting from this year, we will disclose our progress in keeping with the ten Principles in the Global Compact in our annual report. Please see the following table…' (PetroChina, 2008, p. 48).	**Unimportant** **Important** 0 10 20 30 40 50 60 70 80 90 100
Governance, commitments and engagement		
1. General narrative information	'The positions of chairman and president of the Bank are separate' (ICBC, 2008, p. 22).	**Unimportant** **Important** 0 10 20 30 40 50 60 70 80 90 100
2. Specific endeavour in non-quantitative terms	'The Board of Directors has four board committees, namely the Audit Committee, the Investment and Development Committee, the Evaluation and Remuneration Committee, and the Health, Safety and Environment Committee. The Audit Committee is mainly responsible for…' (PetroChina, 2008, p. 9).	**Unimportant** **Important** 0 10 20 30 40 50 60 70 80 90 100

continued

Disclosure type	*Typical example*	*Rating scale*
3. Quantified data	'The Board of Directors is composed of 15 members, including the Chairman, 3 executive directors, 7 nonexecutive directors and 4 independent directors' (Bank of China, 2008, p. 38).	**Unimportant** **Important** 0 10 20 30 40 50 60 70 80 90 100
Performance information (product responsibility)		
1. General narrative information	'The company signed confidentiality agreements with employees from the sales department to keep customer privacy' (BaoSteel, 2008, p. 29).	**Unimportant** **Important** 0 10 20 30 40 50 60 70 80 90 100
2. Specific endeavour in non-quantitative terms	'The key points of the Company's customer relations included dedication in fulfilling contracts, provision of coal quality assurance for customers, improvement in the after-sales service system and customised product development based on customers' needs' (Shenhua Energy, 2008, p. 14).	**Unimportant** **Important** 0 10 20 30 40 50 60 70 80 90 100
3. Quantified performance data	'In 2008, clients' satisfaction score was above 90' (BaoSteel, 2008, p. 30).	**Unimportant** **Important** 0 10 20 30 40 50 60 70 80 90 100
4. Quantified performance data relative to benchmarks	'In 2008, our overall customer satisfaction scores increased to 81.3, compared with 80.8 in 2007 and 79.6 in 2006' (China Mobile, 2008, p. 17).	**Unimportant** **Important** 0 10 20 30 40 50 60 70 80 90 100
5. Quantified performance data at disaggregate level (e.g. plant, business unit, geographic segment)	'Satisfaction investigation was made to 1,800 corporate customers and 3,600 personal customers by preparing and issuing the customer satisfaction questionnaires. According to the investigation, the corporate and personal customer satisfaction rates reached 86.44% and 85.88% respectively' (ICBC, 2008, p. 94).	**Unimportant** **Important** 0 10 20 30 40 50 60 70 80 90 100

Please indicate any additional disclosure type that you feel should be included in the list and assign a weighting to it:

Disclosure type	*Typical example*	*Rating scale*
		Unimportant **Important** 0 10 20 30 40 50 60 70 80 90 100

Part 2 (respondent's profile)

Instructions: Please complete the following question. Your information will be kept strictly confidential.

What is your relationship with the firm that sends you this survey?

Shareholder Creditor Government/Regulator Employee
Customer Supplier Community Media Audit firm
Academic Other (Please specify)

Appendix 5

Rating criteria of the Chinese listed firms' social responsibility ranking list

Aspect	*Weight (%)*	*Item*	*Weight (%)*
Economic conditions	30	Operating revenue	10
		Net asset	10
		Net profit	10
Social responsibility	40	Product safety and service quality	10
		Environmental protection	10
		Labour/management relations	10
		Community relations	10
Social contribution	20	Faithful tax payment	10
		Employee welfare	5
		R&D and innovation	5
Public image	10	Public support on goods/services provided	10

Source: *Southern Weekend*, 2008b.

Appendix 6

Nonparametric tests for context disclosure types

Organisational profile

Kruskal–Wallis test (disclosure types 1, 2 and 3)

Disclosure type	*Obs*	*Rank sum*
1	217	67,517.5
2	217	71,450.5
3	217	73,258

Notes
chi-squared=2.245 with 2 d.f.
probability=0.3255.
chi-squared with ties=3.113 with 2 d.f.
probability=0.2109.

Two-sample Mann–Whitney test (disclosure types 1 and 2)

Disclosure type	*Obs*	*Rank sum*	*Expected*
1	217	45,866.5	47,197.5
2	217	48,528.5	47,197.5
Combined	434	94,395	94,395

Notes
unadjusted variance 1,706,976.25.
adjustment for ties −508,798.72.
adjusted variance 1,198,177.53.
Ho: response(disclosure type =1)=response(disclosure type =2).
z=−1.216.
Prob>|z|=0.2240.

Two-sample Mann–Whitney test (disclosure types 2 and 3)

Disclosure type	*Obs*	*Rank sum*	*Expected*
2	217	46,575	47,197.5
3	217	47,820	47,197.5
Combined	434	94,395	94,395

Notes
unadjusted variance 1,706,976.25.
adjustment for ties −472,286.72.
adjusted variance 1,234,689.53.
Ho: response(disclosure type=2)=response(disclosure type=3).
$z=-0.560$.
Prob>|z|=0.5753.

Report parameter

Two-sample Mann–Whitney test (disclosure types 1 and 2)

Disclosure type	*Obs*	*Rank sum*	*Expected*
1	217	45,406.5	47,197.5
2	217	48,988.5	47,197.5
Combined	434	94,395	94,395

Notes
unadjusted variance 1,706,976.25.
adjustment for ties −477,600.96.
adjusted variance 1,229,375.29.
Ho: response(disclosure type=1)=response(disclosure type=2).
$z=-1.615$.
Prob>|z|=0.1062.

Governance, commitments and engagement

Kruskal–Wallis test (disclosure types 1, 2 and 3)

Disclosure type	*Obs*	*Rank sum*
1	217	66,894.5
2	217	71,446
3	217	73,885.5

Notes
chi-squared=3.281 with 2 d.f.
probability=0.1939.
chi-squared with ties=4.445 with 2 d.f.
probability=0.1083.

Two-sample Mann–Whitney test (disclosure types 1 and 2)

Disclosure type	*Obs*	*Rank sum*	*Expected*
1	217	45,679	47,197.5
2	217	48,716	47,197.5
Combined	434	94,395	94,395

Notes
unadjusted variance 1,706,976.25.
adjustment for ties −429,641.71.
adjusted variance 1,277,334.54.
Ho: response(disclosure type = 1) = response(disclosure type = 2).
$z = -1.344$.
Prob > |z| = 0.1791.

Two-sample Mann–Whitney test (disclosure types 2 and 3)

Disclosure type	*Obs*	*Rank sum*	*Expected*
2	217	46,383	47,197.5
3	217	48,012	47,197.5
Combined	434	94,395	94,395

Notes
unadjusted variance 1,706,976.25.
adjustment for ties −472,429.55.
adjusted variance 1,234,546.70
Ho: response(disclosure type = 2) = response(disclosure type = 3).
$z = -0.733$.
Prob > |z| = 0.4635.
Disclosure type 1 = general narrative, 2 = specific endeavour in non-quantitative terms, and 3 = quantified data.

Appendix 7

Nonparametric tests for performance disclosure types

Economic performance (EC)

Kruskal–Wallis test (disclosure types 1, 2, 3, 4 and 5)

Disclosure type	*Obs*	*Rank sum*
1	38	759
2	38	2,171
3	38	3,631
4	38	5,236
5	38	6,348

Notes
chi-squared=176.979 with 4 d.f.
probability=0.0001.
chi-squared with ties=181.002 with 4 d.f.
probability=0.0001.

Two-sample Mann–Whitney test (disclosure types 1 and 2)

Disclosure type	*Obs*	*Rank sum*	*Expected*
1	38	759	1,463
2	38	2,167	1,463
Combined	76	2,926	2,926

Notes
unadjusted variance 9,265.67.
adjustment for ties −875.27.
adjusted variance 8,390.40.
Ho: response(disclosure type=1)=response(disclosure type=2.)
z=−7.686.
Prob>|z|=0.0000.

Two-sample Mann–Whitney test (disclosure types 2 and 3)

Disclosure type	*Obs*	*Rank sum*	*Expected*
2	38	745	1,463
3	38	2,181	1,463
Combined	76	2,926	2,926

Notes
unadjusted variance 9,265.67.
adjustment for ties −1,164.07.
adjusted variance 8,101.60.
Ho: response(disclosure type=2)=response(disclosure type=3).
$z=-7.977$.
Prob>|z|=0.0000.

Two-sample Mann–Whitney test (disclosure types 3 and 4)

Disclosure type	*Obs*	*Rank sum*	*Expected*
3	38	747	1,463
4	38	2,179	1,463
Combined	76	2,926	2,926

Notes
unadjusted variance 9,265.67.
adjustment for ties −1,327.85.
adjusted variance 7,937.82.
Ho: response(disclosure type=3)=response(disclosure type=4).
$z=-8.036$.
Prob>|z|=0.0000.

Two-sample Mann–Whitney test (disclosure types 4 and 5)

Disclosure type	*Obs*	*Rank sum*	*Expected*
4	38	910	1,463
5	38	2,016	1,463
Combined	76	2,926	2,926

Notes
unadjusted variance 9,265.67.
adjustment for ties −1,642.87.
adjusted variance 7,622.80.
Ho: response(disclosure type=4)=response(disclosure type=5).
$z=-6.334$.
Prob>|z|=0.0000.

Environmental performance (EN)

Kruskal–Wallis test (disclosure types 1, 2, 3, 4 and 5)

Disclosure type	*Obs*	*Rank sum*
1	31	505
2	31	1,455.5
3	31	2,420.5
4	31	3,511.5
5	31	4,197.5

Notes
chi-squared = 143.254 with 4 d.f.
probability = 0.0001.
chi-squared with ties = 146.168 with 4 d.f.
probability = 0.0001.

Two-sample Mann–Whitney test (disclosure types 1 and 2)

Disclosure type	*Obs*	*Rank sum*	*Expected*
1	31	505	976.5
2	31	1,448	976.5
Combined	62	1,953	1,953

Notes
unadjusted variance 5,045.25.
adjustment for ties −517.60.
adjusted variance 4,527.65.
Ho: response(disclosure type = 1) = response(disclosure type = 2).
$z = -7.007$.
Prob > |z| = 0.0000.

Two-sample Mann–Whitney test (disclosure types 2 and 3)

Disclosure type	*Obs*	*Rank sum*	*Expected*
2	31	503.5	976.5
3	31	1,449.5	976.5
Combined	62	1,953	1,953

Notes
unadjusted variance 5,045.25.
adjustment for ties −443.78.
adjusted variance 4,601.47
Ho: response(disclosure type = 2) = response(disclosure type = 3).
$z = -6.973$.
Prob > |z| = 0.0000.

Two-sample Mann–Whitney test (disclosure types 3 and 4)

Disclosure type	*Obs*	*Rank sum*	*Expected*
3	31	506	976.5
4	31	1,447	976.5
Combined	62	1,953	1,953

Notes
unadjusted variance 5,045.25.
adjustment for ties −531.32.
adjusted variance 4,513.93.
Ho: response(disclosure type=3)=response(disclosure type=4).
$z=-7.003$.
Prob>|z|=0.0000.

Two-sample Mann–Whitney test (disclosure types 4 and 5)

Disclosure type	*Obs*	*Rank sum*	*Expected*
4	31	638.5	976.5
5	31	1,314.5	976.5
Combined	62	1,953	1,953

Notes
unadjusted variance 5,045.25.
adjustment for ties −775.13.
adjusted variance 4,270.12.
Ho: response(disclosure type=4)=response(disclosure type=5).
$z=-5.172$.
Prob>|z|=0.0000.

Labour practices performance (LA)

Kruskal–Wallis test (disclosure types 1, 2, 3, 4 and 5)

Disclosure type	*Obs*	*Rank sum*
1	45	1,066.5
2	45	3,056.5
3	45	5,095.5
4	45	7,368.5
5	45	8,838

Notes
chi-squared=207.474 with 4 d.f.
probability=0.0001.
chi-squared with ties=210.978 with 4 d.f.
probability=0.0001.

Two-sample Mann–Whitney test (disclosure types 1 and 2)

Disclosure type	*Obs*	*Rank sum*	*Expected*
1	45	1,066.5	2,047.5
2	45	3,028.5	2,047.5
Combined	90	4,095	4,095

Notes
unadjusted variance 15,356.25.
adjustment for ties −1,240.28.
adjusted variance 14,115.97.
Ho: response(disclosure type=1)=response(disclosure type=2).
z=−8.257.
Prob>|z|=0.0000.

Two-sample Mann–Whitney test (disclosure types 2 and 3)

Disclosure type	*Obs*	*Rank sum*	*Expected*
2	45	1,063	2,047.5
3	45	3,032	2,047.5
Combined	90	4,095	4,095

Notes
unadjusted variance 15,356.25.
adjustment for ties −996.70.
adjusted variance 14,359.55.
Ho: response(disclosure type=2)=response(disclosure type=3).
z=−8.216.
Prob>|z|=0.0000.

Two-sample Mann–Whitney test (disclosure types 3 and 4)

Disclosure type	*Obs*	*Rank sum*	*Expected*
3	45	1,073.5	2,047.5
4	45	3,021.5	2,047.5
Combined	90	4,095	4,095

Notes
unadjusted variance 15,356.25.
adjustment for ties −1,136.88.
adjusted variance 14,219.37.
Ho: response(disclosure type=3)=response(disclosure type=4).
z=−8.168.
Prob>|z|=0.0000.

Two-sample Mann–Whitney test (disclosure types 4 and 5)

Disclosure type	*Obs*	*Rank sum*	*Expected*
4	45	1,332	2,047.5
5	45	2,763	2,047.5
Combined	90	4,095	4,095

Notes
unadjusted variance 15,356.25.
adjustment for ties −2,197.04.
adjusted variance 13,159.21.
Ho: response(disclosure type=4)=response(disclosure type=5).
z=−6.237.
Prob>|z|=0.0000.

Human rights performance (HR)

Kruskal–Wallis test (disclosure types 1, 2, 3, 4 and 5)

Disclosure type	*Obs*	*Rank sum*
1	32	560.5
2	32	1,553
3	32	2,556.5
4	32	3,802
5	32	4,408

Notes
chi-squared=145.115 with 4 d.f.
probability=0.0001.
chi-squared with ties=147.959 with 4 d.f.
probability=0.0001.

Two-sample Mann–Whitney test (disclosure types 1 and 2)

Disclosure type	*Obs*	*Rank sum*	*Expected*
1	32	560.5	1,040
2	32	1,519.5	1,040
Combined	64	2,080	2,080

Notes
unadjusted variance 5,546.67.
adjustment for ties −391.24.
adjusted variance 5,155.43.
Ho: response(disclosure type=1)=response(disclosure type=2).
z=−6.678.
Prob>|z|=0.0000.

Two-sample Mann–Whitney test (disclosure types 2 and 3)

Disclosure type	*Obs*	*Rank sum*	*Expected*
2	32	561.5	1,040
3	32	1,518.5	1,040
Combined	64	2,080	2,080

Notes
unadjusted variance 5,546.67.
adjustment for ties −326.60.
adjusted variance 5,220.06.
Ho: response(disclosure type=2)=response(disclosure type=3).
$z=-6.623$.
Prob>|z|=0.0000.

Two-sample Mann–Whitney test (disclosure types 3 and 4)

Disclosure type	*Obs*	*Rank sum*	*Expected*
3	32	542	1,040
4	32	1,538	1,040
Combined	64	2,080	2,080

Notes
unadjusted variance 5,546.67.
adjustment for ties −406.48.
adjusted variance 5,140.19.
Ho: response(disclosure type=3)=response(disclosure type=4).
$z=-6.946$.
Prob>|z|=0.0000.

Two-sample Mann–Whitney test (disclosure types 4 and 5)

Disclosure type	*Obs*	*Rank sum*	*Expected*
4	32	744	1,040
5	32	1,336	1,040
Combined	64	2,080	2,080

Notes
unadjusted variance 5,546.67.
adjustment for ties −1,047.24.
adjusted variance 4,499.43.
Ho: response(disclosure type=4)=response(disclosure type=5).
$z=-4.413$.
Prob>|z|=0.0000.

Society performance (SO)

Kruskal–Wallis test (disclosure types 1, 2, 3, 4 and 5)

Disclosure type	*Obs*	*Rank sum*
1	36	681
2	36	1,968
3	36	3,258
4	36	4,726.5
5	36	5,656.5

Notes
chi-squared=165.892 with 4 d.f.
probability=0.0001.
chi-squared with ties=168.852 with 4 d.f.
probability=0.0001.

Two-sample Mann–Whitney test (disclosure types 1 and 2)

Disclosure type	*Obs*	*Rank sum*	*Expected*
1	36	681	1,314
2	36	1,947	1,314
Combined	72	2,628	2,628

Notes
unadjusted variance 7,884.00.
adjustment for ties −657.89.
adjusted variance 7,226.11.
Ho: response(disclosure type=1)=response(disclosure type=2).
z=−7.446.
Prob>|z|=0.0000.

Two-sample Mann–Whitney test (disclosure types 2 and 3)

Disclosure type	*Obs*	*Rank sum*	*Expected*
2	36	687	1,314
3	36	1,941	1,314
Combined	72	2,628	2,628

Notes
unadjusted variance 7,884.00.
adjustment for ties −603.13.
adjusted variance 7,280.87.
Ho: response(disclosure type=2)=response(disclosure type=3).
z=−7.348.
Prob>|z|=0.0000.

Two-sample Mann–Whitney test (disclosure types 3 and 4)

Disclosure type	*Obs*	*Rank sum*	*Expected*
3	36	687	1,314
4	36	1,941	1,314
Combined	72	2,628	2,628

Notes
unadjusted variance 7,884.00.
adjustment for ties −603.89.
adjusted variance 7,280.11.
Ho: response(disclosure type=3)=response(disclosure type=4).
z=−7.348.
Prob>|z|=0.0000.

Two-sample Mann–Whitney test (disclosure types 4 and 5)

Disclosure type	*Obs*	*Rank sum*	*Expected*
4	36	859.5	1,314
5	36	1,768.5	1,314
Combined	72	2,628	2,628

Notes
unadjusted variance 7,884.00.
adjustment for ties −1,164.42.
adjusted variance 6,719.58.
Ho: response(disclosure type=4)=response(disclosure type=5).
z=−5.545.
Prob>|z|=0.0000.

Product responsibility performance (PR)

Kruskal–Wallis test (disclosure types 1, 2, 3, 4 and 5)

Disclosure type	*Obs*	*Rank sum*
1	35	678
2	35	1,851.5
3	35	3,080.5
4	35	4,447
5	35	5,343

Notes
chi-squared=158.835 with 4 d.f.
probability=0.0001.
chi-squared with ties=161.092 with 4 d.f.
probability=0.0001.

Two-sample Mann–Whitney test (disclosure types 1 and 2)

Disclosure type	*Obs*	*Rank sum*	*Expected*
1	35	678	1,242.5
2	35	1,807	1,242.5
Combined	70	2,485	2,485

Notes
unadjusted variance 7,247.92.
adjustment for ties −379.67.
adjusted variance 6,868.24.
Ho: response(disclosure type = 1) = response(disclosure type = 2).
z = −6.811.
Prob > |z| = 0.0000.

Two-sample Mann–Whitney test (disclosure types 2 and 3)

Disclosure type	*Obs*	*Rank sum*	*Expected*
2	35	674.5	1,242.5
3	35	1,810.5	1,242.5
Combined	70	2,485	2,485

Notes
unadjusted variance 7,247.92.
adjustment for ties −362.05.
adjusted variance 6,885.87.
Ho: response(disclosure type = 2) = response(disclosure type = 3).
z = −6.845.
Prob > |z| = 0.0000.

Two-sample Mann–Whitney test (disclosure types 3 and 4)

Disclosure type	*Obs*	*Rank sum*	*Expected*
3	35	675	1,242.5
4	35	1,810	1,242.5
Combined	70	2,485	2,485

Notes
unadjusted variance 7,247.92.
adjustment for ties −410.36.
adjusted variance 6,837.55.
Ho: response(disclosure type = 3) = response(disclosure type = 4).
z = −6.863.
Prob > |z| = 0.0000.

Two-sample Mann–Whitney test (disclosure types 4 and 5)

Disclosure type	*Obs*	*Rank sum*	*Expected*
4	35	817	1,242.5
5	35	1,668	1,242.5
Combined	70	2,485	2,485

Notes
unadjusted variance 7,247.92.
adjustment for ties −854.71.
adjusted variance 6,393.21.
Ho: response(disclosure type=4)=response(disclosure type=5).
$z=-5.322$.
Prob>|z|=0.0000.
Disclosure type 1=general narrative, 2=specific endeavour in non-quantitative terms, 3=quantified performance data, 4=quantified performance data relative to benchmarks, and 5=quantified performance data at disaggregate level.

Appendix 8

Importance of SEDI items

No.	*GRI code*	*Importance score*
Strategy and analysis		
1	1.1	2.83
2	1.2	2.42
Organisational profile		
3	2.1	4.00
4	2.2	3.33
5	2.3	2.92
6	2.4	2.17
7	2.5	2.42
8	2.6	2.67
9	2.7	3.00
10	2.8	3.00
11	2.9	2.42
12	2.10	2.67
Report parameters		
13	3.1	4.00
14	3.2	2.08
15	3.3	2.33
16	3.4	3.17
17	3.5	2.42
18	3.6	2.17
19	3.7	1.92
20	3.8	2.42
21	3.9	2.25
22	3.10	2.00
23	3.11	2.17
24	3.12	2.58
25	3.13	2.42
Governance, commitments and engagement		
26	4.1	3.25
27	4.2	2.92
28	4.3	2.92
29	4.4	3.00
30	4.5	2.42

continued

No.	*GRI code*	*Importance score*
31	4.6	2.42
32	4.7	2.42
33	4.8	2.67
34	4.9	2.42
35	4.10	2.42
36	4.11	2.42
37	4.12	2.17
38	4.13	2.08
39	4.14	3.67
40	4.15	3.00
41	4.16	3.67
42	4.17	3.00
Economic performance indicators		
43	EC1	3.92
44	EC2	3.25
45	EC3	3.00
46	EC4	3.00
47	EC5	2.92
48	EC6	3.00
49	EC7	3.00
50	EC8	3.92
51	EC9	2.83
Environmental performance indicators		
52	EN1	3.83
53	EN2	3.00
54	EN3	3.83
55	EN4	3.00
56	EN5	3.83
57	EN6	2.92
58	EN7	2.25
59	EN8	3.83
60	EN9	2.92
61	EN10	3.00
62	EN11	3.00
63	EN12	3.00
64	EN13	2.42
65	EN14	2.25
66	EN15	2.08
67	EN16	3.67
68	EN17	3.00
69	EN18	2.92
70	EN19	3.00
71	EN20	3.00
72	EN21	3.00
73	EN22	3.00
74	EN23	3.00
75	EN24	2.25
76	EN25	2.25
77	EN26	3.00
78	EN27	3.00

No.	*GRI code*	*Importance score*
79	EN28	3.00
80	EN29	2.25
81	EN30	3.92
Social performance indicators		
Labour practices and decent work performance Indicators		
82	LA1	3.67
83	LA2	3.00
84	LA3	3.00
85	LA4	3.00
86	LA5	2.25
87	LA6	2.83
88	LA7	3.92
89	LA8	3.00
90	LA9	2.83
91	LA10	3.00
92	LA11	3.00
93	LA12	3.00
94	LA13	3.00
95	LA14	2.42
Human rights performance indicators		
96	HR1	2.42
97	HR2	2.42
98	HR3	2.83
99	HR4	3.00
100	HR5	3.08
101	HR6	3.17
102	HR7	3.25
103	HR8	2.42
104	HR9	2.42
Society performance indicators		
105	SO1	3.92
106	SO2	3.00
107	SO3	3.00
108	SO4	3.00
109	SO5	3.00
110	SO6	3.67
111	SO7	2.83
112	SO8	3.00
Product responsibility performance indicators		
113	PR1	3.25
114	PR2	3.00
115	PR3	3.00
116	PR4	2.42
117	PR5	3.33
118	PR6	3.58
119	PR7	2.92
120	PR8	2.42
121	PR9	3.00

References

Abercrombie, N., Hill, S. and Turner, B. S. (1984), *Dictionary of Sociology*, Penguin, Harmondsworth, Middlesex.

Abeysekera, I. (2007), *Intellectual Capital Accounting: Practices in a Developing Country*, Routledge, New York.

Abeysekera, I. (2010), 'The influence of board size on intellectual capital disclosure by Kenyan listed firms', *Journal of Intellectual Capital*, vol. 11, no. 4, pp. 504–518.

Abeysekera, I. (2011), *Reputation Building, Website Disclosure, and the Case of Intellectual Capital (Studies in Managerial and Financial Accounting Series, vol. 21)*, Emerald, Bingley, UK.

AccountAbility (1999), *AccountAbility 1000: The Foundation Standard*, AccountAbility, London.

Acs, Z. J. and Dana, L. P. (2001), 'Contrasting two models of wealth redistribution', *Small Business Economics*, vol. 16, no. 2, pp. 63–74.

Adams, C. A. (2002), 'Internal organizational factors influencing corporate social and ethical reporting: beyond current theorizing', *Accounting, Auditing and Accountability Journal*, vol. 15, no. 2, pp. 223–250.

Adams, C. A. (2004), 'The ethical, social and environmental reporting – performance portrayal gap', *Accounting, Auditing and Accountability Journal*, vol. 17, no. 5, pp. 731–757.

Adnan, S. M., Staden, C. van and Hay, D. (2010), 'Do culture and governance structure influence CSR reporting quality: evidence from China, India, Malaysia and the United Kingdom', paper presented at sixth Asia Pacific Interdisciplinary Research in Accounting Conference, Sydney.

Aerts, W. (1994), 'On the use of accounting logic as an explanatory category in narrative accounting disclosures', *Accounting, Organizations and Society*, vol. 19, no. 4/5, pp. 337–353.

Aerts, W. and Cormier, D. (2009), 'Media legitimacy and corporate environmental communication', *Accounting, Organizations and Society*, vol. 34, no. 1, pp. 1–27.

Ahmad, Z., Hassan, S. and Mohammad, J. (2003), 'Determinants of environmental reporting in Malaysia', *International Journal of Business Studies*, vol. 11, no. 1, pp. 69–90.

Al-Tuwaijri, S. A., Christensen, T. E. and Hughes, K. E. (2004), 'The relations among environmental disclosure, environmental performance and economic performance: a simultaneous equations approach', *Accounting, Organizations and Society*, vol. 29, no. 5/6, pp. 447–471.

Anderson, R. H. (1977), 'Social responsibility accounting: time to get started', *CPA Magazine*, February, pp. 28–31.

Andrew, B. H., Gul, F. A., Guthrie, J. E. and Teoh, H. Y. (1989), 'A note on corporate social disclosure practices in developing countries: the case of Malaysia and Singapore', *British Accounting Review*, vol. 21, no. 4, pp. 371–376.

Argenti, J. (1976), *Corporation Collapse: the Causes and Symptoms*, McGraw-Hill, London.

Arndt, M. and Bigelow, B. (2000), 'Presenting structural innovation in an institutional environment: hospitals' use of impression management', *Administrative Science Quarterly*, vol. 45, no. 3, pp. 494–522.

Arnold, P. J. (1990), 'The state and political theory in corporate social disclosure research: a response to Guthrie and Parker', *Advances in Public Interest Accounting*, vol. 3, pp. 177–181.

Bank of China (2008), *CSR Report 2008*, online, available at: www.boc.cn, accessed: 2 April 2009.

Bansal, P. and Kistruck, G. (2006), 'Seeing is (not) believing: managing the impressions of the firm's commitment to the natural environment', *Journal of Business Ethics*, vol. 67, no. 2, pp. 165–180.

BaoSteel (2008), *2008 Sustainability Report*, online, available at: www.baosteel.com, accessed: 2 April 2009.

Barnett, M. L., Jermier, J. M., and Lafferty, B. A. (2006), 'Corporate reputation: the definitional landscape', *Corporate Reputation Review*, vol. 9, no. 1, pp. 26–38.

Barney, J. B. (1986), 'Organizational culture: can it be a source of sustained competitive advantage?', *Academy of Management Review*, vol. 11, no. 3, pp. 656–665.

Beattie, V. and Thomson, S. J. (2007), 'Lifting the lid on the use of content analysis to investigate intellectual capital disclosures', *Accounting Forum*, vol. 31, no. 2, pp. 129–163.

Beattie, V., McInnes, B., and Fearnley, S. (2004), 'A methodology for analysing and evaluating narratives in annual reports: a comprehensive descriptive profile and metrics for disclosure quality attributes', *Accounting Forum*, vol. 28, no. 3, pp. 205–236.

Bebbington, J., Larrinaga, C. and Moneva, J. M. (2008), 'Corporate social reporting and reputation risk management', *Accounting, Auditing and Accountability Journal*, vol. 21, no. 3, pp. 337–361.

Belal, A. R. (2000), 'Environmental reporting in developing countries: empirical evidence from Bangladesh', *Eco-Management and Auditing*, vol. 7, no. 3, pp. 114–121.

Belkaoui, A. (1980), 'The impact of socio-economic accounting statements on the investment decision: an empirical study', *Accounting, Organizations and Society*, vol. 5, no. 3, pp. 263–283.

Belkaoui, A. and Karpik, P. G. (1989), 'Determinants of the corporate decision to disclose social information', *Accounting, Auditing and Accountability Journal*, vol. 2, no. 1, pp. 36–51.

Benson, J. K. (1975), 'The interorganizational network as a political economy', *Administrative Science Quarterly*, vol. 20, no. 2, pp. 229–249.

Berle, Jr. A. and Means, G. (1932), *The Modern Corporation and Private Property*, Macmillan, New York.

Bewley, K. and Li, Y. (2000), 'Disclosure of environmental information by Canadian manufacturing companies: a voluntary disclosure perspective', *Advances in Environmental Accounting and Management*, vol. 1, no. 1, pp. 201–226.

Bhagat, S., Carey, D. and Elson, C. (1999), 'Director ownership, corporate performance, and management turnover', *Business Lawyer*, vol. 54, no. 3, pp. 885–919.

Blacconiere, W. G. and Patten, D. M. (1994), 'Environmental disclosures, regulatory costs and changes in firm value', *Journal of Accounting and Economics*, vol. 18, no. 3, pp. 357–377.

Blumberg, B., Cooper, D. and Schindler, P. (2005), *Business Research Methods*, McGraw-Hill Education, London.

Bolino, M. C., Kacmar, K. M., Turnley, W. H. and Gilstrap, J. B. (2008), 'A multi-level review of impression management motives and behaviors', *Journal of Management*, vol. 34, no. 6, pp. 1080–1109.

Bowman, E. H. and Haire, M. (1975), 'A strategic posture toward corporate social responsibility', *California Management Review*, vol. 18, no. 2, pp. 49–58.

Bowman, E. H. and Haire, M. (1976), 'Social impact disclosure and corporate annual reports', *Accounting, Organizations and Society*, vol. 1, no. 1, pp. 11–21.

Boyd, B. K. (1995), 'CEO duality and firm performance: a contingency model', *Strategic Management Journal*, vol. 16, no. 4, pp. 301–312.

Brace, I. (2004), *Questionnaire Design: How to Plan, Structure and Write Survey Material for Effective Market Research*, Kogan Page, London.

Brannen, J. (2005), 'Mixing methods: the entry of qualitative and quantitative approaches into the research process', *International Journal of Social Research Methodology*, vol. 8, no. 3, pp. 173–185.

Brickley, J. A., Coles, J. L. and Jarrell, G. (1997), 'Leadership structure: separating the CEO and chairman of the board', *Journal of Corporate Finance*, vol. 3, no. 3, pp. 189–220.

Broadbent, J. and Unerman, J. (2011), 'Developing the relevance of the accounting academy: the importance of drawing from the diversity of research approaches', *Meditari Accountancy Research*, vol. 19, no. 1/2, pp. 7–21.

Brown, N. and Deegan, C. (1998), 'The public disclosure of environmental performance information – a dual test of media agenda setting theory and legitimacy theory', *Accounting and Business Research*, vol. 29, no. 1, pp. 21–41.

Bryman, A. (1984), 'The debate about quantitative and qualitative research: a question of method or epistemology', *British Journal of Sociology*, vol. 35, no. 1, pp. 76–92.

Bryman, A. (2006), 'Integrating quantitative and qualitative research: How is it done?', *Qualitative Research*, vol. 6, no. 1, pp. 97–113.

Bryman, A. (2008), *Social Research Methods (third edition)*, Oxford University Press, New York.

Bryman, A. and Bell, E. (2003), *Business Research Methods*, Oxford University Press, Oxford.

Buhr, N. (2007), 'Histories of and rationales for sustainability reporting', in Unerman, J., Bebbington, J. and O'Dwyer, B. (eds), *Sustainability Accounting and Accountability*, Routledge, New York, NY, pp. 57–69.

Cable, D. M. and Graham, M. E. (2000), 'The determinants of job seekers' reputation perceptions', *Journal of Organizational Behavior*, vol. 21, no. 8, pp. 929–947.

Campbell, D. (2004), 'A longitudinal and cross-sectional analysis of environmental disclosure in UK companies – a research note', *British Accounting Review*, vol. 36, no. 1, pp. 107–117.

Campbell, D. and Abdul Rahman, M. R. (2010), 'A longitudinal examination of intellectual capital reporting in Marks and Spencer annual reports, 1978–2008', *British Accounting Review*, vol. 42, no. 1, pp. 56–70.

Carroll, A. B. (1979), 'A three-dimensional model of corporate performance', *Academy of Management Review*, vol. 4, no. 4, pp. 497–505.

Carroll, A. B. (1999), 'Corporate social responsibility: evolution of a definitional construct', *Business and Society*, vol. 38, no. 3, pp. 268–295.

Carter, S. M. (2006), 'The interaction of top management group, stakeholder, and situational factors on certain corporate reputation management activities', *Journal of Management Studies*, vol. 43, no. 5, pp. 1145–1176.

Chalmers, K. and Godfrey, J. M. (2004), 'Reputation costs: the impetus for voluntary derivative financial instrument reporting', *Accounting, Organizations and Society*, vol. 29, no. 2, pp. 95–125.

Chen, M. and Chan, A. (2010), 'Occupational health and safety in China: the case of state-managed enterprises', *International Journal of Health Services*, vol. 40, no. 1, pp. 43–60.

China Mobile (2008), *2008 Corporate Social Responsibility Report*, online, available at: www.chinamobileltd.com, accessed: 2 April 2009.

China National Textile Apparel Council (CNTAC) (2006), *The Report on CSR in China's Textile and Apparel Industries*, CNTAC, Beijing (in Chinese).

China Securities Journal (2009), *290 Listed Firms Disclose Corporate Social Responsibility Reports*, online, available at: www.cs.com.cn/ssgs/02/200905/t20090511_1891772.htm, accessed: 1 September 2009.

China Water (2008), *Water Pollution in China*, online, available at: www.chinawater.net/chinaWaterToday/viewpaper.asp?id=5811, accessed: 12 September 2009.

Chinese Securities and Regulations Commission (CSRC) (2002), *Code of Corporate Governance for Listed Companies in China*, online, available at: www.cninfo.com.cn/finalpage/2002–01–10/571659.html, accessed: 3 September 2009 (in Chinese).

Cho, C. H. (2009), 'Legitimation strategies used in response to environmental disaster: a French case study of Total SA's Erika and AZF incidents', *European Accounting Review*, vol. 18, no. 1, pp. 33–62.

Cho, C. H. and Patten, D. M. (2007), 'The role of environmental disclosures as tools of legitimacy: a research note', *Accounting, Organizations and Society*, vol. 32, no. 7–8, pp. 639–647.

Choi, J. S. (1999), 'An investigation of the initial voluntary environmental disclosures made in Korean semi-annual financial reports', *Pacific Accounting Review*, vol. 11, no. 1, pp. 73–102.

Chow, C. W. and Wong-Boren, A. (1987), 'Voluntary financial disclosure by Mexican corporations', *Accounting Review*, vol. 62, no. 3, pp. 533–541.

Chow, G. C. (2007), 'China's energy and environmental problems and policies', CEPS Working Paper No. 152, Princeton University, Princeton, NJ.

Chua, W. F. (1986), 'Radical developments in accounting thought', *Accounting Review*, vol. 61, no. 4, pp. 601–632.

Clarkson, M. B. E. (1995), 'A stakeholder framework for analyzing and evaluating corporate social performance', *Academy of Management Review*, vol. 20, no. 1, pp. 92–117.

Clarkson, P. M., Li, Y., Richardson, G. D. and Vasvari, F. P. (2008), 'Revisiting the relation between environmental performance and environmental disclosure: an empirical analysis', *Accounting, Organizations and Society*, vol. 33, no. 4/5, pp. 303–327.

Clarkson, P. M., Overell, M. B. and Chapple, L. (2011), 'Environmental reporting and its relation to corporate environmental performance', *ABACUS*, vol. 47, no. 1, pp. 27–60.

Cole, R. and Mehran, H. (1998), 'The effect of changes in ownership structure on performance: evidence from the thrift industry', *Journal of Financial Economics*, vol. 50, no. 3, pp. 291–317.

Commission of the European Communities, (2002), *Corporate Social Responsibility: A Business Contribution to Sustainable Development*, COM 347 final, Brussels.

Construction Bank (2008), *CSR Report 2008*, online, available at: www.ccb.com, accessed: 2 April 2009.

Cooke, T. E. (1989), 'Disclosure in the corporate annual reports of Swedish companies', *Accounting and Business Research*, vol. 19, spring, pp. 113–124.

Cooper, C., Taylor, P., Smith, N. and Catchpole, L. (2005), 'A discussion of the political potential of social accounting', *Critical Perspectives on Accounting*, vol. 16, no. 7, pp. 951–974.

Cooper, S. and Owen, D. (2007), 'Corporate social reporting and stakeholder accountability: the missing link', *Accounting, Organisations and Society*, vol. 32, no. 7–8, pp. 649–667.

Cormier, D. and Gordon, I. M. (2001), 'An examination of social and environmental reporting strategies', *Accounting, Auditing and Accountability Journal*, vol. 14, no. 5, pp. 587–616.

Cormier, D. and Magnan, M. (1999), 'Corporate environmental disclosure strategies: determinants, costs and benefits', *Journal of Accounting, Auditing and Finance*, vol. 14, no. 4, pp. 429–451.

Cormier, D. and Magnan, M. (2003), 'Environmental reporting management: a continental European perspective', *Journal of Accounting and Public Policy*, vol. 22, no. 1, pp. 43–62.

Cormier, D. and Magnan, M. (2007), 'The revisited contribution of environmental reporting to investors' valuation of a firm's earnings: an international perspective', *Ecological Economics*, vol. 62, no. 3–4, pp. 613–626.

Cormier, D., Gordon, I. M. and Magnan, M. (2004), 'Corporate environmental disclosure: contrasting management's perceptions with reality', *Journal of Business Ethics*, vol. 49, no. 2, pp. 143–165.

Cowen, S. S., Ferreri, L. B. and Parker, L. D. (1987), 'The impact of corporate characteristics on social responsibility disclosure: a typology and frequency-based analysis', *Accounting, Organizations and Society*, vol. 12, no. 2, pp. 111–122.

Coy, D., Tower, G. and Dixon, K. (1993), 'Quantifying the quality of tertiary education annual reports', *Accounting and Finance*, vol. 33, no. 2, pp. 121–129.

Craswell, A. and Taylor, S. (1992), 'Discretionary disclosure of reserves by oil and gas companies: an economic analysis', *Journal of Business Finance and Accounting*, vol. 19, no. 2, pp. 295–308.

Creswell, J. W. (2008), *Research Design: Qualitative, Quantitative, and Mixed Methods Approaches (third edition)*, Sage Publications, London.

Dalton, D., Daily, C., Johnson, J. and Ellstrand, A. (1999), 'Number of directors and financial performance: a meta analysis', *Academy of Management Journal*, vol. 42, no. 6, pp. 674–686.

Dasgupta, S., Hong, J. H., Laplante, B. and Mamingi, N. (2006), 'Disclosure of environmental violations and stock market in the Republic of Korea', *Ecological Economics*, vol. 58, no. 4, pp. 759–777.

Davidson, W. N., Jiraporn, P., Kim, Y. S. and Nemec, C. (2004), 'Earnings management following duality-creating successions: ethnostatistics, impression management, and agency theory', *Academy of Management Journal*, vol. 47, no. 2, pp. 267–275.

DeAngelo, L. (1981), 'Auditor size and quality', *Journal of Accounting and Economics*, vol. 3, no. 3, pp. 183–199.

Deegan, C. (2000), *Financial Accounting Theory*, McGraw Hill, Sydney.

Deegan, C. (2002), 'The legitimising effect of social and environmental disclosures – a theoretical foundation', *Accounting, Auditing and Accountability Journal*, vol. 15, no. 3, pp. 282–311.

Deegan, C. (2007), 'Organizational legitimacy as a motive for sustainability reporting', in Unerman, J., Bebbington, J. and O'Dwyer, B. (eds), *Sustainability Accounting and Accountability*, Routledge, New York, NY, pp. 127–149.

Deegan, C. (2009), *Financial Accounting Theory (third edition)*, McGraw Hill, Sydney.

Deegan, C. and Blomquist, C. (2006), 'Stakeholder influence on corporate reporting: an exploration of the interaction between WWF-Australia and the Australian minerals industry', *Accounting, Organizations and Society*, vol. 31, no. 4–5, pp. 343–372.

Deegan, C. and Gordon, B. (1996), 'A study of environmental disclosure practices of Australian corporations', *Accounting and Business Research*, vol. 26, no. 3, pp. 187–199.

Deegan, C. and Rankin, M. (1996), 'Do Australian companies report environmental news objectively? – An analysis of environmental disclosures by firms prosecuted successfully by the Environmental Protection Authority', *Accounting, Auditing and Accountability Journal*, vol. 9, no. 2, pp. 50–67.

Deegan, C. and Rankin, M. (1997), 'The materiality of environmental information to users of annual reports', *Accounting, Auditing and Accountability Journal*, vol. 10, no. 4, pp. 562–583.

Deegan, C. and Rankin, M. (1999), 'The environmental reporting expectations gap: Australian evidence', *British Accounting Review*, vol. 31, no. 3, pp. 313–346.

Deegan, C. and Unerman, J. (2006), *Financial Accounting Theory: European Edition*, McGraw-Hill, Maidenhead.

Deegan, C., Geddes, S. and Staunton, J. (1995), 'A survey of Australian accountants' attitudes on environmental reporting', *Accounting Forum*, vol. 19, no. 2/3, pp. 143–163.

Deegan, C., Rankin, M. and Tobin, J. (2002), 'An examination of the corporate social and environmental disclosures of BHP from 1983–1997: a test of legitimacy theory', *Accounting, Auditing and Accountability Journal*, vol. 15, no. 3, pp. 312–343.

Deegan, C., Rankin, M., and Voght, P. (2000), 'Firms' disclosure reactions to major social incidents: Australian evidence', *Accounting Forum*, vol. 24, no. 1, pp. 101–130.

Deephouse, D. L. (1996), 'Does isomorphism legitimate?', *Academy of Management Journal*, vol. 39, no. 4, pp. 1024–1039.

Deephouse, D. L. and Carter, S. M. (2005), 'An examination of differences between organizational legitimacy and organizational reputation', *Journal of Management Studies*, vol. 42, no. 2, pp. 329–360.

Delgado-Garcia, J. B., Quevedo-Puente, E. de and Fuente-Sabate, J. M. de la (2010), 'The impact of ownership structure on corporate reputation: evidence from Spain', *Corporate Governance: An International Review*, vol. 18, no. 6, pp. 540–556.

Denis, D. and Sarin, A. (1999), 'Ownership and board structures in publicly traded corporations', *Journal of Financial Economics*, vol. 52, no. 2, pp. 187–224.

Dierkes, M. and Preston, L. E. (1977), 'Corporate social accounting reporting for the physical environment: a critical review and implementation proposal', *Accounting, Organizations and Society*, vol. 2, no. 1, pp. 3–22.

Dilley, S. C. and Weygandt, J. J. (1973), 'Measuring social responsibility: an empirical test', *Journal of Accountancy*, vol. 136, no. 3, pp. 62–70.

Disu, A. and Gray, R. H. (1998), 'An exploration of social reporting and MNCs in Nigeria', *Social and Environmental Accounting*, vol. 18, no. 2, pp. 13–15.

Donaldson, T. and Preston, L. E. (1995), 'The stakeholder theory of the corporation: concepts, evidence, and implications', *Academy of Management Review*, vol. 20, no. 1, pp. 65–91.

Dowling, J. and Pfeffer, J. (1975), 'Organizational legitimacy: social values and organizational behaviour', *Pacific Sociological Review*, vol. 18, no. 1, pp. 122–136.

Dye, R. A. (1985), 'Disclosure of nonproprietary information', *Journal of Accounting Research*, vol. 23, no. 1, pp. 123–145.

Elkington, J. (1997), *Cannibals with Forks – The Triple Bottom-line*, Capstone, Oxford.

Elsbach, K. D. (1994), 'Managing organizational legitimacy in the California cattle industry: the construction and effectiveness of verbal accounts', *Administrative Science Quarterly*, vol. 39, no. 1, pp. 57–88.

Elsbach, K. D. and Sutton, R. I. (1992), 'Acquiring organizational legitimacy through illegitimate actions: a marriage of institutional and impression management theories', *Academy of Management Journal*, vol. 35, no. 4, pp. 699–738.

Elsbach, K. D., Sutton, R. I. and Principe, K. E. (1998), 'Averting expected challenges through anticipatory impression management: a study of hospital billing', *Organization Science*, vol. 9, no. 1, pp. 68–86.

Eng, L. and Mak, Y. (2003), 'Corporate governance and voluntary disclosure', *Journal of Accounting and Public Policy*, vol. 22, no. 4, pp. 325–345.

Ernst and Ernst (1972–1978), *Social Responsibility Disclosure Surveys*, Ernst and Ernst, Cleveland, OH.

Fama, E. F. and Jensen, M. C. (1983), 'Separation of ownership and control', *Journal of Law and Economics*, vol. 26, no. 2, pp. 301–325.

Fernandez-Alles, M. and Valle-Cabrera, R. (2006), 'Reconciling institutional theory with organizational theories: how neoinstitutionalism resolves five paradoxes', *Journal of Organizational Change*, vol. 19, no. 4, pp. 503–517.

Fombrun, C. (1996), *Reputation: Realizing Value from the Corporate Image*, Harvard Business School Press, Boston, MA.

Fombrun, C. (2006), 'Corporate governance', *Corporate Reputation Review*, vol. 8, no. 4, pp. 267–271.

Fombrun, C. J. and Rindova, V. (1996), 'Who's tops and who decides? The social construction of corporate reputations', New York University, Stern School of Business, Working Paper.

Fombrun, C. and Shanley, M. (1990), 'What's in a name? Reputation building and corporate strategy', *Academy of Management Journal*, vol. 33, no. 2, pp. 233–258.

Fombrun, C. and Riel, C. van (1997), 'The reputational landscape', *Corporate Reputation Review*, vol. 1, no. 1–2, pp. 5–13.

Fombrun, C. J., Gardberg, N. A. and Barnett, M. L. (2000), 'Opportunity platforms and safety nets: corporate citizenship and reputational risk', *Business and Society Review*, vol. 105, no. 1, pp. 85–106.

Frank, R. H. (1988), *Passions within Reason: The Strategic Role of the Emotions*, W. W. Norton, New York.

Freedman, M. and Wasley, C. (1990), 'The association between environmental performance and environmental disclosure in annual reports and 10Ks', *Advances in Public Interest Accounting*, vol. 3, pp. 183–193.

Freeman, R. E. (1983), 'Strategic management: a stakeholder approach', in Lamb, R. (ed.), *Advances in Strategic Management*, vol. 1, JAI Press, Greenwich, pp. 31–60.

Freeman, R. E. (1984), *Strategic Management: a Stakeholder Approach*, Pitman, Marshall, MA.

Friedman, A. L. and Miles, S. (2001), 'Socially responsible investment and corporate social and environmental reporting in the UK: an exploratory study', *British Accounting Review*, vol. 33, no. 4, pp. 523–548.

Friedman, A. L. and Miles, S. (2002), 'Developing stakeholder theory', *Journal of Management Studies*, vol. 39, no. 1, pp. 1–21.

Frost, G. and Seamer, M. (2002), 'Adoption of environmental reporting and management practices: an analysis of New South Wales public sector entities', *Financial Accountability and Management*, vol. 18, no. 2, pp. 103–127.

Frost, G., Jones, S., Loftus, J. and Laan, S. van der (2005), 'A survey of sustainability reporting practices of Australian reporting entities', *Australian Accounting Review*, vol. 15, no. 1, pp. 89–96.

Gales, L. and Kesner, I. (1994), 'An analysis of the board of director size and composition in bankrupt organizations,' *Journal of Business Research*, vol. 30, no. 3, pp. 271–282.

Gamble, G. O., Hsu, K., Jackson, C. and Tollerson, C. D. (1996), 'Environmental disclosures in annual reports: an international perspective', *International Journal of Accounting*, vol. 31, no. 3, pp. 293–331.

Gao, S. S., Heravi, S. and Xiao, J. Z. (2005), 'Determinants of corporate social and environmental reporting in Hong Kong: a research note', *Accounting Forum*, vol. 29, no. 2, pp. 233–242.

Gardner, W. L. and Martinko, M. J. (1988), 'Impression management in organisations', *Journal of Management*, vol. 14, no. 2, pp. 321–338.

Gibson, R. and Guthrie, J. E. (1995), 'Recent environmental disclosures in annual reports of Australian public and private sector organizations', *Accounting Forum*, vol. 19, no. 2/3, pp. 111–127.

Global Reporting Initiative (GRI) (2002; 2006), *Sustainability Reporting Guidelines*, online, available at: www.globalreporting.org, accessed: 1 September 2009.

Goffman, E. (1959), *The Presentation of Self in Everyday Life*, Doubleday Anchor Books, Garden City, NY.

Gray, R. H. (2002), 'The social accounting project and *Accounting, Organizations and Society*: privileging engagement, imaginings, new accountings and pragmatism over critique?', *Accounting, Organizations and Society*, vol. 27, no. 7, pp. 687–708.

Gray, R. H., Owen, D. L. and Maunders, K. T. (1987), *Corporate Social Reporting: Accounting and Accountability*, Prentice-Hall, Hemel Hempstead.

Gray, R. H., Bebbington, J. and Walters, D. (1993), *Accounting for the Environment*, ACCA, London.

Gray, R. H., Kouhy, R. and Laver, S. (1995a), 'Corporate social and environmental reporting: a review of the literature and a longitudinal study of UK disclosure', *Accounting, Auditing and Accountability Journal*, vol. 8, no. 2, pp. 47–77.

Gray, R., Kouhy, R. and Lavers, S. (1995b), 'Methodological themes: constructing a research database of social and environmental reporting by UK companies', *Accounting, Auditing and Accountability Journal*, vol. 8, no. 2, pp. 78–101.

Gray, R. H., Owen, D. L. and Adams, C. (1996), *Accounting and Accountability: Changes and Challenges in Corporate Social and Environmental Reporting*, Prentice-Hall, London.

Grojer, J. E. and Stark, A. (1977), 'Social accounting: a Swedish attempt', *Accounting, Organizations and Society*, vol. 2, no. 4, pp. 349–386.

Grossman, S. and Hart, O. D. (1983), 'An analysis of the principal-agent problem', *Econometrica*, vol. 51, no. 1, pp. 7–45.

Gul, F. A. and Leung, S. (2004), 'Board leadership, outside directors expertise and voluntary corporate disclosures', *Journal of Accounting and Public Policy*, vol. 23, no. 5, pp. 351–379.

Guo, P. (2005), 'Corporate environmental reporting and disclosure in China', in Welford, R. (ed.), *CSR Asia 2005*, Tsinghua University, Beijing.

Guo, R. (2010), *An Introduction to the Chinese Economy: The Driving Forces Behind Modern Day China*, John Wiley & Sons (Asia) Pty. Ltd., Singapore.

Guthrie, J. E. and Mathews, M. R. (1985), 'Corporate social accounting in Australasia', *Research in Corporate Social Performance and Policy*, vol. 7, no. 1, pp. 251–277.

Guthrie, J. E. and Parker, L. D. (1989), 'Corporate social reporting: a rebuttal of legitimacy theory', *Accounting and Business Research*, vol. 9, no. 76, pp. 343–352.

Guthrie, J. E. and Parker, L. D. (1990), 'Corporate social disclosure practice: a comparative international analysis', *Advances in Public Interest Accounting*, vol. 3, no. 2, pp. 159–176.

Guthrie, J., Petty, R., Yongvanich, K. and Ricceri, F. (2004), 'Using content analysis as a research method to inquire into intellectual capital reporting', *Journal of Intellectual Capital*, vol. 5, no. 2, pp. 282–293.

Hackston, D. and Milne, M. J. (1996), 'Some determinants of social and environmental disclosures in New Zealand companies', *Accounting, Auditing and Accountability Journal*, vol. 9, no. 1, pp. 77–108.

Hafsi, T. and Turgut, G. (2012), 'Boardroom diversity and its effect on social performance: conceptualization and empirical evidence', *Journal of Business Ethics*, April, vol. 112, no. 2, pp. 463–479.

Haniffa, R. M. and Cooke, T. E. (2002), 'Culture, corporate governance and disclosure in Malaysian corporations', *ABACUS*, vol. 38, no. 3, pp. 317–349.

Harte, G. and Owen, D. L. (1991), 'Environmental disclosure in the annual reports of British companies: a research note', *Accounting, Auditing and Accountability Journal*, vol. 4, no. 3, pp. 51–61.

Harte, G., Lewis, L. and Owen, D. (1991), 'Ethical investment and the corporate reporting function', *Critical Perspectives on Accounting*, vol. 2, no. 3, pp. 227–253.

Hasseldine, J., Salama, A. I. and Toms, J. S. (2005), 'Quantity versus quality: the impact of environmental disclosures on the reputations of UK plcs', *British Accounting Review*, vol. 37, no. 2, pp. 231–248.

Hegde, P., Bloom, R. and Fuglister, J. (1997), 'Social financial reporting in India: a case', *International Journal of Accounting*, vol. 32, no. 2, pp. 155–172.

Highhouse, S., Brooks, M. E. and Gregarus, G. (2009), 'An organizational impression management perspective on the formation of corporate reputations', *Journal of Management*, vol. 35, no. 6, pp. 1481–1493.

Hillman, A. J., Keim, G. D. and Luce, R. A. (2001), 'Board composition and stakeholder performance: do stakeholder directors make a difference?', *Business and Society*, vol. 40, no. 3, pp. 295–314.

Hogner, R. H. (1982), 'Corporate social reporting: eight decades of development at US Steel', *Research in Corporate Social Performance and Policy*, vol. 4, no. 1, pp. 243–250.

Holderness, C. and Sheehan, D. (1988), 'The role of majority shareholders in publicly held corporations', *Journal of Financial Economics*, vol. 20, pp. 317–346.

Holsti, O. R. (1969), *Content Analysis for the Social Sciences and Humanities*, Addison-Wesley, London.

Hooghiemstra, R. (2000), 'Corporate communication and impression management – new perspectives why companies engage in corporate social reporting', *Journal of Business Ethics*, vol. 27, no. 1/2, pp. 55–68.

Huang, Y. L. (2008), 'Revamping CSR in China', *Leading Perspectives, CSR in the People's Republic of China*, winter 2007–2008, pp. 3–4.

Hughes, S. B., Anderson, A. and Golden, S. (2001), 'Corporate environmental disclosures: Are they useful in determining environmental performance?', *Journal of Accounting and Public Policy*, vol. 20, no. 3, pp. 217–240.

ICBC (2008), *2008 Corporate Social Responsibility Report*, online, available at: www.icbc.com.cn, accessed: 2 April 2009.

Ilinitch, A. Y., Soderstrom, N. S. and Thomas, T. E. (1998), 'Measuring corporate environmental performance', *Journal of Accounting and Public Policy*, vol. 17, no. 4–5, pp. 383–408.

Information Office of the State Council (2006), *Environmental Protection in China (1996–2005)*, online, available at: www.lawinfochina.com/Wbk/display.asp?id=52&keyword, accessed: 5 August 2009.

Ingram, R. W. (1978), 'An investigation of the information content of (certain) social responsibility disclosures', *Journal of Accounting Research*, vol. 16, no. 2, pp. 270–285.

Ingram, R. W. and Frazier, K. B. (1980), 'Environmental performance and corporate disclosure', *Journal of Accounting Research*, vol. 18, no. 2, pp. 614–621.

Jaggi, B. and Freedman, M. (1982), 'An analysis of the information content of pollution disclosures', *Financial Review*, vol. 19, no. 5, pp. 142–152.

Jaggi, B. and Zhao, R. (1996), 'Environmental performance and reporting: perceptions of managers and accounting professionals in Hong Kong', *International Journal of Accounting*, vol. 31, no. 3, pp. 333–346.

Jenkins, H. and Yakovleva, N. (2006), 'Corporate social responsibility in the mining industry: exploring trends in social and environmental disclosure', *Journal of Cleaner Production*, vol. 14, no. 3–4, pp. 271–284.

John, K. and Senbet, L. (1998), 'Corporate governance and board effectiveness', *Journal of Banking and Finance*, vol. 22, no. 4, pp. 371–403.

Jones, E. E. and Pittman, T. S. (1982), 'Toward a general theory of strategic self-presentation', in Suls, J. (eds), *Psychological Perspectives on the Self*, Lawrence Erlbaum, Hillsdale, NJ, pp. 231–262.

Jones, K. and Alabaster, T. (1999), 'Critical analysis of corporate environmental reporting scoring systems', *Journal of Environmental Assessment Policy and Management*, vol. 1, no. 1, pp. 27–60.

Jones, T. M. and Wicks, A. C. (1999), 'Convergent stakeholder theory', *Academy of Management Review*, vol. 24, no. 2, pp. 206–221.

Jose, A. and Lee, S. M. (2007), 'Environmental reporting of global corporations: a content analysis based on website disclosures', *Journal of Business Ethics*, vol. 72, no. 4, pp. 307–321.

Kaplan, S. (1989), 'The effects of management buyouts on operating performance and value', *Journal of Financial Economics*, vol. 24, no. 2, pp. 217–254.

Keim, G. (1978), 'Managerial behavior and the social responsibilities debate: goals versus constraints', *Academy of Management Journal*, vol. 21, pp. 57–68.

King, B. G. (2008), 'A political mediation model of corporate response to social movement activism', *Administrative Science Quarterly*, vol. 53, no. 3, pp. 395–421.

King, B. G. and Whetten, D. A. (2008), 'Rethinking the relationship between reputation and legitimacy: a social actor conceptualization', *Corporate Reputation Review*, vol. 11, no. 3, pp. 192–207.

Kisenyi, V. and Gray, R. H. (1998), 'Social disclosure in Uganda', *Social and Environmental Accounting*, vol. 18, no. 2, pp. 16–18.

Klare, M. T. (2001), *Resource Wars: The New Landscape of Global Conflict*, Henry Holt and Co, New York.

KPMG (2002), *KPMG International Survey of Environmental Reporting 2002*, KPMG Environmental Consulting, De Meern, Netherlands.

KPMG (2005), *KPMG International Survey of Corporate Responsibility Reporting 2005*, KPMG Global Sustainability Services, Amsterdam, Netherlands.

Krippendorff, K. (2004), *Content Analysis: An Introduction to Its Methodology (second edition)*, Sage Publications, London.

Kuhn, T. (1970), *The Structure of Scientific Revolutions (second edition)*, University of Chicago Press, Chicago.

Laan Smith, J. van der, Adhikari, A. and Tondkar, R. H. (2005), 'Exploring differences in social disclosures internationally: a stakeholder perspective', *Journal of Accounting and Public Policy*, vol. 24, no. 2, pp. 123–151.

Laurence, J., Gao G. P. and Paul, H. (1995), 'Confucian roots in China: a force for today's business', *Management Decision*, vol. 33, no. 10, pp. 29–34.

Leary, M. R. and Kowalski, R. M. (1990), 'Impression management: a literature review and two-component model', *Psychological Bulletin*, vol. 107, no. 1, pp. 34–47.

Lehman, C. and Tinker, T. (1987), 'The "real" cultural significance of accounts', *Accounting, Organizations and Society*, vol. 12, no. 5, pp. 503–522.

Li, J. (2006), *Law on Product Quality Control and Product Liability in China*, William S. Hein & Co., Buffalo.

Lindblom, C. K. (1993), 'The implications of organizational legitimacy for corporate social performance and disclosure', paper presented at Critical Perspectives on Accounting Conference, New York, NY.

Linowes, D. F. (1972), 'Social-economic accounting', *Journal of Accountancy*, vol. 133, pp. 37–42.

Little, P. L. and Little, B. L. (2000), 'Do perceptions of corporate social responsibility contribute to explaining differences in corporate price-earnings ratios? – A research note', *Corporate Reputation Review*, vol. 3, no. 2, pp. 137–142.

Liu, X. and Anbumozhi, V. (2009), 'Determinant factors of corporate environmental information disclosure: an empirical study of Chinese listed companies', *Journal of Cleaner Production*, vol. 17, no. 6, pp. 593–600.

Loderer, C. and Martin, K. (1997), 'Executive stock ownership and performance: tracking faint traces', *Journal of Financial Economics*, vol. 45, no. 2, pp. 223–255.

Lodge, M. (1981), *Magnitude Scaling: Quantitative Measurement of Opinions*, Sage, Thousand Oaks, CA.

Logsdon, J. M. (1985), 'Organizational responses to environmental issues: oil refining companies and air pollution', in Preston, L. E. (ed.), *Research in Corporate Social Performance and Policy*, vol. 7, JAI Press, New York, NY, pp. 47–72.

Lorraine, N. H. J., Collison, D. J. and Power, D. M. (2004), 'An analysis of the stock market impact of environmental performance information', *Accounting Forum*, vol. 28, no. 1, pp. 7–26.

Lynn, M. (1992), 'A note on corporate social disclosure in Hong Kong', *British Accounting Review*, vol. 2, no. 2, pp. 105–110.

McGuire, J. B., Sundgren, A. and Schneeweis, T. (1988), 'Corporate social responsibility and firm financial performance', *Academy of Management Journal*, vol. 31, no. 4, pp. 854–872.

McKinstry, S. (1996), 'Designing the annual reports of Burton plc from 1930 to 1994', *Accounting, Organizations and Society*, vol. 21, no. 1, pp. 89–111.

MacMillan, K., Money, K., Downing, S. and Hillenbrand, C. (2004), 'Giving your organization SPIRIT: an overview and call to action for directors on issues of corporate governance, corporate reputation and corporate responsibility', *Journal of General Management*, vol. 30, no. 2, pp. 15–42.

Magness, V. (2002), 'The value relevance of environmental disclosures – an event study in the Canadian mining industry', Working Paper, Ryerson University.

Magness, V. (2006), 'Strategic posture, financial performance and environmental disclosure: an empirical test of legitimacy theory', *Accounting, Auditing and Accountability Journal*, vol. 19, no. 4, pp. 540–563.

Marston, C. L. and Shrives, P. J. (1991), 'The use of disclosure indices in accounting research: a review article', *British Accounting Review*, vol. 23, no. 3, pp. 195–210.

Mathews, M. R. (1984), 'A suggested classification for social accounting research', *Journal of Accounting and Public Policy*, vol. 3, no. 3, pp. 199–221.

Mathews, M. R. (1993), *Socially Responsible Accounting*, Chapman and Hall, London.

Mathews, M. R. (1997), 'Twenty-five years of social and environmental accounting research: is there a silver jubilee to celebrate?', *Accounting, Auditing and Accountability Journal*, vol. 10, no. 4, pp. 481–531.

Mathews, M. R. and Perera, M. H. B. (1995), *Accounting Theory and Development*, third edition, Thomas Nelson Australia, Melbourne.

Maunders, K. T. and Burritt, R. L. (1991), 'Accounting and the ecological crisis', *Accounting Auditing and Accountability Journal*, vol. 4, no. 3, pp. 9–26.

Mazzola, P., Ravasi, D. and Gabbioneta, C. (2006), 'How to build reputation in financial markets', *Long Range Planning*, vol. 39, no. 4, pp. 385–407.

Merchants Bank (2008), *2008 Corporate Social Responsibility Report*, online, available at: www.cmbchina.com, accessed: 2 April 2009.

Merriam, S. B. (1998), *Qualitative Research and Case Study Applications in Education*, Jossey-Bass Inc., San Francisco.

Milne, M. and Chan, C. (1998), 'Narrative corporate social disclosures: how much difference do they make to investment decision-making?' *British Accounting Review*, vol. 31, no. 4, pp. 439–457.

Milne, M. J. and Adler, R. W. (1999), 'Exploring the reliability of social and environmental disclosures content analysis', *Accounting, Auditing and Accountability Journal*, vol. 12, no. 2, pp. 237–256.

Milne, M. J. and Patten, D. M. (2002), 'Securing organizational legitimacy: an experimental decision case examining the impact of environmental disclosures', *Accounting, Auditing and Accountability Journal*, vol. 15, no. 3, pp. 372–405.

Mingers, J. and Gill, A. (1997), *Multimethodology: The Theory and Practice of Combining Management Science Methodologies*, Wiley, Chichester.

Ministry of Health (2006), *Ministry of Health Notification about the 2005 Nationwide Health Monitoring Work Status (in Chinese)*, online, available at: www.gov.cn/zwgk/2006–07/18/content_338541.htm, accessed: 18 August 2009.

Mobley, S. C. (1970), 'The challenges of socio-economic accounting', *Accounting Review*, vol. 45, no. 4, pp. 762–768.

Mohamed, A. A. and Gardner, W. L. (2004), 'An exploratory study of interorganizational defamation: an organizational impression management perspective', *Organization Analysis*, vol. 12, no. 2, pp. 129–145.

Mohamed, A. A., Gardner, W. L. and Paolillo, J. G. P. (1999), 'A taxonomy of organizational impression management tactics', *Advances in Competitiveness Research*, vol. 7, no. 1, pp. 108–130.

Moore, G. (2001), 'Corporate social and financial performance: an investigation in the UK supermarket industry', *Journal of Business Ethics*, vol. 34, no. 3/4, pp. 299–315.

Morgan, D. L. (2007), 'Paradigms lost and pragmatism regained: methodological implications of combining qualitative and quantitative methods', *Journal of Mixed Methods Research*, vol. 1, no. 1, pp. 48–76.

Murray, A., Sinclair, D., Power, D. and Gray, R. (2006), 'Do financial markets care about social and environmental disclosure? – Further evidence and exploration from the UK', *Accounting, Auditing and Accountability Journal*, vol. 19, no. 2, pp. 228–255.

Musteen, M., Datta, D. K. and Kemmerer, B. (2010), 'Corporate reputation: do board characteristics matter?', *British Journal of Management*, vol. 21, no. 2, pp. 498–510.

Myers, M. D. (2009), *Qualitative Research in Business and Management*, Sage Publications, London.

Nasi, J., Nasi, S., Phillips, N. and Zyglidopoulos, S. (1997), 'The evolution of corporate social responsiveness: an exploratory study of Finnish and Canadian forestry companies', *Business and Society*, vol. 36, no. 3, pp. 296–321.

National Energy Administration (2007), *News Conference*, online, available at: www.gov.cn/jrzg/2008-08/20/content_1075206.htm, accessed: 21 August 2009.

Neibecker, B. (1984), 'The validity of computer-controlled magnitude scaling to measure emotional impact of stimuli', *Journal of Marketing Research*, vol. 21, no. 3, pp. 325–331.

Neu, D. and Wright, M. (1992), 'Bank failures, stigma, management and the accounting establishment', *Accounting, Organizations and Society*, vol. 17, no. 7, pp. 645–665.

Neu, D., Warsame, H. and Pedwell, K. (1998), 'Managing public impressions: environmental disclosures in annual reports', *Accounting, Organizations and Society*, vol. 23, no. 3, pp. 265–282.

Neuman, W. L. (2006), *Social Research Methods: Qualitative and Quantitative Approaches (seventh edition)*, Pearson, Boston.

Newson, M. and Deegan, C. (2002), 'Global expectations and their association with corporate social disclosure practices in Australia, Singapore and South Korea', *International Journal of Accounting*, vol. 37, no. 2, pp. 183–213.

OCLC (2009), *Online Catalogs: What Users and Librarians Want*, online, available at: www.oclc.org, accessed: 25 November 2011.

O'Connor, L. (2006), 'Empirical research in social and environmental accounting: a meta-review', online, available at: www.vuw.ac.nz/sacl/about/csear2006/papers/oconnor,larry.pdf, accessed: 3 August 2009.

O'Donovan, G. (2002), 'Environmental disclosures in the annual report: extending the applicability and predictive power of legitimacy theory', *Accounting, Auditing and Accountability Journal*, vol. 15, no. 3, pp. 344–371.

O'Dwyer, B. (2002), 'Managerial perceptions of corporate social disclosure: an Irish story', *Accounting, Auditing and Accountability Journal*, vol. 15, no. 3, pp. 406–436.

Ogden, S. and Clarke, J. (2005), 'Customer disclosures, impression management and the construction of legitimacy: corporate reports in the UK privatised water industry', *Accounting, Auditing and Accountability Journal*, vol. 18, no. 3, pp. 313–345.

Owen, D. (2008), 'Chronicles of wasted time? – A personal reflection on the current state of, and future prospects for, social and environmental accounting research', *Accounting, Auditing and Accountability Journal*, vol. 21, no. 2, pp. 240–267.

Pang, C. K., Roberts, D. and Sutton, J. (1998), 'Doing business in China – the art of war?', *International Journal of Contemporary Hospitality Management*, vol. 10, no. 7, pp. 272–282.

Parker, L. D. (2005), 'Social and environmental accountability research: a view from the commentary box', *Accounting, Auditing and Accountability Journal*, vol. 18, no. 6, pp. 842–860.

Patten, D. M. (1991), 'Exposure, legitimacy and social disclosure', *Journal of Accounting and Public Policy*, vol. 10, no. 4, pp. 297–308.

Patten, D. M. (1992), 'Intra-industry environmental disclosures in response to the Alaskan oil spill: a note on legitimacy theory', *Accounting, Organizations and Society*, vol. 17, no. 5, pp. 471–475.

Patten, D. M. (2002), 'The relation between environmental performance and environmental disclosure: a research note', *Accounting, Organizations and Society*, vol. 27, no. 8, pp. 763–773.

PetroChina (2008), *2008 Corporate Social Responsibility Report*, online, available at: www.petrochina.com.cn, accessed: 2 April 2009.

Pfeffer, J. and Salancik, G. R. (1978), *The External Control of Organizations: A Resource Dependence Perspective*, Harper & Row, New York.

Power, M. (1991), 'Auditing and environmental expertise: between protest and professionalisation', *Accounting, Auditing and Accountability Journal*, vol. 4, no. 3, pp. 30–42.

Preston, A. M., Wright, C. and Young, J. J. (1996), 'Imaging annual reports', *Accounting, Organizations and Society*, vol. 21, no. 1, pp. 113–137.

Puxty, A. (1986), 'Social accounting as immanent legitimation: a critique of a technicist ideology', *Advances in Public Interest Accounting*, vol. 1, pp. 95–111.

Qu, W. and Leung, P. (2006), 'Cultural impact on Chinese corporate disclosure – a corporate governance perspective', *Managerial Auditing Journal*, vol. 21, no. 3, pp. 241–264.

Radbourne, J. (2003), 'Performing on boards: the link between governance and corporate reputation in nonprofit arts boards', *Corporate Reputation Review*, vol. 6, no. 3, pp. 212–222.

Ramanathan, K. V. (1976), 'Toward a theory of corporate social accounting', *Accounting Review*, vol. 51, no. 3, pp. 516–528.

Rao, A., Schmidt, S. M. and Murray, L. H. (1995), 'Upward impression management: goals, influence strategies, and consequences', *Human Relations*, vol. 48, no. 2, pp. 147–167.

Rediker, K., and Seth, A. (1995), 'Board of directors and substitution effects of alternative governance mechanisms', *Strategic Management Journal*, vol. 16, no. 2, pp. 85–99.

Remenyi, D., Williams, B., Money, A. and Swartz, E. (1998), *Doing Research in Business and Management*, Sage Publications, London.

Richardson, A. J. (1985), 'Symbolic and substantive legitimation in professional practice', *Canadian Journal of Sociology*, vol. 10, no. 2, pp. 139–152.

Richardson, A. J. (1987), 'Accounting as a legitimating institution', *Accounting, Organizations and Society*, vol. 12, no. 4, pp. 341–355.

Richardson, A. J. and Welker, M. (2001), 'Social disclosure, financial disclosure and the cost of equity capital', *Accounting, Organizations and Society*, vol. 26, no. 7/8, pp. 597–616.

Rindova, V. and Fombrun, C. J. (1999), 'Constructing competitive advantage: the role of firm-constituent interactions', *Strategic Management Journal*, vol. 20, no. 8, pp. 691–710.

Rindova, V. P., Williamson, I. O., Petkova, A. P. and Sever, J. M. (2005), 'Being good or being known: an empirical examination of the dimensions, antecedents, and consequences of organizational reputation', *Academy of Management Journal*, vol. 48, no. 6, pp. 1033–1049.

Roberts, C. B. (1991), 'Environmental disclosures: a note on reporting practices in mainland Europe', *Accounting, Auditing and Accountability Journal*, vol. 4, no. 3, pp. 62–71.

Roberts, R. W. (1992), 'Determinants of corporate social responsibility disclosure: an application of stakeholder theory', *Accounting, Organizations and Society*, vol. 17, no. 6, pp. 595–612.

Robertson, D. and Nicholson, N. (1996), 'Expressions of corporate responsibility in UK firms', *Journal of Business Ethics*, vol. 15, no. 10, pp. 1095–1106.

Rockness, J. W. (1985), 'An assessment of the relationship between US corporate environmental performance and disclosure', *Journal of Business Finance and Accounting*, vol. 12, no. 3, pp. 339–354.

Rosenfeld, P., Giacalone, R. A. and Riordan, C. A. (1995), *Impression Management in Organizations*, Routledge, London.

Ross, G. H. B. (1971), 'Social accounting: measuring the unmeasurables', *Canadian Chartered Accountant*, July, pp. 46–54.

Rowbottom, N. and Lymer, A. (2009), 'Exploring the use of online corporate sustainability information', *Accounting Forum*, vol. 33, no. 2, pp. 176–186.

Rowe, A. L. (2007), 'Corporate environmental reporting: informal institutional Chinese cultural norms', presented at fifth Asia Pacific Interdisciplinary Research in Accounting Conference, Auckland.

Ryan, B., Scapens, R. W., and Theobald, M. (1992), *Research Method* and *Methodology in Finance and Accounting*, Academic Press, London.

Saunders, M. N. K., Lewis, P. and Thornhill, A. (2009), *Research Methods for Business Students (fifth edition)*, Pearson Education Limited, Essex.

Savage, A. A. (1994), 'Corporate social disclosure practices in South Africa: a research note', *Social and Environmental Accounting*, vol. 14, no. 1, pp. 2–4.

Schlenker, B. R. (1980), *Impression Management: The Self-concept, Social Identity, and Interpersonal Relations*, Brooks/Cole, Monterey, CA.

Schneider, A. and Samkin, G. (2008), 'Intellectual capital reporting by the New Zealand local government sector', *Journal of Intellectual Capital*, vol. 9, no. 3, pp. 456–486.

Scott, W. R. (2004), 'Institutional theory' in Ritzer, G. (eds) *Encyclopedia of Social Theory*, Sage, Thousand Oaks, CA, pp. 408–414.

Shane, P. B. and Spicer, B. H. (1983), 'Market response to environmental information produced outside the firm', *Accounting Review*, vol. 58, no. 3, pp. 521–538.

Shenhua Energy (2008), *CSR Report 2008*, online, available at www.csec.com, accessed: 2 April 2009.

Silverman, D. (2009), *Doing Qualitative Research (third edition)*, Sage Publications Ltd, London.

Singh, D. R. and Ahuja, J. M. (1983), 'Corporate social reporting in India', *International Journal of Accounting*, vol. 18, no. 2, pp. 151–169.

Singleton, R. A. and Straits, B. C. (2005), *Approaches to Social Research (fourth edition)*, Oxford University Press, New York.

Smith, J. K. (1983), 'Quantitative versus qualitative research: an attempt to clarify the issue', *Educational Researcher*, vol. 12, no. 3, pp. 6–13.

Smith, M., Yahya, K. and Amiruddin, A. M. (2007), 'Environmental disclosure and performance reporting in Malaysia', *Asian Review of Accounting*, vol. 15, no. 2, pp. 185–199.

Solomon, L. D. and Palmiter, A. R. (1994), *Corporations: Examples and Explanations (second edition)*, Little, Brown and Co., Boston.

Southern Weekend (2008a), *2008 Chinese Stock-listed Firms' Social Responsibility Ranking List*, online, available at: http://finance.sina.com.cn/hy/20081218/13315654249.shtml, accessed: 26 March 2009 (in Chinese).

Southern Weekend (2008b), *Rating Criteria of the Chinese Stock-listed Firms' Social Responsibility Ranking List*, online, available at: www.infzm.com/content/17501, accessed: 26 March 2009 (in Chinese).

Southern Weekend (2009), *2009 Chinese Stock-listed Firms' Social Responsibility Ranking List*, online, available at: http://finance.sina.com.cn/hy/20100916/10408667713.shtml, accessed: 25 September 2010 (in Chinese).

Spence, C. (2007), 'Social and environmental reporting and hegemonic discourse', *Accounting Auditing and Accountability Journal*, vol. 20, no. 6, pp. 855–882.

Staden, C. J. van and Hooks, J. (2007), 'A comprehensive comparison of corporate environmental reporting and responsiveness', *British Accounting Review*, vol. 39, no. 3, pp. 197–210.

State Environmental Protection Administration (SEPA) (2003), *Regulations of Environmental Inspection on Companies Accessing to or Refinancing on the Stock Market*, online, available at: www.sepa.gov.cn, accessed: 2 September 2009 (in Chinese).

State Environmental Protection Administration (SEPA), the People's Bank of China (PBC), and the China Banking Regulatory Commission (CBRC) (2007), *Notes on Reducing Loan Risk by Enforcing Environmental Protection Policies and Regulations*, online, available at: www.sepa.gov.cn, accessed: 2 September 2009 (in Chinese).

State-owned Assets Supervision and Administration Commission of the State Council (SASAC) (2008), *Guidelines on Central State-owned Enterprises Fulfilling Social Responsibilities*, online, available at: www.sasac.gov.cn, accessed: 2 September 2009 (in Chinese).

Staw, B. M., McKechnie, P. I. and Puffer, S. M. (1983), 'The justification of organisational performance', *Administrative Science Quarterly*, vol. 28, no. 4, pp. 582–600.

Steenkamp, N. and Northcott, D. (2007), 'Content analysis in accounting research: the practical challenges', *Australian Accounting Review*, vol. 17, no. 3, pp. 12–25.

Stone, D. (1995), 'No longer at the end of the pipe, but still a long way from sustainability: a look at management accounting for the environment and sustainable development in the United States', *Accounting Forum*, vol. 19, no. 2/3, pp. 95–110.

Strauss, A., Schatzman, L., Ehrich, D., Bucher, R. and Sabshin, M. (1973), 'The hospital and its negotiated order', in Salaman, G. and Thompson, K. (eds), *People and Organizations*, Longman, London.

Suchman, M. C. (1995), 'Managing legitimacy: strategic and institutional approaches', *Academy of Management Review*, vol. 20, no. 3, pp. 571–610.

SustainAbility/UNEP (1997), *Engaging Stakeholders: the 1997 Benchmark Survey – The 3rd International Progress Report on Company Environmental Reporting*, SustainAbility, London.

SustainAbility (2007), *China: New Landscapes*, SustainAbility, London.

Tashakkori, A. and Teddlie, C. (2003), *Handbook of Mixed Methods in Social and Behavioral Research*, Sage, Thousand Oaks, CA.

Taylor, D. and Shan, Y. G. (2007), 'What drives the fledging practice of social and environmental reporting by Chinese companies listed in Hong Kong', *Accounting, Accountability and Performance*, vol. 13, no. 2, pp. 55–86.

Tedeschi, J. T., Ed. (1981), *Impression Management Theory and Social Psychological Research*, Academic Press, New York.

Tedeschi, J. T. and Melburg, V. (1984), 'Impression management and influence in the organization', in Bacharach, S. B. and Lawler, E. J. (eds), *Research in the Sociology of Organizations*, JAI, Greenwich, CT, pp. 31–58.

Teoh, H. Y. and Thong, G. (1984), 'Another look at corporate social responsibility and reporting: an empirical study in a developing country', *Accounting, Organizations and Society*, vol. 9, no. 2, pp. 189–206.

Tilt, C. A. (2007), 'External stakeholders' perspectives on sustainability reporting' in Unerman, J., Bebbington, J. and O'Dwyer, B. (eds), *Sustainability Accounting and Accountability*, Routledge, New York, NY, pp. 104–126.

Tilt, C. A. and Symes, C. F. (1999), 'Environmental disclosure by Australian mining companies: environmental conscience or commercial reality?', *Accounting Forum*, vol. 23, no. 2, pp. 137–154.

Tinker, A. M. (1985), *Paper Prophets: A Social Critique of Accounting*, Holt, Reinhart and Winston, Eastbourne.

Tinker, A. M., Lehman, C. and Neimark, M. (1991), 'Corporate social reporting: falling down the hole in the middle of the road', *Accounting Auditing and Accountability Journal*, vol. 4, no. 1, pp. 28–54.

Tinker, T. and Gray, R. (2003), 'Beyond a critique of pure reason: from policy to politics to praxis in environmental and social research', *Accounting, Auditing and Accountability Journal*, vol. 16, no. 5, pp. 727–761.

Toms, J. S. (2002), 'Firm resources, quality signals and the determinants of corporate environmental reputation: some UK evidence', *British Accounting Review*, vol. 34, no. 3, pp. 257–282.

Tozer, L. E. and Mathews, M. R. (1994), 'Environmental auditing: current practice in New Zealand', *Accounting Forum*, vol. 18, no. 3, pp. 47–69.

Trotman, K. T. (1979), 'Social responsibility disclosures by Australian companies', *Charted Accountant in Australia*, vol. 49, no. 8, pp. 24–28.

Trotman, K. T. and Bradley, G. W. (1981), 'Associations between social responsibility disclosure and characteristics of companies', *Accounting, Organizations and Society*, vol. 6, no. 4, pp. 355–362.

Tsang, E. W. K. (1998), 'A longitudinal study of corporate social reporting in Singapore: the case of the banking, food and beverages and hotel industries', *Accounting, Auditing and Accountability Journal*, vol. 11, no. 3, pp. 624–635.

Turnley, W. H. and Bolino, M. C. (2001), 'Achieving desired images while avoiding undesired images: exploring the role of self-monitoring in impression management', *Journal of Applied Psychology*, vol. 86, no. 2, pp. 351–360.

Ullmann, A. E. (1976), 'The corporate environmental accounting system: a management tool for fighting environmental degradation', *Accounting, Organizations and Society*, vol. 1, no. 1, pp. 71–79.

Ullmann, A. E. (1985), 'Data in search of a theory: a critical examination of the relationships among social performance, social disclosure and economic performance of US firms', *Academy of Management Review*, vol. 10, no. 3, pp. 540–557.

Unerman, J. (2000), 'Methodological issues: reflections on quantification in corporate social reporting content analysis', *Accounting, Auditing and Accountability Journal*, vol. 13, no. 5, pp. 667–680.

Unerman, J. (2007), 'Stakeholder engagement and dialogue', in Unerman, J., Bebbington, J. and O'Dwyer, B. (eds), *Sustainability Accounting and Accountability*, Routledge, New York, NY, pp. 86–103.

Unerman, J. (2008), 'Strategic reputation risk management and corporate social responsibility reporting', *Accounting, Auditing and Accountability Journal*, vol. 21, no. 3, pp. 362–364.

Unerman, J. and Bennett, M. (2004), 'Increased stakeholder dialogue and the internet: towards greater corporate accountability or reinforcing capitalist hegemony?', *Accounting, Organizations and Society*, vol. 29, no. 7, pp. 685–707.

Unerman, J., Guthrie, J. and Striukova, L. (2007), *UK Reporting of Intellectual Capital*, Institute of Chartered Accountants in England and Wales, London.

United Nations Economic and Social Commission for Asia and the Pacific (UNESCAP) (2000), *State of Environment in Asia and the Pacific 2000*, online, available at: www.unescap.org/esd/environment/soe/2000/documents/CH08.PDF, accessed: 12 September 2009.

UNESCAP (2010), *Creating Business and Social Value: the Asian Way to Integrate CSR into Business Strategies (Studies in Trade and Investment 68)*, United Nations Publications, New York.

UN Global Compact (2010), *Setting up a Multi-Stakeholder Panel as a Tool for Effective Stakeholder Dialogue*, online, available at: www.unglobalcompact.org/docs/issues_doc/human_rights/Resources/Stakeholder_Panels_Good_Practice_Note.pdf, accessed: 12 December 2011.

Verrecchia, R. E. (1983), 'Discretionary disclosure', *Journal of Accounting and Economics*, vol. 5, no. 1, pp. 179–194.

Villiers, C. de and Staden, C. J. van (2006), 'Can less environmental disclosure have a legitimizing effect? – evidence from Africa', *Accounting, Organizations and Society*, vol. 31, no. 8, pp. 763–781.

Voon, P. K. (2007), 'China's Energy Needs and Economic Relations with reference to Southeast Asia', paper presented at China in the World, the World in China International Conference, University of Malaya, online, available at: http://ics.um.edu.my/images/ics/aug2007/voonpk.pdf, accessed: 26 August 2009.

Walden, W. D. and Schwartz, B. N. (1997), 'Environmental disclosures and public policy pressure', *Journal of Accounting and Public Policy*, vol. 16, no. 2, pp. 125–154.

Walker, K. (2010), 'A systematic review of the corporate reputation literature: definition, measurement, and theory', *Corporate Reputation Review*, vol. 12, no. 4, pp. 357–387.

Wallace, R. S. O., Naser, K. and Mora, A. (1994), 'The relationship between the comprehensiveness of corporate annual reports and firm characteristics in Spain', *Accounting and Business Research*, vol. 25, no. 97, pp. 41–53.

Wang, J. and Dewhirst, H. D. (1992), 'Boards of directors and stakeholder orientation', *Journal of Business Ethics*, vol. 11, no. 2, pp. 115–123.

Wang, L. and Juslin, H. (2009), 'The impact of Chinese culture on corporate social responsibility: the harmony approach', *Journal of Business Ethics*, vol. 88, no. 3, pp. 433–451.

Wartick, S. L. and Mahon, J. F. (1994), 'Toward a substantive definition of the corporate issue construct: a review and synthesis of the literature', *Business and Society*, vol. 33, no. 3, pp. 293–311.

Weber, R. P. (1990), *Basic Content Analysis (second edition)*, Sage Publications, Newbury Park, CA.

Wei, Z. H. (2004), 'Economic Development and Energy Issues in China', working paper prepared for first KEIO-UNU-JFIR Panel Meeting, online, available at: http://coe21-policy.sfc.keio.ac.jp/ja/event/file/s2–6.pdf, accessed: 26 August 2009.

Wheeler, D., Colbert, B. and Freeman, R. E. (2003), 'Focusing on value: reconciling corporate social responsibility, sustainability and a stakeholder approach in a network world', *Journal of General Management*, vol. 28, no. 3, pp. 1–28.

Whetten, D. A., Felin, T. and King, B. G. (2009), 'The practice of theory borrowing in organizational studies: current issues and future directions', *Journal of Management*, vol. 35, no. 3, pp. 537–563.

White, H. (1980), 'A heteroscedasticity-consistent covariance matrix estimator and a direct test for heteroscedasticity', *Econometrica*, vol. 48, no. 4, pp. 817–838.

Williams, S. M. (1999), 'Voluntary environmental and social accounting disclosure practices in the Asia-Pacific region: an international empirical test of political economy theory', *International Journal of Accounting*, vol. 34, no. 2, pp. 209–238.

Wilmshurst, T. D. and Frost, G. R. (2000), 'Corporate environmental reporting: a test of legitimacy theory', *Accounting, Auditing and Accountability Journal*, vol. 13, no. 1, pp. 10–26.

Wiseman, J. (1982), 'An evaluation of environmental disclosures made in corporate annual reports', *Accounting, Organizations and Society*, vol. 7, no. 1, pp. 53–63.

Woodward, D., Edwards, P. and Birkin, F. (2001), 'Some evidence on executives' views of corporate social responsibility', *British Accounting Review*, vol. 33, no. 3, pp. 357–397.

World Bank (2004), *Opportunities and Obstacles for Corporate Social Responsibility in Developing Countries*, World Bank, Washington, DC.

Wu, Y. L. (2004), 'The impact of public opinion on board structure changes, director career progression, and CEO turnover: evidence from CalPERS' corporate governance program', *Journal of Corporate Finance*, vol. 10, no. 1, pp. 199–227.

Xiao, H. and Yuan, J. (2007), 'Ownership structure, board composition and corporate voluntary disclosure: evidence from listed companies in China', *Managerial Auditing Journal*, vol. 22, no. 6, pp. 604–619.

Xinhua News Agency (2008), *Pollution Poisons Guangxi Villagers*, online, available at: www.chinadialogue.net/blog/show/single/en/2460-Pollution-poisons-Guangxi-villagers, accessed: 20 October 2008.

Yermack, D. (1996), 'Higher market valuation of companies with a small board of directors', *Journal of Financial Economics*, vol. 40, no. 2, pp. 185–211.

Zahra, S. A. and Pearce, J. A. (1989), 'Boards of directors and corporate financial performance: a review and integrative model', *Journal of Management*, vol. 15, no. 2, pp. 291–334.

Zeghal, D. and Ahmed, S. A. (1990), 'Comparison of social responsibility information disclosure media used by Canadian firms', *Accounting, Auditing and Accountability Journal*, vol. 3, no. 1, pp. 38–53.

Zeis, C., Regassa, H., Shah, A. and Ahmadian, A. (2001), 'Goodness-of-fit tests for rating scale data: applying the minimum chi-square method', *Journal of Economic and Social Measurement*, vol. 27, no. 1–2, pp. 25–39.

Zhi, S. (2003), 'Occupational health and safety legislation and implementation in China', *International Journal of Occupational Environment and Health*, vol. 9, no. 4, pp. 302–308.

Zhou, W. D. (2006), 'Will CSR work in China?', *Leading Perspectives, CSR in the People's Republic of China*, summer 2006, pp. 5–7.

Index

For Product Safety Concerns and Information please contact our EU representative GPSR@taylorandfrancis.com Taylor & Francis Verlag GmbH, Kaufingerstraße 24, 80331 München, Germany